Pauline Politics

Pauline Politics

An Examination of Various Perspectives

PAUL AND THE
UPRISING OF THE DEAD,
VOLUME 1

Daniel Oudshoorn

Foreword by Neil Elliott

CASCADE *Books* • Eugene, Oregon

PAULINE POLITICS
An Examination of Various Perspectives

Paul and the Uprising of the Dead, Volume 1

Cascade Books
An Imprint of Wipf and Stock Publishers
199 W. 8th Ave., Suite 3
Eugene, OR 97401

www.wipfandstock.com

PAPERBACK ISBN: 978-1-5326-7521-8
HARDCOVER ISBN: 978-1-5326-7522-5
EBOOK ISBN: 978-1-5326-7523-2

Cataloguing-in-Publication data:

Names: Oudshoorn, Daniel.

Title: Pauline politics : an examination of various perspectives. / Daniel Oudshoorn.

Description: Eugene, OR: Cascade Books, 2020. | Series: Paul and the Uprising of the Dead, Volume 1. | Includes bibliographical references.

Identifiers: ISBN 978-1-5326-7521-8 (paperback) | ISBN 978-1-5326-7522-5 (hardcover) | ISBN 978-1-5326-7523-2 (ebook)

Subjects: LCSH: Paul, the Apostle, Saint—Political and social views. | Bible. Epistles of Paul—Criticism, interpretation, etc. | Politics in the Bible.

Classification: BS2655.P64 O93 2020 (print) | BS2655.P64 (ebook)

Manufactured in the U.S.A.   JANUARY 14, 2020

TABLE OF CONTENTS

TABLE OF CONTENTS

LIST OF TABLES

FOREWORD

THE LAST SIXTY-PLUS YEARS have seen dramatic and tumultuous changes in scholarship on the apostle Paul. It is nevertheless still common to pick up the latest monograph on this or that aspect of Paul's thought and see on the cover one or another oil portrait of the apostle painted by the seventeenth-century master Rembrandt van Rijn.

In any of several paintings, Paul sits at a heavy wooden desk, quill pen in hand, the folio-sized parchment of his next letter laid out before him. In one portrait from 1657, he strokes his forehead and looks into the middle distance, apparently laboring, almost neuralgically, to form just the right phrase to express a sublime thought. In another from two years later, *An Elderly Man as Saint Paul*, the apostle gazes off, pensively, at an angle from the viewer. His emblematic sword lies idle against his cot in *St. Paul in Prison* (1627); the cot is weighed down by a heavy codex of his letters, even as the gray-haired apostle prepares another, staring blankly into space, hand to lips, as if to capture the *mot juste*. At last, in *The Apostle Paul* (1633), the saint, now white-haired, locks eyes with the viewer. He sits, turned away from another heavy codex, the arm holding his quill at rest; his gaze seems to invite the viewer to contemplate his oeuvre (symbolized by a library of leather-bound codices on the desk in front of him). Despite their differences, in each painting Paul is presented as a solitary thinker, absorbed with the products of his own genius—not least in one of Rembrandt's own self-portraits, from 1661, in which he has depicted himself in the guise of the apostle, heavy parchment volume in hand.

So also with the academic study of Paul, the habit is engrained in many of us—especially those who labor at desks, producing books—to understand Paul as a thinker of deep and profound thoughts. That is, we think of Paul as we would like to think of ourselves, and we present ourselves to others as uncommonly gifted to untangle what would otherwise remain impenetrable in his thought.

Daniel Oudshoorn's vital work in these three volumes is all the more remarkable for that reason. It is not just that his effort is directed, not toward displaying his own cleverness as an interpreter, but at getting to the point—his surveys of scholarship on diverse questions are as bracing as they are lucid—but that he chafes against the common pressure to conform Paul to the role of religious genius. He writes more often of "the Pauline faction," calling attention to the evident reality that Paul strove to achieve his purposes always alongside colleagues and collaborators. Oudshoorn's apostle is also every ounce an activist, a revolutionary, dedicated to proclaiming and mobilizing the "uprising" of those society has left for dead. This is a gritty comprehension of Paul, informed by the experience of those society has abandoned.

In earlier work, I observed how useful a single passage in Paul's letters—the injunction to "be subject to the governing authorities" (Rom 13:1–7)—had proved to be to the powers in various periods of oppression or tyranny. Regardless of the erudition of scholars who have exercised their wits on that passage, it remains the device of choice for deflecting criticism of "zero-tolerance" policies that tear children from their parents' arms at the US-Mexico border. In this and myriad other ways, the apostle Paul remains a blunt instrument in the hands of the powerful. How very important it is, then, to see the figure of the apostle, the praxis of his "faction," and the letters that were instruments of that praxis brought to life over against the death-dealing logic of neoliberalism. Oudshoorn's strategic choices of phrase continue to haunt my own reading of Paul's letters; I believe they should haunt the assumed verities of our political economy as well, and fuel our own uprising against them.

Neil Elliott

PREFACE

IN *PAUL AND THE Uprising of the Dead*, I attempt a comprehensive study of the Pauline epistles, paying especial attention to socioeconomic and theopolitical matters. I survey a broad range of positions, and note how presuppositions related to the socioeconomic status of the early Jesus loyalists as well as presuppositions about Pauline eschatology heavily influence the conclusions that diverse parties draw in relation to these themes. I begin by surveying four prominent positions taken in relation to "Paul and politics," and then explore the socioeconomic and general eschatological arguments that are made to support these positions (volume 1: Pauline Politics). I then turn to examining Pauline apocalyptic eschatology in more detail and relate it to the realized eschatology of Rome, while studying the ideo-theology of Roman imperialism more generally (volume 2: Pauline Eschatology). This leads to a presentation of Paulinism that focuses especially upon the themes of living as members of the transnational family of God, embracing shame in solidarity with the crucified, engaging in sibling-based practices of economic mutuality, and loyally and lovingly gospeling the justice of God in treasonous, law-breaking, and law-fulfilling ways, within the newly assembled body of the Anointed (volume 3: Pauline Solidarity). This presentation is distinct, in many ways, from the most prominent conservative, liberal, and radical readings of the Pauline epistles. Ultimately, what is presented is an understanding of Paulinism as a faction within a movement that is actively working to organize the oppressed, abandoned, vanquished, and left-for-dead, into a body that experiences Life in all of its abundance and goodness. This body necessarily exists in conflict with dominant (imperial) death-dealing ways of organizing life in the service of Death. The Pauline faction, then, are those who help to organize this resistance to Death—and all the ways in which Death is structured into social, economic, political, and religious organizations—within assemblies where justice is understood

xi

to be that which is life-giving and life-affirming, especially for those who have been deprived of life and left for dead.

ACKNOWLEDGMENTS

I BEGIN BY ACKNOWLEDGING the various sovereign Indigenous peoples who have allowed me to live and work and play and complete this project on the lands to which they belong—from the Wendat, Petun, and Mississaugas, to the Musqueam, Squamish, and Tsleil-Waututh, to the Attawandaron, Wendat, Lenape, Haudenosaune, and Anishinaabe—I lift my hands to them and thank them for the care that they have shown the land and for allowing me and my children and other loved ones to live, work, and struggle alongside of them. In many ways, my ability to complete this project is related to my own status as a white, cishet, male settler, of Christian European descent. It is precisely people like me who have benefited most from the ongoing and genocidal process of Canadian colonialism. Thus, when I acknowledge various sovereign Indigenous peoples, as I am doing now, I do so with a sense of my own interconnectedness, liability, accountability, and responsibility. I hope that this work contributes to the ongoing process of decolonization and the uprising of those whom my people have left for dead in these territories. Were I to begin this project again, I would be more interested in writing about Paulinism as it relates to militant Indigenous movements pursuing solidarity, resistance, and liberation, within the overarching context of colonialism. The parallels, to me, are striking and I believe that kind of study could be very enriching and, perhaps, help bring together two groups of people who are often at odds with each other.

I acknowledge my children, Charlie and Ruby, and my partner, Jessica Marlatt. You each played central roles in my own *anastasis* from the dead. Thank you for giving me the gifts of wonder, gratitude, gentleness, love, joy, kindness, fatherhood, companionship, and life—new creation life, abundant life, resurrection life. You are all marvels and wonders and I love you with all of my everything.

I acknowledge those scholars who showed me that we have to figure these things out in the streets, on the barricades, in our homes, in squats, in physical altercations with riot police, and in the midst of the struggle. Thank you, Charles and Rita Ringma, and Dave and Teresa Diewert. Nobody else whom I have known who bothers talking about Paul has ever come close to embodying Paulinism in the ways that you all have and do. Bob Ekblad and Don Cowie also helped me a great deal in this regard. Thank you also to all those involved in the fight who may or may not have cared one bit about Paul but who helped teach me (personally or from a distance) what it means to serve Life and fight against Death—thank you, Jody Nichols, Nicky Dunlop, Andrea Earl, Jan Rothenburger, Anthony Schofield, Ivan Mulder, Stanislav Kupferschmidt, Alex Hundert, Ann Livingston, Harsha Walia, John Clarke, Mechele te Brake, Haley Broadbent, Richard Phillips, as well as all the people at Boy'R'Us (Vancouver) and SafeSpace London, everyone involved in creating overdose prevention sites across Canadian-occupied territories, and the old warrior from AIM who gave me his bandana late one night at a bar in Vancouver's downtown eastside. Indeed, it is Indigenous peoples who have spent generations organizing against colonialism, capitalism, patriarchy, and the devastation of Turtle Island—from the Wet'suwet'en camp, to Elsipogtog, to Amjiwnaang, to Kanehsatake, to Ts'peten, to Aazhoodena, to Esgenoopititj, to the Tiny House Warriors—who, to my mind, show us the closest example of what something akin to Paulinism might look like today. I lift my hands to them.

I acknowledge my brothers, Joshua, Judah, and Abram, who have shown me how wonderful, transformative, and good, sibling relationships can be. And my nephews and nieces—Evan and Wyatt, Emery and Selah, Ben and Chris and Daniella—who gave me life at a time when I was separated from my own children. Without their love, the joy they experienced playing silly games with me, and the ways that made me feel okay in the midst of a very not-okay time, this project would never have been completed.

I acknowledge all of those who encouraged me to complete this project at various times over these years. Apart from those already mentioned, thank you Daniel Imburgia, Chris Graham, Nathan Colquhoun, Daniel Slade, Danielle Firholz, Chris Tilling, Nicole Luongo, Mark Van Steenwyk, John Stackhouse, Christian Amondson, Audrey Molina, Larry Welborn, Ward Blanton, Roland Boer, and my ever loving, ever gentle, ever patient, mother (I love you, mama!). Thank you, Neil Elliott, for agreeing to be the first reader of this project. It is a great joy to be able to work with you (it is like a dream come true for me after I first read *Liberating Paul* all those years ago). And thank you, Regent College (Vancouver), for allowing me to bring this project to completion after all this time and all these words. I appreciate the graciousness you have shown me. Thank you also, to Steve Thomson (the Silver Fox) for making me read Paul in new and suddenly exciting ways when I was first an undergraduate student, and to Ms. Lane, my high school writing teacher, who believed I had a special gift for writing at a time when I had recently been deprived of housing (i.e., made homeless) by my parents and did not believe anything good about myself.

Finally, I also acknowledge the great multitude of those whom I have known who lost their homes, health, happiness, well-being, children, and, in many cases, their lives, because the Law of Sin and of Death continues to be enforced by the blind and corrupt rulers of this present evil age. I miss you and love you all. You are the song in my heart and the fire in my blood. And, since the system that killed you or left you for dead will not burn down by itself, I offer the following work as a spark.

1

INTRODUCTION

Paul and the Anastasis of the Dead

OF ALL THE VOICES found within the Christian Scriptures, the one ascribed
to Paul is perhaps the most wildly contested. Over the centuries, various
social, political, and academic factions have found it useful to discover or
produce and then attempt to enforce or promote a hegemonic perspective on Paul that aligns with their values and interests. The view of Paul
as a conservative and spiritual voice dominated much of English-speaking
scholarship for the latter two-thirds of the twentieth century. Although
much of this is in keeping with the significantly longer history of Christian
imperialism, this recent forceful retrenchment of Paul as a conservative
or spiritual voice was a reaction to prominent scholars in the nineteenth
and early twentieth centuries, who understood Paul and Marx to be allies in a common struggle (and who, themselves, were reacting against the
bourgeois readings of Paul that became dominant in post-Reformation
Protestantism and Roman Catholicism).[1] In response to a surge of interest
in Paul as a leader of the revolutionary proletariat, conservative Christian
scholars—mostly through sheer strength of numbers—forcibly reasserted
Paul as the apostle of White, middle-class morals and heteronormative
family values. However, by the end of the twentieth century, liberal aca-
demics had displaced conservatives in prominent academic seats, and this
opened spaces for different perspectives on Paul and the reconsideration of

1. See Deissmann, *Light from the Ancient East*; Kautsky, *Foundations of Christianity*.

old questions (sometimes in light of new data, sometimes in light of new sensibilities). Increasingly, Paul was presented as an apostle who embodied the proclamation of a counter-imperial and subversive way of structuring communal life under the ever-watchful and threatening eye of the empire.

Interestingly, and perhaps not coincidentally, the conservative understanding of Paul was dominant while Christianity itself was intimately connected with the ruling classes of the English-speaking West. Now that the sociopolitical influence of Christianity has waned (as in most of Western Europe) or is rapidly waning (as in Canadian and American occupied territories on Turtle Island), Paul is being reread in increasingly "counter-cultural" or "counter-imperial" ways. This immediately raises the question: are we continually allowing our understanding of Paul to be shaped by our own sociopolitical contexts, or are some of us just now becoming re-sensitized to elements of Pauline writings that we have previously overlooked due to the relation of scholars to dominant populations' experiences of socioeconomic power?[2] The answer, I suspect, contains at least a bit of both, although the emphasis of what follows will fall on the latter.

In this series, I will explore some of the diverse and contradictory ways in which Paulinism has been understood, and I will assert that the Pauline faction presents us with a particularly creative and subversive combination of eschatology, economics, and political ethics—a combination that abolishes the combination favored by empires, both then and now. I believe that it is crucial to engage in a detailed exploration of Paulinism in this way, both because the Pauline faction is a valuable resource for countering the oppressive imperial ideologies of our day, and because Paulinism itself has so often been co-opted by imperial ideologies. All too often, Paulinism has been appropriated by oppressive rulers who have placed it in the service of Death.[3] I am therefore hoping to contribute to the recovery of the Pauline

2. On this note, it is interesting to observe that, over the years, I have often discussed this project with people experiencing oppression—youth experiencing housing deprivation (i.e., homelessness), refugees, sex workers, criminalized populations (such as illicit drug users), and so on—and the presentation of a counter-imperial Paul or Jesus has consistently made a lot more immediate sense to them than when I have discussed this project with folks like me (cishet, middle-class, White Christian settlers) who tend to be extremely skeptical or entirely unconvinced.

3. On this subject, see Elliott, *Liberating Paul*, 3–24. Wes Howard-Brook shows how far back this goes in Christian history (Howard-Brook, *Empire Baptized*). As I will argue below, I believe Paul himself was already struggling against parties who were keen to initiate this project. Other key figures in Christian history—notably Luther, Calvin, and the Magisterial Reformers—are prime examples of this. This trajectory of compromise

faction which anticipated the resurrection (in Greek: *anastasis*) of the dead, and did so by helping to organize an uprising (again, in Greek: *anastasis*) among those who were left for dead within the society of their day.[4]

However, given that Paul and his coworkers were members of colonized, vanquished, enslaved, and oppressed populations, and given that people from these populations continue to be their focus, facilitating this kind of uprising, at strategic locations within the body politic of their world's greatest superpower, takes a considerable amount of skill, intelligence, and quick thinking—all of which are required in order to survive, counter threats from multiple fronts, and thrive as proof that they are, here and now, beneficiaries of the abundant life God promised to them. But, as the Pauline faction says, much of this takes place in a veiled manner, out of sight, in the cracks, spreading rhizomatically beneath the skin of Caesar's body, slowly multiplying until their numbers hit a tipping point. It is these cracks that social theorists refer to as "interstitial spaces," and when we go looking for Paul and his coworkers, this is where I believe we find them. In the interstitial spaces of the empire, something is happening, something is growing, something is spreading, something that should not be, is. Behold, the dead are rising, the Spirit of Life is moving, Death is being swallowed up in victory, and the new creation of all things has begun.

Difficulties in Studying the Pauline Faction

However, studying Paulinism is no easy task for at least five reasons—first, because any (manageable) study of this sort must possess some limitations; second, because Paulinism is not as coherent and systematic as we might want it to be; third, because all the various elements of the lived experiences

---

and betrayal of the vision of the founders is not surprising when one studies the history of revolutionary movements. If the empire cannot simply liquidate the key figures and legacies of such movements (both from life and from memory), the empire rapidly appropriates and bleaches those memories and histories in order to ensure that they are not threatening to the status quo. The ways in which Martin Luther King Jr. and Mahatma Gandhi are celebrated by Western liberals are prime examples of this. For examples of those who challenge the bleached-out remembrance of these figures, see Churchill, *Pacifism as Pathology*; Gelderloos, *How Nonviolence Protects the State*; Gelderloos, *Failure of Nonviolence*. I believe that conservatives, liberals, and most self-avowed "radicals" have bleached Paulinism in a similar way.

4. I am indebted to Alain Badiou for translating *anastasis* not only as "resurrection" but also as "uprising," and for using this translation with intentionally political overtones. See Badiou, *St. Paul*, 68.

and writings of the Pauline faction are deeply interconnected and weave through each other in ways that are difficult to unravel; fourth, because we now live at a great distance from the Pauline faction; and, fifth, because we often possess a great deal of naïveté regarding our own contexts, which hinders efforts to understand the possible contemporary relevance of Paulinism.

Limitations

A study of the Pauline faction is complicated because so many have written so much about Paul. One could easily spend a lifetime (as many do) simply covering everything that has been written on a particular subtopic, a specific letter, a single motif in that letter, and so on. Therefore, I have limited this study in several ways.

The Seven Non-Contested Letters

It is common practice within the study of Paulinism to focus on the seven non-contested letters—the letters that scholars on all sides agree were authored, at least in part, by Paul himself (specifically: 1 Thessalonians, 1 and 2 Corinthians, Galatians, Romans, Philippians, and Philemon). I have chosen to follow suit largely for pragmatic reasons—it would take far too much space and time to cover all of the Deutero-Pauline letters and the issues that would need to be addressed in order to engage those letters properly.[5]

However, there are both benefits and costs to eliminating the deutero-Pauline epistles from our study. The benefits are rather obvious—for example, this selection allows us to narrow the subject matter being discussed, and it also allows us to focus upon what we are fairly certain Paul had a part in writing, instead of having our reading of Paulinism manipulated by later exegetes or writers who may have written in Paul's name.

In this regard, contemporary counter-imperial readings of Paul often argue that our understanding of Paulinism has been corrupted because we are reading the non-contested letters through the lenses imposed by the deutero-Pauline epistles. Thus, for example, John Dominic Crossan

5. I do recognize that some strong arguments have been made for Colossians and 2 Thessalonians as Pauline, and find James D. G. Dunn to be useful on this point (*Beginning from Jerusalem*, 99–100). N. T. Wright pushes this matter even further and argues that Ephesians is also "thoroughly and completely Pauline" (*Justification*, 43–44).

and Jonathan Reed argue that the New Testament reflects a drift from the original "radical" Paul, to a "liberal" Paul (in Colossians and Ephesians), to a "conservative" and "reactionary" Paul (in the Pastorals).[6] Others, including Neil Elliott, Paula Fredriksen, Robin Scroggs, and Arthur Dewey, make similar arguments, asserting in one way or another that the deutero-Pauline epistles attempt to domesticate Paulinism and blunt the radical edge (and implications) of the life and work of Paul and his original co-conspirators.[7] Focusing on the non-contested letters allows for the prioritization of the proper passages and helps contemporary readers approach Pauline interpreters through lenses provided by Paul and his coworkers, rather than approaching Paul and his coworkers through lenses provided by later Pauline interpreters.

Of course, by limiting Paulinism in this way, I recognize that I am making a somewhat contested move (at least when it comes to some conservative Evangelical and Roman Catholic readings of Paul). Indeed, it seems conveniently advantageous to those who engage in counter-imperial readings to marginalize the significance of the seemingly more conservative deutero-Pauline epistles. Not surprisingly, then, those who wish to propose a more conservative understanding of Paulinism want to prioritize the latter epistles as genuinely Pauline or, at the very least, as accurate interpretations of what Paul and his coworkers were doing. I believe this issue can only be resolved by careful and critical readings of both the non-contested and the contested letters. Suffice to say that parties on both sides of the debate regarding "Paul and politics" seem to have been not entirely fair to the contested epistles—those who favor counter-imperial readings have almost completely disregarded them, and those who favor conservative readings have all too often used them to marginalize what is written in the non-contested letters. So, while I find myself in general agreement with those who focus on the seven non-contested letters, there are a few more issues that problematize this approach and should be noted before we proceed.

For example, affirmation of the deutero-Pauline epistles as pseudepigraphical makes these epistles something of an anomaly within their genre—especially given that they follow so immediately after Paul's life.[8]

6. Crossan and Reed, *In Search of Paul*, xiii; Crossan, *God and Empire*, 145.

7. Elliott, *Liberating Paul*, 25–27, 31, 85; Fredriksen, *From Jesus to Christ*, 171; Scroggs, *Paul for a New Day*, 2–3; Dewey, "EIS THN SPANIAN," 321.

8. For some discussion of the prevalence of forged documents in the first century

Additionally, one must note that some of the traditional cornerstones used to classify the deutero-Pauline epistles as pseudepigraphical—stylistic, syntactical and lexical differences between the letters—are increasingly being called into question.[9] Given that we possess the records of only a very few letters co-authored by Paul, and given that a person's style, syntax, and lexicon can change fairly significantly in a short amount of time, use of these differences to distinguish between authentically Pauline and pseudepigraphical writings may be overly hasty.

This issue is only further problematized when one recalls that all of the Pauline letters, with the exception of Romans, give credit to multiple authors—and even Romans later pulls several other people into the orbit of Paul's words (Rom 16:21–23). Thus, 1 Thessalonians is authored by Paul, Silas, and Timothy (1 Thess 1:1); 1 Corinthians is authored by Paul and Sosthenes (1 Cor 1:1); 2 Corinthians, Philippians, and Philemon are authored by Paul and Timothy (2 Cor 1:1; Phil 1:1; Phlm 1), and Galatians is authored by Paul and "all the siblings with [him]" (Gal 1:1). Additionally, Paul and his companions sometimes relied upon a scribe to record their letters—Tertius is recorded as the scribe who wrote Romans for Paul (Rom 16:22)—and Paul's reference to writing with "large letters" in Gal 6:11 suggests that he might not actually have been that literate or that comfortable writing his own correspondences.[10]

see Ehrman, *Jesus, Interrupted*, 112–23. That said, the Pauline letters are unique in other ways—notably in length. Larry Hurtado concludes that the average letter in Paul's day was 87 words in length, and few letters exceeded 200 words. Even letters by the prolific authors Cicero and Seneca only range from 22–2530 words and 149–4134 words, respectively. Paul's shortest known letter, Philemon, is 395 words, and Romans is 7101 words, by Hurtado's count. Hurtado concludes that it would take Paul days to compose his letters, which he finds rather stunning since Paul was not a professional writer or a member of the leisure class (*Destroyer of the Gods*, 120–29). While one might question the classism implicit in Hurtado's analysis (I have personally known many truly brilliant people who lacked formal education and lived on the street or in other liminal places), the point is that the letters we ascribe to Paul appear unique on a number of points, so we need to be cautious about rushing to this or that conclusion based strictly upon the criterion of uniqueness. Furthermore, if, as I argue, Paulinism arose out of apocalyptic elements of Second Temple Judaism(s), then the members of the movement would be more accustomed than most people to pseudepigraphical texts, making their use a more obvious tool for appropriating the Pauline tradition than first meets the eye.

9. See, for example, Jewett, *Thessalonians Correspondence*, 3–18; Malherbe, *Letters to the Thessalonians*, 364–70; Dunn, *Epistles to the Colossians*, 35–39; O'Brien, *Letter to the Ephesians*, 4–47; Hoehner, *Ephesians*, 2–61.

10. For more on the possible influence of scribes and co-authors on the content of first-century letters, see Richards, *Paul and First-Century Letter Writing*; also Schreiner,

Observing this should, therefore, make us especially cautious about drawing any conclusions about authorship based on stylistic, syntactical, and lexical differences. It is difficult to know if those differences reflect differences between Paul and those who write in Paul's name, or if they are simply differences reflected within Paul's internal circle of co-authors and scribes. Indeed, given that Ephesians, Titus, and 1 and 2 Timothy claim no author apart from Paul, those who see these letters as Pauline could make the argument that differences in style and lexicon are due to the fact that Paul is the only author of these letters! Conversely, the fact that Paul is named as the sole author could be used as an argument against their authenticity, since all of the letters of Paul are in some way co-authored, and to not write collectively may go against Paul's understanding of community, leadership, and so on. We thus see something of the unavoidable ambiguity related to arguments of this nature.

Keeping these objections in mind, however, I believe that the thematic differences (which I take to be contradictions) between the seven non-contested letters and the deutero-Pauline epistles—especially the Pastorals, but also significant portions of Colossians and Ephesians—are significant enough to warrant an explanation that is at least akin to the popular pseudepigraphical argument.[11]

Lastly, these observations about the authorship of the seven non-contested letters raises a larger and more urgent question: if all of these letters (with the possible but not certain exception of Romans) are written by multiple authors, isn't it somewhat misleading to speak of these letters as "Pauline"? Perhaps much of what we ascribe to Paul owes its origin or inspiration to Timothy, Sosthenes, Silas, Paul's unnamed companions, or even Tertius, not to mention Phoebe, Prisca and Aquila, Andronicus and Junia, and others Paul mentions as having some kind of relationship with him as friends, siblings, peers, and coworkers.[12] Certain New Testament

---

Romans, 2; Dunn, *Beginning from Jerusalem*, 592–95.

11. Then again, perhaps the deutero-Pauline epistles are not as conservative as parties on all sides imagine. Just as the conservative Paul has been thrown into question, perhaps it is time to more seriously question the conservative nature of the latter epistles. Unfortunately, such an endeavor falls outside the scope of this series. However, Harry O. Maier starts to explore this in a book I enjoyed very much, even if I did not agree with all of his conclusions (see Maier, *Picturing Paul in Empire*).

12. Frequently referred to as "Priscilla," the name "Prisca" is more technically accurate. In Romans and 1 Corinthians, both references are to Prisca. I understand that Priscilla is a diminutive form of Prisca but that variation is only used in Acts so I'm trying to stick with the name as it appears in the Pauline material.

scholars are particularly attuned to this idea given post-Marxist criticisms of "hero cults" or "the cult of the leader" that can negatively influence how revolutionary movements both develop and come to be remembered (and therefore imitated).[13] I believe that this is an important point. Contra scholars such as E. P. Sanders (who argues against an emphasis on corporate authorship because he feels this "obscures Paul" and the ways in which the epistles reveal "a religious genius at work"), I believe that the corporate nature of writing was an example of one of the ways in which Paul and his co-workers sought to undercut the establishment of standard hierarchies of power within the assemblies of Jesus loyalists with whom they were involved.[14] What follows in this study will be offered as evidence to support this statement.

However, there are at least two reasons why it remains reasonable to continue to speak of these epistles as "Pauline." First and most obviously, Paul is the only author common to all seven letters. Second, stories about Paul's personal experiences dominate several places in the letters. For example, Gal 1:11–2:16, can reasonably be assumed to be a narration of Paul's experiences (and not the experiences of the group or the exclusive experience of one of the anonymous siblings mentioned in the opening of the letter). The same argument applies to passages like 1 Cor 3:1–15 and 2 Cor 10:1–2, and can reasonably be assumed to apply to other passages like 2 Cor 11:22–12:18 (though here Paul's "I" statements return to "we" language by the final verse, presumably referring to both Paul and Timothy). Therefore, even if some (much?) of what is found in the seven non-contested letters does not originate with Paul personally, it was surely embraced by Paul. Paul, in turn, can be assumed to be an especially important representative of a particular group within the early Jesus movement. It is important to think of Paul in this way—as one member within a broader movement, and not as an isolated trail-blazing individual—and we will return to this point later. For now, we need to remember that when we speak of something as

13. See, for example, Jennings, *Outlaw Justice*, 226.

14. Sanders, *Paul: The Apostle's Life*, 154–55. Sanders asserts that Paul dictated the letters himself and did not substantially revise them, thus seeing the letters as revealing Paul's "mind at work" (155). Sanders appeals to the presence of features such as *anacolutha* (where an abrupt change in the text renders a thought inconsistent or dubious) as evidence of this (169). This strongly contradicts the position taken not only by those who emphasize corporate authorship but also by Hurtado (noted above in n. 8), who argues that letters of the length of the epistles required considerable time to compose.

"Pauline" we are referring to a corporate entity, a specific sub-faction of the early Jesus movement composed of Paul *and his coworkers*.

The Book of Acts

By choosing to focus on the seven non-contested letters, I have also limited this study by largely avoiding the book of Acts and the scholarly debate regarding its relation to the Pauline faction and their writings. Acts appears to present a Paul who is much more compatible with empire than the Paulinism we find in the non-contested letters. In Acts, Paul is always vindicated by the magistrates, the Judeans appear to always be the problem, the Jesus movement is presented as neither criminal nor dangerous, and so on.[15] However, as C. Kavin Rowe has shown, there may be more counter-imperialism in Acts than first meets the eye—Paulinism and the author of Acts may not be as opposed to each other as some make them out to be.[16] If the author of Acts is trying to blunt Paul's radicality, then they do not entirely succeed—especially since Paul is presented as regularly getting into trouble with religious, civic, business, and imperial authorities.[17] Furthermore, if we assume that the same author(s) wrote the Gospel according to Luke, then it seems to me that attempting to present an entirely bleached out and inoffensive Paul would be somewhat anachronistic, given that Luke's Gospel consistently subverts the standards, norms, structures, and values of Roman society.[18]

However, I have mostly avoided engaging this debate, and though I am quite familiar with the Paul presented to us in Acts, I have not relied

15. For scholars who see sharp opposition between Acts and Paul, see Crossan and Reed, *In Search of Paul*, 28–34; Crossan, *God and Empire*, 149–52; Ehrman, *Jesus, Interrupted*, 53–58; Fredriksen, *From Jesus to Christ*, 53–55, 171–73; Blanton, *Materialism for the Masses*, 18–33; Sanders, *Paul*, 15–17. Other problems with Acts relate to the ways in which Acts depicts the early stages of Paul's life in a way that appears to contradict what we find in the Pauline Epistles (see Sanders, *Paul*, 19–20).

16. Rowe, *World Upside Down*. For an alternative perspective and a helpful review of this debate, see Dunn, *Beginning from Jerusalem*, 73–98. See also Rhoads et al., *Luke-Acts and Empire*.

17. Is it that the author of Acts cannot completely eradicate the radical memory of Paul, or is it that the author of Acts is sympathetic to that memory in some ways? Or is there some kind of complex hybridity, of the sort highlighted by postcolonial scholars, going on in Acts just as much as in Paul?

18. For a compelling subversive reading of Luke's Gospel, see Green, *Gospel of Luke*. See also Rhoads et al., *Luke-Acts and Empire*.

on Acts to draw conclusions regarding Paul. In this regard, I am following the trend among contemporary Pauline scholarship, which is itself reacting against previous scholars who tended to give Acts (a non-Pauline source) an undeserved degree of influence over our understanding of Paulinism.[19]

Having said that, it is important to note that I do, in fact, refer to Acts, at times making strategic and supplementary uses of it. Indeed, it seems quite odd to me that scholars are comfortable referring to (among other things) Greco-Roman historians, Stoic philosophers, Roman poets, and all sorts of other literary, architectural, epigraphic, and numismatic materials when studying Paulinism, while altogether avoiding Acts and the deutero-Pauline epistles. While I do believe that many of these other sources are critical to understanding the Pauline faction and their context, we cannot altogether neglect sources that we know have at least some proximity to them (even if those sources put their own ideological spin on Paulinism). It strikes me as both odd and potentially irresponsible to, for example, read Paul in light of Virgil while simultaneously ignoring Acts and the deutero-Pauline epistles.

Secondary Literature

A third limit upon this study is my choice to restrict myself to studying scholars who have written about Paul during the last 150 years (and even then, given the vast amount of recent literature on Paul, I have mostly limited myself to engaging pivotal or representative texts, or voices who directly engage topics I have prioritized). Although I very occasionally touch on what patristic, medieval, and Reformation-era voices have said about Paul, time and space prevent me from engaging these voices in any detail. Furthermore, even in the (relatively) recent scholarship I have studied, I have relied most heavily upon those who have written about Paul in more general terms, relying less heavily on detailed commentaries. This is not to say that I have avoided the commentaries, nor is it to suggest that those who write about Paul more generally do not also engage in detailed exegesis; it simply reflects the fact that this study is seeking a "big picture" presentation of Paulinism.

---

19. It should be noted, however, that we cannot be certain that Paul is in the right on the points where his narrative disagrees with that of Acts—after all, Paul is writing quite passionately and utilizing his story to achieve certain ends (see Dunn, *Beginning from Jerusalem*, 52).

I understand that this focus on contemporary scholarship runs counter to a recent trend in much (conservative or Evangelical) scholarship—that of privileging patristic voices. While I can appreciate the value of listening to voices from different eras, and while I have been personally influenced in some ways by patristic sources (notably on matters related to faith and wealth), I am suspicious of granting voices from any era of history authority over those of any other era.[20] Indeed, it seems to me that, in many ways, patristic voices—just like voices from every other era of history—accommodate and frequently corrupt the witness of Paul and his coworkers. Hence, for example, within the patristics we see a (far from harmless) shift from the Pauline (and Judean) apocalyptic eschatological orientation to a Greek focus upon ontological matters, and so on and so forth.

In this regard, I cannot help but wonder if conservative and Evangelical scholars are finally admitting to some of the implications of the sustained historical-critical, socio-rhetorical, and political exegetical approaches to their Scriptures. Scripture, it seems, is far more messy, difficult, and perhaps even contradictory than conservative readings have allowed. In light of the evidence, conservative conclusions become increasingly difficult to maintain. Consequently, a flight from historical evidence to patristic voices and hermeneutical methods strikes me as a tactical move deployed to recover some sort of clear authoritative (and conservative) voice to which one can and must submit with little or no questioning.[21]

That said, largely for pragmatic reasons, I have chosen to focus on relatively contemporary voices. This is not because they are the most authoritative, but because they are most accessible and, generally speaking, better informed by the history of the interpretation of Paulinism and about the Pauline context itself.[22]

The reader will also notice that I quote a wide variety of authors. One will encounter a whole range of New Testament scholars and theologians, as well as many social theorists, economists, and philosophers, not to mention anarchists, indigenous scholars, and revolutionaries. My use of most of these voices is strategic and not systematic. Consider this text a bricolage. With many of these voices, I do not fully agree with all of what they say, but

20. See González's study of patristic sources, *Faith and Wealth*. However, Howard-Brook problematizes much of this perspective on patristic voices in *Empire Baptized*.

21. For a recent example of this, see Carter, *Interpreting Scripture*.

22. In this regard, I must admit that I think there is no going back to a pre-historical-critical, or pre-literary-critical, or pre-political (as if such a thing existed) reading of Paul.

I believe that bringing these voices into dialogue with each other can help "fund the imagination" and create the "short circuits" that are essential to approaching Paulinism in our context.[23]

Non-Systematic Writings

Seeking a "big picture" presentation of Paulinism that is coherent—without neglecting this or that aspect of the life and writings of the Pauline faction, or without being overly vague—is a difficult task, because Paul and his coworkers are not systematic thinkers in the rational, post-Enlightenment sense. This is a point that has been made many times over in recent scholarship.[24] However, it is a point that is worth repeating, because all too often in the history of Christianity (even up until the present day in certain circles), Paul has been treated as if he were a systematic theologian expounding timeless truths in tightly structured propositional arguments. This is implausible. The Pauline faction was writing occasional, narrative-based, deeply contextual, action-oriented, and community-focused letters to particular people, who inhabited particular places, at a particular moment in history. Of course, recovering this narrative-based and occasional understanding of the Pauline letters does not require us to deny that the letters possess theological content—we need not posit a false antithesis between "theological" and "occasional" letters.[25] What it does require is the exercise of caution about simply inserting Paulinism into some sort of previously established theological system (not least because of the limits within which the contemporary discipline of "theology" is understood).

We are confronted, then, with the question of the coherence of the experiences, goals, actions, and writings of the Pauline faction. Given that

23. I owe the language of "funding the imagination" to Walter Brueggemann, *Texts Under Negotiation*, 1–25. A "short circuit," according to Slavoj Žižek, is a "faulty connection in the network," though only from "the standpoint of the network's smooth functioning" (*Puppet and the Dwarf*, vii). Bringing various texts together is a means of "crossing wires" and "short circuiting" current networks of power and privilege, as well as the ways in which those networks dominate our reading of texts like the Pauline letters.

24. See Cousar, *Introduction to the New Testament*, 7–8; Fee, *God's Empowering Presence*, 2; Hays, *Moral Vision*, 16–17; Ladd, *Theology of the New Testament*, 556; Longenecker, *Ministry and Message of Paul*, 87–90; Marxsen, *New Testament Foundations*, 214; Meeks, *Writings of Saint Paul*, 442; Perrin, *New Testament*, 97; Roetzel, *Paul*, 39; Schnackenburg, *Moral Teaching*, 273; Weiss, *Earliest Christianity*, 2:650.

25. See Schrage, *Ethics of the New Testament*, 186–91; Wright, *Climax of the Covenant*, 259–62.

they are not systematic theologians, how are we to fit all of this into some sort of coherent framework for interpretation? One finds many answers in response to this question. At one extreme, we find scholars who argue that it is impossible to find a coherent framework for Paul's life and writings because Paul himself was incoherent.[26] At the other extreme, we find scholars who argue that Paul was completely consistent and coherent.[27] In between we find some who argue that Paul is not entirely consistent—there are some tensions and inconsistency in Paul's own life and letters—but that he is mostly coherent.[28] Thus, for example, scholars such as J. Christaan Beker and James D. G. Dunn argue that there is an ongoing, and not entirely resolvable, dialectic between coherence and contingency found in Paulinism.[29] It is this position that I, personally, find most convincing. It seems to me that all who live and write are negotiating this dialectic, and I have yet to encounter a person whose actions and ideals are perfectly consistent. Furthermore, when a situation is tense, when an actual or perceived risk is present, and when emotions are running high, it seems to me that people are more likely to say or do things that are inconsistent with their general approach to life. This is an important point because the letters composed by Paul and his co-authors generally reflect situations that have escalated in some way. It should therefore come as no surprise to us that there are also tensions and even contradictions to be found in Paul.

Having recognized this dialectic in Paulinism, many scholars attempt to negotiate Paul by positing various "centers" of his life and writings. Thus, just to name of a few, we have Paul's life and writing centered on:

- salvation by faith through grace (Luther);

- being in Christ (Schweitzer);

- anthropology (Bultmann);

- the cross and resurrection of Jesus (Meeks);

- the triumph of God in the death and resurrection of Jesus (Beker);

---

26. For varying degrees of this attitude, see Deissmann, *Paul*, 215; Dibelius, *Paul*, 40–45; Goguel, *Primitive Church*, 447–50; Räisänen, *Paul and the Law*, 266–69; Sanders, *Paul*, 34–39, 91–98.

27. For an example—as well as a helpful breakdown of this discussion—see Thielman, *Theology of the New Testament*, 219–29.

28. See, for example, Dunn, "Diversity in Paul," 118.

29. See Beker, *Paul the Apostle*, 11; Dunn, *Theology of Paul the Apostle*, 23.

- a fourfold center focused on the church, eschatology, Easter, and Jesus (Fee);

- redemptive history (Ridderbos);

- God's glory in Christ (Schreiner); and

- God's graciousness towards weak and sinful creatures (Thielman).[30]

From this multitude of centers, two lessons can be learned. First, it demonstrates to us just how often the quest for a center to Paulinism can be an exercise in overcoding—a way of imposing one's own ideological paradigms onto Paul.[31] Second, and more significantly, I think that this multitude of centers helps us to realize that searching for a central idea or thesis statement to Paul's life and writings is trying to fit Paul into a way of thinking that is foreign to him. To search for a center in Paul's life and thought is to continue to impose the template of the systematic, post-Enlightenment theologian onto Paul.

Instead of looking for some supposed central theme or motif to Paulinism, some have argued that it is more beneficial to look for a central *story*. Rather than focusing on theoretical concepts, Paulinism is said to be rooted within a particular narrative.[32] What, then, is this story? Often some variation of the following: the story of YHWH's engagement with the cosmos and with Israel, now radically reworked around the life, death, resurrection, and *parousia* of Jesus of Nazareth. This is presented as a climactic part of the story of the God of creation and salvation, overcoming all the forces of destruction and damnation. The reader is therefore urged to relate the individual parts of the letters back to this larger story. When viewed in this way, some elements of Paulinism become more representative than other parts. Thus, for example, Phil 2:5–11, is often understood as a

---

30. Luther, *Galatians*; Schweitzer, *Mysticism of Paul the Apostle*; Bultmann, *Theology of the New Testament*, 1:191; Bultmann, *Existence and Faith*, 149–50; Meeks, *First Urban Christians*, 191; Beker, *Paul's Apocalyptic Gospel*, ix; Beker, *Paul the Apostle*, 88; Fee, *God's Empowering Presence*, 12–13; Fee, *Paul, the Spirit*, 6–7; Ridderbos, *Paul*, 39; Schreiner, *Paul*, 20–22; Thielman, *Theology of the New Testament*, 232, 477–79. Note that significant differences still appear between scholars who are very closely ideologically related to each other. For example, Fee, Ridderbos, Schreiner, and Thielman can all be classified as conservative or "Evangelical" scholars, but they all posit different centers for Paulinism.

31. For more on overcodings, see Deleuze and Guattari, *Anti-Oedipus*.

32. See Horrell, *Introduction*, 58–61; Strom, *Reframing Paul*, 73–74; Dunn, *Theology of Paul*, 18; Wright, *Justification*, 34–35.

shorthand description of the climactic part of the story.[33] Meanwhile, other passages—say, those governing matters like head coverings or the length of one's hair—can be regarded as more tangential. Indeed, the Pauline faction makes this distinction in their writings, granting their own words more or less value (e.g., 1 Cor 7:6, 10, 12, 25, 40).

This narrative-based approach is presented as part of overcoming a gap that earlier scholars created between Pauline "beliefs" and Pauline "ethics." However, as I will seek to show in what follows, this narrative-based approach is still too oriented around conceptualizations and a logocentrism that fails to capture the way in which the life and work and writings of the Pauline faction are oriented around a central *project*—that of loyally, lovingly, and lawlessly gospeling among the left-for-dead.[34] This project—and not, ultimately, the theses, concepts, or narratives used to support it—is at the heart of Paulinism.

The Integrated Nature of Paul's Life and Writings

As mentioned above, it used to be quite common to create a sharp divide between Paul's "beliefs" and his "ethics," or between his "theology" and his "paraenesis."[35] However, that divide has been increasingly challenged and a new consensus has emerged among scholars: Paul's belief, ethics, theology, and paraenesis are all deeply intertwined and cannot be separated from each other.[36] Therefore, to study the words and deeds of the Pauline faction from a particular angle does not mean we can simply cherry-pick bits and pieces—say, the pieces that strike us as the most "spiritual" or "political" in nature—from the letters. As any researcher will quickly discover, one cannot talk about Pauline politics without also talking about theology, one cannot address the Pauline understanding of power without also exploring crucifixion, one cannot engage Pauline ethics without also engaging eschatology, and so on. As a result, any comprehensive study of Paulinism can

33. See, for example, Gorman, *Cruciformity*.

34. I will develop this understanding of "gospeling" in volume 3.

35. See, for example, Dibelius, *From Tradition to Gospel*, 238–40; Betz, *Galatians*, 254, 292.

36. See Barclay, *Obeying the Truth*, 223–24; Cadoux, *Early Church and the World*, 78–79; Furnish, *Theology and Ethics in Paul*, 210–13; Hays, *Moral Vision*, 18; Sampley, *Walking Between the Times*, 2–3; Schrage, *Ethics of the New Testament*, 167; Wright, *New Testament*, 120; Engberg-Pedersen, *Paul and the Stoics*, 301.

quickly lead the researcher down a million different rabbit holes. I myself have fallen into a good many of these holes, but I hope that this text is richer because of this.

Distance from Paul

Another obvious challenge when studying an ancient person like Paul is the considerable amount of distance that exists between him and the contemporary researcher. For example, I am separated from Paul on many levels: I live in the twenty-first century CE, Paul lived in the first century CE; I am Caucasian, Paul was Semitic; I am a Canadian, Paul was a diaspora Judean; I live in a post-industrial urban center, Paul traveled between pre-industrial cities; I enjoy relative affluence, Paul was poor; I write in English, the Pauline faction wrote in Koine Greek; I am a settler colonizing stolen land, Paul was living in exile as a result of the colonization of his land; my world is dominated by global capitalism, Paul's world was dominated by the Roman Empire, and so on. Given this great distance between myself and Paul, there is every possibility that, despite my best efforts, I will misunderstand what the Pauline faction wrote.

This is a problem facing all contemporary readers of the Pauline letters—especially those who have been raised in Christian environments and who are trained to treat Paul with familiarity. It is essential that such readers recover the alterity of Paulinism. We must recover our distance from the Pauline faction and not bridge that gap in an overly hasty manner. No matter what our background or faith tradition has taught us, we cannot afford to assume that we already know what the Pauline faction is talking about.[37]

Therefore, it is absolutely essential that we learn everything we can about the contexts of Paulinism, because contexts provide words with their meanings. Words without contexts are ambiguous at best, or nonsensical at worst.[38] If we hope to understand the words we have received from Paul, we

37. As Wright has written, "History is where we have to go if, as we say, we want to listen to Scripture itself rather than either the venerable traditions of later church leaders or the less venerable footnotes of more recent scholars. . . . It's time to get back to reading with first-century eyes and twenty-first century questions" (Wright, *Justification*, 37). I am not convinced that Wright does this well—or that "history" is any less ideological than "theology."

38. Wright has made a similar point in response to John Piper's desire to minimize the importance of situating Paul's words within the first-century context (*Justification*,

must understand the contexts in which they were written. Two examples of this may be helpful. I once had a person approach me and ask: "Do you know where I can find some Latin?" Now, if I was being asked this question in a library, I would assume that the person was asking me about the location of some Latin language books, or books by Latin authors. However, I was not in a library when asked this question—in fact, I was in a part of downtown Vancouver frequented by johns and sex workers. In that context, the sentence meant something very different—it meant that the fellow asking me was a john looking for a woman of Latin American origin (he was speaking the *argot* common to those involved in this subculture—an *argot* designed to protect "insiders" from "outsiders" and from the police). Thus, we see how this sentence can mean entirely different things depending on the context in which it is spoken.[39] To take a second example, we can look at a great deal of the language Paul uses. Terms like "Savior," "gospel," and "*parousia*" (and several others to be explored in this series) can carry a variety of meanings. As we shall see, some exegetes assume that these are strictly spiritual or apolitical terms, while other exegetes note the ways in which Paul's language echoes that of the imperial Roman ideology and conclude that Paul is engaging in something more politically subversive than many have recognized. Therefore, if we are to determine which meaning we are to privilege (is Paul speaking the *argot* of revolutionaries—an insider language designed to protect those revolutionaries from outsiders—or the apolitical language of a transcendental religion?), we must inform ourselves as much as we can about the contexts in which Paul uses this language.

Naïveté of Our Own Context(s)

Understanding the contexts related to the Pauline faction is only one half of the contemporary reader's task. The other half of this task—which is especially crucial if exegesis is performed with application in mind (as I intend it to be)—is to engage in a proper study of our own contexts. Unfortunately, this is almost entirely neglected by New Testament scholars. Within the guild of Biblical Studies, a good many courses are devoted to

---

46–51). I am thinking of Wittgenstein in this use of the word "nonsensical." See Nordman, *Wittgenstein's Tractatus*, 159–202.

39. On another occasion, a person looking for illicit drugs in Toronto's now rapidly gentrifying Regent Park asked me, "Do you know where I can find some food?" The "food" being sought was crack cocaine.

properly understanding the contexts of the texts, but almost no effort is made to arrive at a proper understanding of our own contexts. It seems as though scholars are operating on the assumption that we already have a proper understanding of the world in which we live, simply because we live in it. Unfortunately, this is a potentially fatal assumption—not, perhaps, fatal to the one making that assumption, but certainly fatal to those who experience the kinds of violence that have been justified by those who favor imperial iterations of Paulinism. We can no more assume that we understand our own contexts than we can assume that we understand those of Paul and his coworkers. If we are to study Paulinism with an eye towards its contemporary relevance, we must exegete our own situation.[40]

The Scholar as Partisan

No one among us is situated within our contemporary context in a detached, unbiased way. Furthermore, given the philosophical and ethical problems associated with post-Enlightenment and Eurocentric notions of objectivity, I do not see detachment as desirable.[41] It must be observed that this book is an exercise in openly partisan scholarship. However, there is nothing particularly new or unique about this. The Pauline faction certainly did not hide their partisanship. In fact, *all* scholars have always been partisan, and the notion of the scholar as a detached, apolitical, or objective observer has now been thoroughly rejected.[42] It is important that we recognize this, because the rhetoric of "detachment" and "objectivity" has all too often been employed to disguise the fact that scholars are writing from particular contexts with the hope of persuading their readers to accept certain beliefs along with their concomitant actions. The language of detached objectivity all too often masks this. As David Goldberg observes: "One cannot teach . . . by assuming this neutral 'view from nowhere,' for it

---

40. A task I had originally intended to perform in more detail in this series but which, alas, has been pushed off because it is already plenty long enough!

41. For criticisms of these problems arising within that same European tradition, see Foucault, *Archaeology of Knowledge*, and Foucault, *Power/Knowledge*. For an example of criticisms arising from outside a Eurocentric tradition, see Smith, *Decolonizing Methodologies*.

42. See Bauckham, *Bible in Politics*, 1; Elliott, "Paul and the Politics of Empire," 17; Fowl and Jones, *Reading in Communion*, 17; Gorringe, "Eschatology and Political Radicalism," 87–92; Schüssler-Fiorenza, *Rhetoric and Ethic*, 19; Wright, *Paul*, 15.

is no view at all. In other words, the Assumption of a View from Nowhere is the projection of local values as neutrally universal ones."[43]

To openly embrace and proclaim partisanship is not the same as blinding oneself to all opposing arguments. One can be partisan and remain open to dialogue and to confronting the possibility that one's allegiances may be mistaken.[44] To highlight the scholar as partisan is simply to honestly confront the fact that all of us are committed to various allegiances within the diverse aspects of our lives. Neutrality is an illusion, and to confess partisanship is to get those allegiances out in the open and enable genuine dialogue between various parties.

On the other hand, the partisanship I stress within this series differs from much of the focus of other partisan biblical scholars because my emphasis falls on *performing specific actions* and not on *confessing certain propositions*.[45] That is to say, many biblical scholars exhibit an obvious partisanship when it comes to confessing certain beliefs or doctrines, but spend little time explicating how the confession of those things relates to concrete historical and political activity. For example, while some biblical scholars may do their utmost to persuade us that the confession of Jesus as Lord was fundamental to the early Christian movement, these same scholars may show little regard for how this confession might impact our contemporary political, economic, racial, gendered, or class-based allegiances.

Unfortunately, scholars who neglect the connection between confession and action or downplay economic and political partisanship in pursuit of some sort of mythical "detached objectivity" often end up serving the interests of the death-dealing rulers of our age.[46] The fact is that it is conducive to the dynamics of the status quo to produce scholars who are able to distance themselves from the context of oppression and see both sides of the situation. Unfortunately, this is a hard pill for many scholars to swallow, for confessing the current context of oppression might require them to realize that they are situated on the side of the oppressors rather than on the side of the oppressed.

43. Goldberg, *Multiculturism,* 19. Indeed, for Badiou, truth itself is partisan (*Being and Event,* 345–61).

44. Indeed, having personally grown up as a middle-class, cishet, white, male, Christian settler, this was a lesson I needed to learn many times.

45. In fact, as I will argue in volume 3, this is a very Pauline mode of partisanship.

46. See Eagleton, "Critic as Partisan," 78; Brueggemann, *Prophetic Imagination,* 24–25; Walsh and Keesmaat, *Colossians Remixed,* 120.

We would therefore do well to follow the example of Terry Eagleton, who redefines objectivity and disinterestedness not as detachment but as abandoning egoism in order to be open to the needs and experiences of others.[47] This connects objectivity to love, because "genuinely caring for someone is not what gets in the way of seeing their situation for what it is, but what makes it possible. . . . It is because love involves a radical acceptance that it allows us to see others for what they are."[48] Therefore:

> Disinterestedness means not viewing the world from some sublime Olympian height, but a kind of compassion or fellow-feeling. It means trying to feel your way imaginatively into the experience of another, sharing their delight and sorrow without thinking of oneself. . . . You do not need to rise majestically above the fray to decide that in a specific situation, somebody else's interests should be promoted over yours. On the contrary, to judge this accurately involves being in the thick of the affray, assessing the situation from the inside, not loitering in some no man's land where you would be incapable of knowing anything. . . . Objectivity does not mean judging from nowhere. On the contrary, you can only know how the situation is if you are in a *position* to know.[49]

The result of this is that, as Eagleton notes, some political and economic locations are better suited for honestly confronting the reality of our contemporary situation. Notably, those in positions of power and privilege tend to view the world in a way that permits them to maintain that power and privilege, whereas those experiencing marginality, oppression, and suffering are more in touch with what actually makes things tick.[50] The logical conclusion to this diagnosis is this:

> Objectivity and partisanship are allies, not rivals. . . . It is the liberal who falls for the myth that you can only see things aright if you don't take sides. . . . The liberal has difficulty with situations in which one side has a good deal more of the truth than the other—which is to say, all the key political situations. . . . True judiciousness means taking sides.[51]

47. Eagleton, *After Theory*, 131–37.

48. Eagleton, *After Theory*, 131.

49. Eagleton, *After Theory*, 133–35; also Eagleton, "Critic as Partisan," 78.

50. Eagleton, *After Theory*, 132, 135–36.

51. Eagleton, *After Theory*, 136–37. This demonstrates how "objectivity" fits quite well with the notion of practicing a "preferential option" for and with the poor, as has been advanced by several Latin American Liberation theologians. See, for example, Boff

Indeed, to assume that we can avoid taking sides simply means that we have become so deeply rooted in the ideology of oppression that we have lost an awareness of our own complicity.[52]

I will argue that Pauline scholars should be concretely rooted in communities that are both committed to the pursuit of Life and liberation and opposed to the powers of Death and bondage. It is not just that a study of Paulinism drives us to such communities; it is also that our rootedness in such communities enables us to properly understand Paulinism. Indeed, I cannot help but wonder if the academy is itself one of the largest obstacles to a proper understanding of what exactly Paul and his coworkers were doing.

Having heeded this warning many years ago when I first began to read the Latin American liberation theologians, my own reading of Paul is informed not only by the academy but by my rootedness within various communities engaging in the pursuit of solidarity, resistance, and liberation. As much as this book is informed by what New Testament scholars have written, it is also informed by dinners shared with sex workers in Vancouver's downtown eastside; by joking around with crack dealers in Toronto's alleys late at night; by the youth who slept on my couch after the shelter I worked at kicked them out; by conversations at funerals for loved ones killed by prohibition laws; by tending to the abscesses of crystal meth users deprived of housing; and by everyone who masked up, wore black, and charged the riot police because the streets are ours, the people united will never be defeated, and without justice there will be no peace. I did not simply seek out those communities because I believed what I believed, I also believed what I did (and what I do) because I am or have been rooted in those communities.[53] It is my contention in what follows that Paul and his coworkers also understood this rootedness and its central importance. Sadly, most Pauline scholars do not—and even if they gesture towards it, they make no serious efforts to embody it. It is no wonder, then, that they

and Boff, *Introducing Liberation Theology*, 43–63; Gutierrez, *Theology of Liberation*, 287–302; Gutierrez, *We Drink from Our Own Wells*, 95–106; Gutierrez, *Power of the Poor*, 169–221; Sobrino, *No Salvation Outside the Poor*, 35–76.

52. So says Miranda, *Marx and the Bible*, xi.

53. It is these liberation theologians who have been telling us that theology must be understood as critical reflection on praxis. See Gutierrez, *Theology of Liberation*, 6–13; Boff and Boff, *Introducing Liberation Theology*, 4–9, 22–23; Walsh and Keesmaat, *Colossians Remixed*, 128–29. The truth is that *all* theology is critical reflection upon praxis of one kind or another—it is just that some are more honest about this than others!

are usually at a loss when it comes to finding cracks in the Death-dealing practices of contemporary structures. The Spirit of Life is rarely present where they choose to remain, so the answers are not to be found where they seek them.

Outline

Having addressed these introductory matters, it is worth providing a brief overview of how this study of Paulinism will progress. Volume 1 will prepare the way for an engaged socioeconomic and political reading of Paul. Chapter 1 will briefly survey and analyze what I take to be the four main political readings of Paul: (1) the conservative or spiritual Paul; (2) Paul, the founder of a Christian subculture; (3) the no-longer-directly-applicable Paul; and (4) the counter-imperial Paul. The importance of how we understand the socioeconomic status of Paul, his coworkers, and other Jesus loyalists—as well as the importance of the eschatology we ascribe to them—will become apparent through this survey. Our understanding of these factors plays a very significant role in how we interpret the politics of Paulinism. Therefore, chapter 2 will examine the question of the socioeconomic status of Paul and the early assemblies of Jesus loyalists. This chapter will begin with reconstructions of Paul's own background, then turn to examining day-to-day economic life in the eastern portion of the Roman Empire during the Julio-Claudian dynasty. This information will then be used to examine arguments made for the presence of wealthy or high-status members in the assemblies of Jesus loyalists associated with the Pauline faction. The theme of suffering and persecution is relevant to this discussion, and will be examined here. Chapter 3 will then take up the topic of eschatology and what I understand to be Paul's "apocalyptic eschatology." The chapter will begin with some necessary ground-clearing work in order to establish what we are talking about when we talk about "eschatology" or "apocalypticism." It will then explore various perspectives on Paul's apocalyptic eschatology and its central themes.

Volume 2 will spend considerable time examining the ideo-theology of the Roman Empire as it relates to the context of Paul and his coworkers. Chapter 1 will extend and complete our study of apocalyptic eschatology by examining what I take to be the apocalyptic eschatology of the Roman Empire—a very significant element of Paul's context that tends to be neglected in scholarly discussions of Pauline eschatology. Chapter 2 will engage in a fuller examination of the multifaceted beliefs and practices that justified and perpetuated Roman imperialism, specifically, the household unit, cultural constructions of honor and shame, the practice of patronage, and traditional Roman religiosity. It will then explore key themes and figures of the Roman imperial cult, in which many of these cultural elements found expression.

Volume 3 will return us to Paul and the uprising of the dead, examining each of the cornerstones of Roman imperialism as they are reworked, resisted, or rejected by Paul and his coworkers. Chapter 1 will explore the household unit as it is redefined in a transnational family of God. Chapter 2 will turn to the theme of honor and shame, exploring the Pauline embrace of shame in the company of the crucified. Chapter 3 will take up the rejection of patronage and benefaction within a new sibling-based economy of grace that posits economic mutuality over against hierarchical models of charity (as exemplified in the famous Pauline Collection, as well as practices of hospitality, table fellowship, sharing against private property, and caring for "the poor"). This chapter will be followed by a brief excursus on the question of how Paul understood or used his "authority" within the assemblies of Jesus loyalists. Finally, chapter 4 will examine the assembling of the gospel of the Anointed Jesus over against the assembled gospel of the August Caesar and the central themes and terms of the imperial cult. This chapter addresses several core themes in the Pauline letters—such as loyalty, the Law, and love—and concludes with a critical rereading of Rom 13:1–7. It is only at the end of this study that I believe we will be equipped to understand and engage a passage that has haunted political readings of Paul throughout the ages.

This is a lengthy work but, I hope, the shortest it can be in order to present a not only plausible but compelling and comprehensive picture of the aims, objectives, and ideology of Paulinism. Thus, while the key points of my own "unique contributions" to Paulinism (whatever they are worth) could be presented in a smaller single-volume work, I believe such a work would be little more than "preaching to the choir." Those who are already predisposed to view Paulinism in a counter-imperial manner may enjoy it and add it to their libraries, but those predisposed to other views could easily ignore it because it would not adequately address a number of the background matters that make various political interpretations of Paulinism more or less plausible or compelling. Therefore, I have written this longer work to deal comprehensively with the broader contextual issues that heavily influence these things. Engaging in this more sustained kind of project does not always rush the reader (or writer!) to the most exciting "capture points" but, I believe, the payoff in the end is much greater. I am not interested in simply preaching to the choir (and, for the most part, I do not think the choir needs me to preach to it). I am more interested in recruiting new members to the choir (and making other choirs sound more off-key). In this area, there is still much work to be done.

2

POLITICAL READINGS OF PAUL: THE MAIN ALTERNATIVES

> It's easy to read the story of Paul one-sidedly and to overlook latent elements within him. No one understood him, one might say, but then no one completely misunderstood him either.[1]
>
> —Jacob Taubes, *The Political Theology of Paul*

BEFORE ENGAGING IN A more detailed study of Paulinism, it is worth exploring the various approaches taken by scholars in relation to "Paul and politics." In this chapter, I will look at four broad approaches: (1) the Conservative or Spiritual Paul; (2) Paul, the Founder of a Christian Subculture; (3) the No-Longer-Directly-Applicable Paul; and (4) the Counter-Imperial Paul. I will summarize each position, note some of the nuances and internal differences involved in each, and then provide some questions and criticisms.

As with any system of classification that covers a broad (but by no means exhaustive) range of scholars, some individual perspectives fit more or less well into each of these categories. Some straddle the lines between categories. I have done my best to find categories that best reflect the schools of thought at work in scholarship, and I have done my best not to disrespect the texts or thoughts of any given author, but I understand if some wish to contest this-or-that scholar's placement within this-or-that category. However, I trust that beginning with an exploration of these broad scholarly

---

1. Taubes, *Political Theology of Paul*, 57.

trends will enable us to gain a sense of the terrain we are covering and assist us with critical questions about the matters at hand. While engaging in this task, it is worth recalling the words of N. T. Wright:

> Nobody who wants to think about Christianity can ignore [Paul]; but they can, and do, abuse him, misunderstand him, impose their own categories on him, come to him with the wrong questions and wonder why he doesn't give a clear answer, and shamelessly borrow material from him to fit into other schemes of which he would not have approved.[2]

Many people misuse the work of paul

Therefore, while considering the various approaches surveyed in this chapter, we must ask ourselves: does this reading abuse or misunderstand Paulinism? How are we to know if it does? Does it impose false categories and ask the wrong questions? Again, how can we know this? Is it simply slotting Paulinism into a previously constructed political perspective or ideology? And, once more, how can we know this? Furthermore, what makes certain readings seem more true or plausible or appealing to me, the specific reader of this text, at this moment in history? Questions like these should be brought to any reading—including my own.

The Conservative or Spiritual Paul—Summary

Perhaps the reading of Paul that is most dominant at the popular level today (both within and outside of Christian circles) is the presentation of Paul as a voice of conservative moral and political values. Directly associated with this reading of Paul is the presentation of Paul as a "spiritual," "religious," or "theological" voice—wherein things like "spirituality," "religion," and "theology" are understood as apolitical matters focused on that which is transcendent, internal to the subject, or otherworldly. This spiritual Paul, then, was focused on "planting churches" (which, from this perspective, is a distinctly religious practice, not to be confused with building any kind of sociopolitical movement), "preaching the gospel" (which is focused on propositional religious doctrines rather than lived trajectories or actions related to things like economics or politics), and the inner life of a person (which frequently leads to a marked indifference to the material situations

---

2. Wright, *What Saint Paul Really Said*, 11. Wright is, of course, much better at identifying how others do this than he is at identifying how he does this, but that is probably true of most of us.

of others).[3] Faith, in this context, is a cognitive thing. It is a matter of a proper understanding—of believing the correct theses.[4] Therefore, when Paul speaks of the cross and _anastasis_ of Jesus—or employs other terms that could have political overtones—these things are treated as cosmic, religious, or spiritual.[5] Thus, for example, Ethelbert Stauffer argues that, although both Christianity and the imperial cult were on the rise in the first century, Christianity triumphed precisely because it did not confuse religion with politics and "came with no political programme . . . scorned all political means to power . . . avoided all political provocation, and even renounced any form of political protest."[6] F. C. Grant is even blunter, arguing against what he takes to be overly subjective and "melodramatic" Marxist accounts of the development of Christianity:

> It is less and less possible, to represent early Christianity as a revolutionary social (or social-economic) movement . . . it is clear that Christianity was from the very beginning a purely religious movement, a cult, a body of beliefs and practices centred on something else than the economic welfare or well-being of any racial, national, or social group.[7]

It is important to observe that this presentation of Paul as an apolitical religious figure has significant political consequences in the lives of those who read Paul in this way. An apolitical Paul tends to lead the Christians

3. See Coggan, *Paul,* 156–58; Marshall, *Concise New Testament Theology,* 164; Weiss, *Earliest Christianity,* 2:563–64; Wrede, *Paul,* 13–15, 25–28.

4. See, for example, Engberg-Pedersen, *Paul and the Stoics,* 109, 120. For Engberg-Pedersen and many others in this camp, sin is also understood in a very depoliticized, individualized manner, wherein being "under sin" (as per Rom 3:9) means being at risk of sinning and Sin (with a capital "S") is not in any way understood as a key structural element of the socioeconomic and political realms (see Engberg-Pedersen, *Paul and the Stoics,* 207).

5. For one example of this, see Keck, *Paul and His Letters,* 37, 43, 48–49, 58–59.

6. Stauffer, *Christ and the Caesars,* 212–13; cf. 205–21. Thus, Werner Georg Kümmel argues—and many others do the same—that Paul's real significance is that he is the first theological thinker in Christianity (Kümmel, *Introduction to the New Testament,* 139; see also Dunn, *Theology of Paul the Apostle,* 2–12).

7. Grant, "Economic Background," 101. Grant repeats this point, again targeting Marxist readings of early Christianity: "Christianity was not a social revolution disguised as a cult . . . It was a religion, pure and simple" (114). Without anticipating the remainder of this book in too much detail, it is worth noting that we need not posit a "social revolution" and a "cult" as if they are mutually exclusive things—especially, as we will see, in the first-century context of the eastern portion of the Roman Empire.

who claim him to embody a political quietism that either does not disrupt the status quo (because it does not care about the status quo) or defends the status quo against any others who wish to propose change (because those who pursue change here and now are pursuing the wrong goals). Consequently, the conservative Paul and the spiritual Paul work together hand-in-glove.

Arguments in favor of Paul as a conservative and spiritual voice tend to stress one or more the following things: (a) Paul himself affirmed and propagated conservative and bourgeois morals; (b) Paul was focused on internal spiritual liberation and detachment, not historical and material liberation; (c) Paul was focused on the spiritual future and the imminent end of the world, so the political realm did not matter to him; and (d) Paul was a conservative who focused on the spiritual because he was a part of a politically powerless group. I will briefly outline these arguments here.

Paul the Teacher of Conservative and Bourgeois Morals

The understanding of Paul as a teacher of conservative and bourgeois morals is probably the most common understanding of Paul among non-scholars in the English-speaking West, whether within or outside of Christian environments. This Paul is a patriarchal figure who is unconcerned with matters related to slavery, patriarchy, political oppression, or altering the world order—after all, these things are ephemeral and inconsequential in light of the deeper spiritual reality of "the Gospel."[8] The following passages, among others, are often brought forward as proofs of this perspective:[9]

- 1 Cor 7:17–24. "let each of you lead the life that the Lord has assigned, to which God called you. This is my rule in all the [assemblies] . . . Were you a slave when called? Do not be concerned about it. Even if you gain your freedom, make use of your present condition now more than ever . . . In whatever condition you were called, [siblings], there remain with God."

---

8. For some examples of scholars who have argued along these lines, see: Lietzmann, *Beginnings of the Christian Church*, 113–30; Bultmann, *History and Eschatology*, 230–31; Käsemann, *New Testament Questions*, 208–9; Sanders, *Paul: The Apostle's Life*, 211; Schreiner, *Paul*, 412–13.

9. Other passages, largely from the deutero-Pauline epistles, also provide virtue and vice lists that potentially reflect a conservative ethic. See Gal 5:19–23; Eph 4:25–32; 5:1–5; Col 3:5–17; 1 Tim 3:2–11; Titus 1:6–9.

- 1 Cor 11:7–9. "For a man ought not to have his head veiled, since he is the image and reflection of God; but woman is the reflection of man. Indeed, man was not made from woman, but woman from man. Neither was man created for the sake of woman, but woman for the sake of man."

- Rom 13:1–2. "Let every person be subject to the governing authorities; for there is no authority except from God, and those authorities that exist have been instituted by God. Therefore, whoever resists authority resists what God has appointed, and those who resist will incur judgment."

- 2 Thess 3:6–10. "keep away from believers who are living in idleness . . . Anyone unwilling to work should not eat."

- Col 3:18—4:1. "Wives be subject to your husbands, as is fitting in the Lord . . . Children obey your parents . . . Slaves obey your earthly masters . . . "

- Eph 5:21—6:9. "Wives, be subject to your husbands as you are to the Lord. For the husband is the head of the wife . . . Children, obey your parents in the Lord, for this is right . . . Slaves, obey your earthly masters with fear and trembling, in singleness of heart as you obey [the Anointed] . . . "

- 1 Tim 2:10–11. "Let a woman learn in silence with full submission. I permit no woman to teach or to have authority over a man; she is to keep silent."

- 1 Tim 6:1–2. "Let all who are under the yoke of slavery regard their masters as worthy of all honor . . . Those who have believing masters must not be disrespectful to them on the ground that they are members of the church; rather they must serve them all the more."

- Titus 2:9. "Tell slaves to be submissive to their masters and to give satisfaction in every respect."

- Titus 3:1. "Remind them to be subject to rulers and authorities, to be obedient."

In summary, the role of Christians is to obey the state, uphold the social order, stay in one's place, and exhibit a good work ethic in whatever they do.[10]

---

10. See Bammel, "Romans 13," 374; Bultmann, *Existence and Faith*, 307; Ridderbos, *Paul*, 315–16.

Indeed, according to this Paul, those who focus on such things as fighting against poverty or resisting oppression are making the mistake of "banking on the present world for happiness."[11] Nevertheless, this Paul's teachings have a significant impact upon society. Scholars who read Paul in this way disagree on whether this impact is positive or negative.

The Conservative Paul as a Positive Influence on Society

Some argue that this Paul had a positive, reforming effect on the world by altering attitudes and perspectives, instilling society with a new spirit of freedom for service, and the hard work of loyal citizens. This allowed the Pauline faction to act as a leaven within society and participate in the ongoing process of God's new creation.[12] From this perspective, Paul affirmed the conservative and bourgeois morals of the society in which he lived, but he rooted those morals within a new spirit and ended up reforming society.[13] Here, in nascent form, we discover the "Protestant work ethic" described by Max Weber as "the Spirit of Capitalism."[14]

While I will reserve most points of criticism until later, it is worth noting how the scholars in this camp often apply the language of "revolution" and "radicality" to their conservative readings of Paul. Herman Ridderbos,

11. Schreiner, *Paul*, 414.

12. See Bultmann, *Existence and Faith*, 308; Käsemann, *New Testament Questions*, 211; Ridderbos, *Paul*, 317; Schreiner, *Paul*, 438.

13. The argument that Pauline ethics differ more in terms of motivation than content from the ethics proposed by Second Temple Judaism, especially in the diaspora, and by Greco-Roman culture more generally, has often been repeated by scholars writing about Pauline ethics. For a discussion of what New Testament scholars do in this regard, see Horrell, *Solidarity and Difference*, 12–15, 19–24. Horrell concludes: "at a number of points, the content of Paul's moral exhortation exhibits similarity with, and probably the influence of, contemporary Greco-Roman as well as Jewish moral traditions. Nor is it to be denied, in contrast, that Paul gives to his ethical instruction a distinctively Christian, theological basis and motivation. What remains open to debate is the *extent* to which this theological basis shapes and forms the character and content of Pauline ethics, or, put the other way around, the extent to which they reproduce what was morally commonplace or presume a model essentially derived from other ancient traditions" (24). In his subsequent exploration (155–63), Horrell concludes that Paul provides "distinctive motivations," but "the substance of what Paul considers right and wrong, and the language in which he expresses what is vice and what is virtue, represent not a particular discourse which distinguishes his ethics from those of 'the world' but rather, to a considerable extent, a shared moral vocabulary" (162–63).

14. Weber, *Protestant Work Ethic*. Developed further by Tawney, *Religion and the Rise*.

having stressed that "[t]he gospel does not make its appearance in the form of a new social program," goes on to say that his understanding of Paul's gospel still has "'revolutionary' implications" and carries "deep and radical social significance."[15] Similarly, Thomas Schreiner's reading of Paul stresses that Christians must "avoid trying to make earth into heaven" and that "any utopian schemes must be jettisoned," because Paul "was no revolutionary—the social pattern of the Greco-Roman society is maintained."[16] However, he then goes on to write that Paul's understanding of social status (specifically, its ephemerality) is, itself, "revolutionary."[17] Ben Witherington and Gordon Fee similarly apply the language of radicality to readings of Paul that uphold a generally conservative ethic (Witherington) or almost entirely neglect politics (Fee).[18] No wonder, then, that Emil Brunner—who also reads Paul as a politically conservative agent of reform—can speak of Paul "revolutionizing the idea of revolution"![19]

There are various ways of understanding the use of this language. On the one hand, one could observe that scholars in all camps—including those who see Paul as affirming the status quo, supporting patriarchal structures, and admiring the Roman Empire as a force of stability which restrains the forces of evil (as some interpret 2 Thess 2:1–12, wherein the empire is seen as that which keeps the "man of evil" at bay[20])—recognize that there is something fundamentally revolutionary and radical at work in Paul's life and writings. Despite many scholars' best efforts to root Paul thoroughly within the conservative camp, it appears that he cannot quite be made to fit.

On the other hand, one could read the use of this language by conservative scholars as an act of overcoding, wherein the coding (i.e., the application of meaning or value) of a particular discursive field is applied to the code of another discursive field in order to weaken alternative readings or uses of that discourse.[21] Stated more simply, the use of this language

15. Ridderbos, *Paul*, 317.

16. Schreiner, *Paul*, 412–14, 244.

17. Schreiner, *Paul*, 434.

18. Witherington, *Paul Quest*, 202; Fee, *God's Empowering Presence*, 8.

19. Brunner, *Eternal Hope*, 61–65.

20. See, for example, Cadoux, *Early Church and the World*, 88–89.

21. For more on this, see Deleuze and Guattari, *Anti-Oedipus*, 260 and throughout. Here, Deleuze and Guattari are engaging the writings of Michel Foucault—see especially *Archaeology of Knowledge*.

can be understood as an ideological tool used to subvert or dominate other readings of Paul. Here, the use of revolutionary or radical language is applied to subvert the ways in which Marxist readings of Paul began to use those terms in relation to the early Jesus movement.[22] Adding to this is the seeming susceptibility of scholars to the temptation to appear to be "radical" or "cutting-edge" to their students, their peers, and themselves. Whatever the case may be, when people on all sides of a debate are using the same words ("radical!" "revolutionary!"), we must pause and question why and to what purpose those terms are being deployed.

The Conservative Paul as a Negative Influence on Society

There are other scholars who affirm that Paul was a teacher of moral and political conservatism but deny him any revolutionary impact. Instead, they see him as a person who, at best, blunted the radical edge of the early Jesus movement and, at worst, deliberately oppressed already marginalized populations in order to build churches that were actively invested in reproducing the dynamics of an oppressive status quo. Thus, for example, in the readings proposed by both Gerd Theissen and Elizabeth Schüssler-Fiorenza, Paul is seen as ignoring the radical character of Jesus's organizing and tempering the more radical early traditions (whose social implications were either rejected or interiorized), in order to affirm a conservative ethic.[23] For Theissen, Paul's attitude toward these things is the result of Paul being "fully integrated" in the "political texture of the Roman Empire," which leads him to accept its structures "without reservation."[24] In Theissen's view, this is necessary because "moderate forms of assimilation" permitted early Christianity to sustain its viability (a viability which the "prophetic radicalism" of the movement jeopardized).[25]

---

22. For an obvious example of such an ideological tool at work, recall how, in 2004, *TIME Magazine* named George W. Bush the person of the year and dubbed him an "American Revolutionary" and a "radical" (Gibbs and Dickerson, "Person of the Year"). Of course, there is nothing at all revolutionary about George Bush. Rather, *TIME* is both appropriating and undercutting the whole discourse of "revolution" by using that language. One cannot help but wonder if the same thing is occurring in many so-called "revolutionary" readings of Paul.

23. Theissen, *Fortress Introduction*, 53; Schüssler-Fiorenza, *In Memory of Her*, 192, 218–21.

24. Theissen, *Social Setting of Pauline Christianity*, 36.

25. Theissen, *Religion of the Earliest Churches*, 36.

Schüssler-Fiorenza sees things in a less positive light. While she praises Paul for continuing the early Christian tradition of speaking about equality and freedom, she argues that Paul corrupts these notions in order to create a "Christian patriarchalism" and a "kyriarchical" form of community based on a rigid hierarchy, wherein women in particular are marginalized and even vilified.[26] Thus, rather than seeing the cross of the Anointed as a political event, Paul uses it to justify the suffering of the oppressed and to encourage silence and submission, as he seeks to consolidate his own power and authority.[27] However, while some scholars conclude that Paul had ill intent, Schüssler-Fiorenza argues that Paul had good intentions, as the practice of wholesale emancipation would have been detrimental to the advance of "the gospel" and the way in which "his churches" appeared to outsiders.[28]

Of course, there are other readings of Paul that apply criticisms like these to other areas of Paul's social interactions—Paul the oppressor of slaves, Paul the misogynist, Paul the racist xenophobe, Paul the authoritarian, and so on. Indeed, most people outside of Christian circles tend to view Paul in this way—thanks in no small part to the oppressive, enslaving, misogynistic, racist, xenophobic, and authoritarian actions and attitudes of many people who claim to follow in his footsteps today. To provide an example of one such perspective, it is worth mentioning the thoughtful work of the Jewish scholar, Daniel Boyarin. According to Boyarin, Paul is motivated by a "Hellenistic desire for the One" and operates with the admirable intention of founding "a non-differentiated, non-hierarchical humanity."[29] However, Paul's project is deeply flawed because this leads to the eradication of cultural specificity and achieves little more than integration into the dominant culture, even as equality is confused with sameness.[30] Therefore, Boyarin concludes, this Pauline universalism fits comfortably with the coercive and racialized violence of the Roman imperial order.[31]

---

26. Schüssler-Fiorenza, *In Memory of Her*, 223–24, 233, 236; Schüssler-Fiorenza, *Rhetoric and Ethic*, 119; Schüssler-Fiorenza, "Paul and the Politics," 40–57.

27. Schüssler-Fiorenza, *In Memory of Her*, 199, 231–33; Schüssler-Fiorenza, *Rhetoric and Ethic*, 119, 121.

28. Schüssler-Fiorenza, *In Memory of Her*, 207, 233.

29. Boyarin, *Radical Jew*, 7–8.

30. Boyarin, *Radical Jew*, 8–9.

31. Boyarin, *Radical Jew*, 228–33.

PAUL'S FOCUS ON THE INTERNAL AND SPIRITUAL FREEDOM

Given this general conservative understanding of Paulinism, one naturally asks how to make sense of frequent references to freedom. One thinks especially of passages like Gal 5:1 ("for freedom [the Anointed] has set us free. Stand firm, therefore, and do not submit again to a yoke of slavery") and 2 Cor 3:17 ("Now the Lord is the Spirit, and where the Spirit of the Lord is there is freedom"), and asks how these fit with an apostle said to affirm the oppressive status quo of the Roman Empire. The proposed solution is that Paul was speaking of internal, personal, and spiritual freedom (or detachment) and was most definitely not speaking of the experience of external, material, and tangible freedom (or engagement).[32] Freedom is thus understood as freedom from "the world," "sin," and "death" (which are, themselves, understood in a strictly religious or spiritual way) and not as related to one's historical circumstances.[33] Furthermore, the freedom described in Gal 3:28 is found in one's spiritual status *before God*, which has little impact on one's material status *before other people*. In this view, one must continue to both follow and respect the Rule of Law even as one maintains an internal sense of superiority over such worldly things.[34] Thus, Pauline freedom is the freedom of religious individualism that finds expression in the religious sphere, with no consideration of freedom or equality in the political realm.[35] As Günther Bornkamm aptly states: "Faith is ours in the present . . . life in the future."[36]

Understood in this sense, Paul preaches freedom not only from "sin" and "death," but also from the (Jewish) law or "Judaism" understood especially as a failed form of "legalistic works' righteousness" (and never associated with the Rule of Law as such)—a view that is, at least in part, indebted

32. See, for example, Bruce, *Apostle of the Heart*, 18; Bultmann, *Primitive Christianity*, 207; Keck, *Paul and His Letters*, 57; Schoeps, *Paul*, 211; Schweitzer, *Mysticism of Paul the Apostle*, 312; Troeltsch, *Social Teachings*, 1:77, 83–85; Richardson, *Paul's Ethic of Freedom*, 99–125.

33. See Bruce, *Apostle of the Heart*, 18; Case, *Social Origins of Christianity*, 128–39; Conzelmann, *Outline of the Theology*, 15–16; Weiss, *Earliest Christianity*, 1:192.

34. See Bruce, *Apostle of the Heart*, 224–26; Keck, *Paul and His Letters*, 54; Bultmann, *Primitive Christianity*, 205–6; Dibelius, *Paul*, 90, 104.

35. See Troeltsch, *Social Teachings*, 1:70–76.

36. Bornkamm, *Paul*, 226–27; Bornkamm, *Early Christian Experience*, 81. Thus, Conzelmann describes "the Church" as those set free under the lordship of Jesus, but he then asserts that Jesus's lordship is only visible in the propositional confession that "Jesus is Lord" (*Outline of the Theology*, 255–56).

to the ongoing influence of Martin Luther and his commentary on Galatians.[37] Thus, Donald Coggan refers to Paul as both a "Revolutionary" and a "Freedom-Fighter" because, according to Coggan, he liberates the personality from the restraints imposed by the Jewish law.[38] The result of this—for Coggan and many others—is the liberation of the individual from the supposed legalism of the (Jewish) law.[39] Furthermore, for scholars such as Stauffer, Paul can also be seen as liberating the early Jesus loyalists from the illusions sustained by Jewish messianic utopianism.[40] In other words, Paul liberates people from their hope for (tangible) liberation.

PAUL'S FOCUS ON AN IMMINENT END AND DISREGARD FOR THE WORLD

A further rationale for this view of Paul as a conservative is the argument that Paul gave political, social, and material areas of life little (if any) attention because he believed the world would soon end. Scholars in this camp argue that Paul believed in the imminent and triumphant return of Jesus, which would result in the cataclysmic end of the material realm and the full arrival of the kingdom of heaven. Paul therefore focused on saving souls, without getting distracted by more mundane things or getting caught up in an over-realized eschatology.[41] Thus, in a revealing passage, Rudolph Bultmann writes:

> The new people of God has no real history, for it is the community of the end-time, an eschatological phenomenon. How could it have a history now when the world-time is finished and the end is imminent! . . . Therefore neither the Christian community, nor the individuals within it have any responsibility for the present world and its order . . . no social programme can be developed but only negative ethics of abstinence and sanctification.[42]

37. Luther, *Galatians*. For a recent examination of this Lutheran reading of Paul, see Westerholm, *Perspectives Old and New*.

38. Coggan, *Paul*, 133–35.

39. Coggan, *Paul*, 137–54; cf., Grant, *Early Christianity and Society*, 20; Longenecker, *Paul, Apostle of Liberty*, x; Weiss, *Earliest Christianity*, 2:564–65.

40. As Stauffer argues in *Christ and the Caesars*, 196–97.

41 See, for example, Keck, *Paul and His Letters*, 93; Pilgrim, *Uneasy Neighbors*, 8–22, 33; Weiss, *Earliest Christianity*, 1:76–77, 2:594; Troeltsch, *Social Teachings*, 1:77; Bultmann, *Primitive Christianity*, 207–8; Schreiner, *Paul*, 412.

42. Bultmann, "History and Eschatology," 36–37.

It is here that we first begin to observe the foundational importance of eschatology for our understanding of Pauline ethics and politics.

PAUL WAS POLITICALLY CONSERVATIVE
BECAUSE HE WAS SOCIALLY POWERLESS

While the scholars mentioned thus far have tended to focus on theological reasons for Paul's conservatism, some scholars emphasize a sociological element. This group argues that Paul was primarily addressing a politically powerless minority within the Roman Empire—a group for whom the only realistic political option was to keep quiet and try to impress the authorities. To try and do otherwise would have been both useless and suicidal.[43] Therefore, when confronted with the choice of either living on the terms set by the political powers or dying in an effort to violently overthrow those powers, Paul strategically chose the former option and rejected the latter.[44]

SEYOON KIM ON PAUL AND POLITICS

Before we conclude this section, it is worth mentioning Seyoon Kim's contribution to this portrait of Paul.[45] Most of the pivotal voices in the development of this perspective (Troeltsch, Bultmann, Conzelmann, etc.) predate a considerable amount of research pertaining to the Pauline faction, the Greco-Roman world, and Pauline interaction with Roman imperialism. In recent years, many conservative scholars have maintained their position by strategically ignoring these developments or by treating them as though they are not even worth engaging. Kim takes a different approach. He states he was initially impressed with the scholarship that has been building around a counter-imperial presentation of Paul, and therefore chose to engage the best-known voices presenting this perspective.[46] In the end, however, he is unconvinced, and therefore reaffirms the conservative presentation of Paul.

43. See, for example, Bauckham, *Bible in Politics*, 3; Coggan, *Paul*, 156–58; Deissmann, *Light from the Ancient East*, 339–40; Dunn, *Theology of Paul the Apostle*, 679–80. As mentioned above, Theissen and Schüssler-Fiorenza also highlight this point.

44. Bauckham, *Bible in Politics*, 3; Bryan, *Render to Caesar*, 92–93; Dunn, *Theology of Paul the Apostle*, 680.

45. Kim, *Christ and Caesar*.

46. Kim, *Christ and Caesar*, xi.

Kim begins by presenting what he considers to be the major methodological problems of counter-imperial readings. First, he argues that such readings are driven by a "parallelomania" that is eager to find overlaps between Paul's language and the language of the imperial ideology, even when the passages where that language is found show no clear anti-imperial intention.[47] Second, Kim argues that such counter-imperial readings are based on deductions rooted in faulty assumptions. He particularly criticizes the following moves: stressing the all-pervasive nature of the Roman imperial cult; rooting Paul in a Jewish apocalypticism that was opposed to empires; assuming the memory of Jesus's crucifixion would be understood as anti-Roman; thinking that the language of *ekklesia* is inherently political; seeing Paul's refusal of patronage in Corinth as more generally anti-imperial; and seeing Paul's persecution by the ruling authorities as related to transgression of the imperial order.[48] Kim challenges the validity of all these "assumptions" (although not in much detail) and accuses those who operate with them of engaging in proof-texting and of "desperately" appealing to some sort of "coding" in order to try and force Paul to say what Paul never actually intended.[49]

Having addressed methodology, Kim goes on to mention several other factors that make an anti-imperial reading of Paul difficult. First, Kim argues that Paul—especially when compared with John's Apocalypse—neither makes specific criticisms of the empire nor explicitly references the imperial cult (or any conflicts with it). Here, Kim draws on Rom 13 to argue that Paul sees the Roman authorities in a positive light.[50] Second, adding to the suggestion that Paul saw the authorities positively, Kim argues that Paul had positive interactions with the Roman courts before which he was falsely charged. According to Kim, the observation that Paul is repeatedly acquitted by the courts (according to Acts) demonstrates that Paul's gospel is politically innocuous.[51] Third, Kim argues that Paul was driven by a belief in the imminent return of Jesus, and that this led Paul to: (a) maintain the status quo; (b) focus on preaching the (spiritual) message of the gospel without getting entangled in material things; (c) focus on persevering under suffering rather than changing the situation that caused suffering;

47. Kim, *Christ and Caesar*, 28–30.
48. Kim, *Christ and Caesar*, 30–31.
49. Kim, *Christ and Caesar*, 31–33.
50. Kim, *Christ and Caesar*, 34–43.
51. Kim, *Christ and Caesar*, 43–50.

and (d) pursue transcendental salvation.[52] Finally, Kim points out that anti-imperial readings of Paul run aground on the fact that the early Church did not read Paul in this way. Therefore, Kim concludes, "there is no anti-imperial intent to be ascertained in the Pauline epistles." Instead, Paul calls others to "live a life of quietude, earning the respect of the non-Christian community."[53] According to Kim, the "stumbling block" or "offense" caused by Paul's gospel is precisely that it offers no political stumbling block and is completely inoffensive—the "scandal of the cross" is that it is not politically scandalous![54]

The Conservative or Spiritual Paul— Questions and Criticisms

Having summarized the main arguments employed by those who understand Paul as a conservative and spiritual voice, it is worth raising a few questions and points of criticism before turning to the next position. First, one must ask how a characterization of Paul as focused exclusively on spiritual matters can be said to make sense within the first-century contexts in which Paul lived. Divisions between religion and politics or between social engagement and spirituality are distinct characteristics of the post-Enlightenment, post-industrial world of modernity. It could well be that the retrojection of such divisions into Paul's pre-Enlightenment, pre-industrial, and pre-modern world is to make a fundamental methodological error.[55]

The same set of questions and criticisms apply to those who wish to talk about a Paul who is focused upon *internal* freedom, *individual* salvation, and *personal* detachment. Again, such a view of one's self or others reflects the mentality of the modern and postmodern eras. It does not capture the common view within Paul's contexts, wherein the external, communal, and corporate areas of life were far more significant than the internal, individual, and personal.

52. Kim, *Christ and Caesar*, 50–60.

53. Kim, *Christ and Caesar*, 68, 71.

54. Kim, *Christ and Caesar*, 58, 201.

55. Indeed, given the nitty-gritty, day-to-day matters addressed in the Pauline letters—matters related to everything from food and sex to community integration and economic matters—it seems obvious that the Pauline faction saw spirituality as intimately connected to daily life and the activities associated with it.

Similarly, to see Pauline talk of freedom as limited to freedom from the so-called "Jewish law" raises the question of how one understands that law—and whether or not current readers of Paul are imposing post-Reformation lenses onto Paul's Second Temple Judean context and thereby mistaking the Judaism(s) of Paul's day for medieval Roman Catholicism as understood via Luther and Calvin. Indeed, as scholars such as Krister Stendahl, E. P. Sanders, and other advocates of the "New Perspective on Paul" have demonstrated, it seems unlikely that Paul and other first-century Judeans were plagued by guilty consciences or longing for freedom from a legalistic form of works' righteousness.[56] Furthermore, that so many of the Christians who argue against the supposed "legalism" of the "Jewish Law" are keen to affirm and enforce the contemporary Rule of Law makes one wonder how much their position on "Paul and the Law" remained rooted in the history of Christian anti-Semitism.

Related to this point, one must ask whether some of the scholars in this camp have a well-informed understanding of Second Temple Judean eschatologies. Is positing an imminent, cataclysmic world-end consistent with views that would be held by people like Paul and his coworkers, or are later eschatologies being imposed upon them? If later eschatologies are being imposed, how might this affect how we read and understand what the Pauline faction has to say about ethical and political matters?

Two further methodological concerns have been mentioned previously but bear repeating here. The first is the way in which several scholars read the universally agreed-upon non-contested letters through the lenses of the deutero-Pauline epistles.[57] The second is the way in which many of these scholars simply assume that Pauline language—terms such as "the cross" or "faith," "lord," "gospel," "*parousia*," and so on—is theological or spiritual language. Again, while this understanding of Pauline language may seem obvious to contemporary readers, it may well be the case that those terms carry overtones and meanings that are not as noticeable to those of us who are two thousand years removed from Paul.

One wonders, therefore, what picture of Paul might result if we: (a) do not posit a divide between religion and politics in Paul's day; (b) accept that people in Paul's day were focused on the external, communal,

56 See Stendahl, *Paul Among Jews and Gentiles,* 1–96; Sanders, *Paul and Palestinian Judaism,* 33–238; Wright, *What Saint Paul Really Said,* 113–33; Dunn, *Theology of Paul the Apostle,* 128–61.

57. Note, for example, that only three of the ten passages quoted at the opening of this section come from non-contested Pauline Epistles.

and corporate elements of life; (c) examine Second Temple Judaism(s) on its own terms, especially in relation to eschatology and the Law; (d) do not allow our reading of the non-contested letters to be determined by the deutero-Pauline epistles; and (e) look at the resonance Pauline terms had in their contexts, rather than ours.

Paul, the Founder of a Christian Subculture—Summary

An alternative picture of Paul presents him as the founder of a Christian subculture. This is probably the presentation of Paul that has the most support among contemporary scholars (whom I would mostly identify as "liberal"). This camp tends to focus on the culturally distinctive ways in which the Pauline faction approached matters related to relationships, values, and ethics in the communities associated with them. These scholars draw attention to the particular (though not always entirely unique) ways in which Paul addresses ethnicity, gender, and social rank or status. Significantly, from this perspective, these matters tend to be treated as cultural rather than political matters. This is one of the key ways in which scholars in this camp differ from those who read Paul in a more counter-imperial way.

This perspective often employs Gal 3:28—"There is no longer [Judean] or Greek, there is no longer slave or free, there is no longer male and female; for all of you are one in [Anointed] Jesus"—as a foundation or summary text. The following passages are also frequently referenced.

On ethnicity and race:

- Rom 1–3. The leveling of the playing field between Judeans and people from other regions due to the universality of sin, climaxing in Rom 3:29–30: "Or is God the God of [Judeans] only? Is he not the God of [foreign nationals] also? Yes, of [foreign nationals] also, since God is one; and [God] will justify the circumcised on the ground of faith and the uncircumcised through that same faith."

- Rom 9–11. The story of salvation for both Judeans and people from other nations.

- Rom 14:1—15:13. The call to respect one another's diets and calendars, and for Judeans and other nationalities to welcome each other.

- 1 Cor 1:18–25. The leveling of the playing field between Judeans, Greeks, and people from other regions due to the way the crucified

Anointed overturns both their expectations. This leads Paul to write: "For [Judeans] demand signs and Greeks desire wisdom, but we proclaim the Anointed crucified, a stumbling block to [Judeans] and foolishness to [foreign nationals], but to those who are called, both [Judeans] and Greeks, [the Anointed] the power of God and the wisdom of God" (1 Cor 1:22–24).

- 1 Cor 10:23–33. The call to respect various diets and share in table fellowship across ethnic boundaries.

- Galatians. The sustained emphasis that both Judeans *as* Judeans and foreign nationals *as* foreign nationals are fully welcomed into the people of God now (re)constituted around Jesus the Anointed.

- Phil 3:2–9. A passionate and polemical passage emphasizing that both Judeans and people of other nationalities are welcomed into the people of God.

On gender:

- Various passages mentioning Paul's female coworkers, female deacons, and female apostles. In several of these, Paul not only ascribes a position of authority to women but he also speaks of them as his equals. It is possible that some of them may have served as patrons to him.

  » Rom 16:1–15. Greetings sent to several significant women (Prisca is also mentioned in 1 Cor 16:19 and Acts 18:1–3, 18–19).

  » Phil 4:2–3. The prominent role of Euodia and Syntyche.

  » Acts 16:11–15. The importance of Lydia.

  » Acts 17:4, 12. The mention of "leading women."

  » Acts 21:9. Prophetic offices exercised by the four daughters of Agabus.

- 1 Cor 7:3–4. When speaking of marriage, Paul does not simply grant a husband authority over his wife's body, but also grants a wife authority over her husband's body.

- 1 Cor 7:10–11. Paul urges both wives and husbands not to divorce their spouses (which, in Paul's day, was a harder injunction for men to follow than women).

- 1 Cor 7:39. While women often had their marriage determined by (male) family members, Paul states that a widow is "free to marry anyone she wishes."

On social rank and status:

- Phil 2:5–11. A central passage, in which the Philippians are called to imitate the downward mobility and surrender of status exemplified by Jesus.

- Rom 12:16; 1 Cor 1:18—2:5; 4:8–13; 9:19–23; 12:22–26; 2 Cor 4:7–12; 4:16—5:4; 6:4–10; 11:16–33; 12:10; Phil 3:4–8; 1 Thess 2:1–2. Paul often provides himself as an example of one who has pursued a Jesus-like surrender of status, emphasizing that he has embraced folly, suffering, and shame—in the company of others who are foolish and lowly—for the cause of the Anointed.

- Philemon. Paul calls Philemon to treat his former slave, Onesimus, not as a slave but as a brother—thereby overturning the underpinnings of slavery within the Christian community.

- 1 Cor 7:21. Several scholars in this camp contest the conservative translation of this passage as encouraging slaves not to pursue freedom if given the opportunity. Noting difficulties with translating the Greek in this passage, these scholars argue that Paul is actually encouraging slaves to pursue freedom if given the opportunity.

- 1 Cor 11:17–34. The Corinthians are rebuked for (re)instating social divisions between the wealthy and the poor, and between those with higher and lower status, when celebrating the Lord's Supper.

There are two things worth noting about this list of passages. First, both the number of passages and the length of some of these passages significantly outweigh the key passages employed by those who appeal to Paul as a socio-political conservative. Second, with the exception of a few references from Acts, all of the passages come from the non-disputed letters.

Based on these passages, scholars in this camp conclude that Paul was developing a subculture in which distinctly egalitarian relationships of love and mutuality overturned a number of social norms and conventions. However, the focus is almost entirely internal to the "community of faith"— there is little interest expressed in either spreading these new standards into society more broadly or of confronting the dominant values in any way. Thus, Leander Keck, a pivotal figure in scholarship related to Pauline ethics, argues that Paul's focus is solely on "intra-communal issues," though Keck notes that this must also impact the way in which a person acts "extra-communally."[58] Specifically, Keck argues that the primary extra-communal goals of "Paul's churches" were to make a good impression on others and "participate in community life as responsible citizens."[59] In a similar vein, Margaret MacDonald asserts that Paul's communities existed as part of a "conversionist sect" that was set apart from the evil world. They were, there-fore, not "protest groups," but rather groups that maintained the existing social order out of their twin desires to be separate and to maintain social respectability.[60] Likewise, J. Christiaan Beker argues that Paul understands "the Church" as a "beachhead," holding values that have the potential to be revolutionary but that do not meet this revolutionary potential because the focus is on the "internal religious-social life" of the church rather than influencing the social institutions of Paul's world.[61] Consequently, Paul exhibits a "social conservatism" that does not extend the "ecclesial revo-lution" but rather demonstrates "religious accommodation to the social sphere."[62] The result of this, according to Douglas Harink's reading of one such understanding of Paul, is a "revolutionary subordination" wherein a "Christoform culture" is created as a part of a new "social project" that fo-cuses especially on the mutual accommodation of Jews and gentiles to one another.[63] It should be noted that these are statements made by scholars who choose to even acknowledge the possibility of Paul engaging the politi-cal order. Others, such as Richard Longenecker in his book *New Testament Social Ethics for Today*, do not even raise the political issue but focus solely on matters such race ("the cultural mandate"), slavery ("the social man-date"), and gender ("the sexual mandate").[64] In contrast to the bourgeois conservative Paul, this might be considered the bourgeois liberal Paul.

Paul's eschatology and the social status of the members of "Paul's churches" play an important role in supporting this view. Regarding social

---

58. Keck, *Paul and His Letters*, 79–80, 90.

59. Keck, *Paul and His Letters*, 90.

60. MacDonald, *Pauline Churches*, 37–42.

61. Beker, *Paul the Apostle*, 318–23.

62. Beker, *Paul the Apostle*, 325–26.

63. Harink, *Paul Among the Postliberals*, 148–49, 213, 223–24.

64. Longenecker, *New Testament Social Ethics*. See also Matera's take on Paul's apoliti-cal morality which is said to be focused upon linking the individual to the community of faith in *New Testament Ethics*.

status, Adolf Deissmann argues that "political interest and political activity were on the whole remote from the class to which [Paul] belonged."[65] Consequently, instead of pursuing political change, Paul developed a cult that exhibited "a new moral earnestness."[66] Connecting this to eschatology, Deissmann argues that this new earnestness was due in part to the expectation of the Anointed's imminent *parousia*.[67] Charles Cousar follows this line of thought, arguing that Paul's churches were likely too insignificant to be interested in converting or influencing the structures of the Roman Empire, and instead focused upon defining themselves as "God's eschatological vanguard" within the world.[68] The present order is understood as insignificant and fleeting, so the church must simply begin to embody the new order within itself as the old passes away.[69]

Like some scholars who view Paul as a conservative, some scholars in this camp argue that Paul's intra-communal and subcultural focus still ended up having a positive impact upon society more broadly. Ben Witherington, for example, argues that Paul was "placing the leaven of the gospel in a particular subculture in the Greco-Roman world" so that the broader structures of society would eventually be "transformed by grace within the context of the Christian community," transforming society as a whole.[70] Beker makes a similar point when he argues that the church was a "seed for social reform" that created pockets of a new lifestyle that would go on to penetrate society.[71]

Paul, the Founder of a Christian Subculture— Questions and Criticisms

The strength of this position should not be denied. It is firmly rooted in the non-contested letters, and it finds support in a good many lengthy passages. In my opinion, it convincingly demonstrates that the early assemblies of Jesus loyalists associated with Paul and his coworkers were creating and

65. Deissmann, *Light from the Ancient East*, 339–40.

66. Deissmann, *Light from the Ancient East*, 390.

67. Deissmann, *Light from the Ancient East*, 398.

68. Cousar, *Letters of Paul*, 141–45.

69 Cousar, *Letters of Paul*, 160.

70. Witherington, *Paul Quest*, 174. Witherington's presentation of Paul straddles the line between this position and the one explored previously.

71. Beker, *Paul the Apostle*, 236.

implementing new standards and values related to ethnicity, gender, and social status. However, it is worth posing a few critical questions about this perspective.

First, one must question the divide that is created between the "social and cultural" and the "economic and political." To what extent can groups like the assemblies of Jesus loyalists remain apolitical when they are exhibiting such subcultural norms and practices? What is the dividing line between a subculture that focuses on its own distinct identity and a counterculture that actively subverts and resists the dominant culture of Greco-Roman society? Given the purported accumulation of alternative practices in these assemblies—and given the ways in which racialized, gendered, and class-based forms of oppression were deeply embedded in Greco-Roman socioeconomic political, and familial practices—does it make better sense of Paulinism to understand it as both culturally distinct and politically subversive? Again, one wonders if contemporary notions of the divide between "culture" and "politics" are being imposed on a context where those things were much more intimately related.

Further, even if one grants the poor and marginalized status of most or all Jesus loyalists and pairs that with the expectation of Jesus's imminent return, must these things lead to an apolitical praxis? Is there not a long history of political resistance among people experiencing poverty and oppression?[72] Although a broad socioeconomic group may have felt powerless, could not an event occur—like one taken to be the outpouring of the eschatological Spirit of Life—that would lead that same group to gain a new sense of power and pursue more active engagement? Similarly, must the expectation of an imminent *parousia* lead to political apathy?[73] If the assemblies associated with the Pauline faction understood themselves as an eschatological vanguard, then is it not just as likely that they would seek to see God's new creation break in to all areas of life? If God is Lord of *all*, and the eschaton was to bring the new creation of *all* things, is it not just as

72. See, for example: Scott, *Domination and the Arts*; Scott, *Weapons of the Weak*; Venturi, *Roots of Revolution*; James, *Black Jacobins*; Bloom and Martin, *Black Against Empire*; Hill, *500 Years of Resistance*; Grubačić and O'Hearn, *Living at the Edges*. Think also of the various liberation theologies that have arisen among, or in conversation with, poor and marginalized populations around the world. Various Indigenous resurgence movements on Turtle Island—from the Oceti Sakowin Camp, to the Unist'ot'en Camp, to Idle No More (to name but a few)—also illustrate this quite vividly.

73. One only need to think of more recent groups (like the Branch Davidians) to realize that the sense of an imminent apocalypse may very well be tied to extreme political action.

likely that the early Jesus loyalists desired to see that new creation occurring in all realms of life and in the lives of all people—even if the time remaining was short? Arguing that Paul had no desire to get bogged down in the technicalities of political structures may miss the point that Paul longed for the day when God would be "all in all" (1 Cor 15:28) and expressed that longing by actively working to attain that goal. We need to be careful not to leap to conclusions when a plurality of conclusions is possible based on the evidence put forward.

Second, we need to remember that Paul was pursuing these alternate values within the context of first-century, Greco-Roman urban centers, wherein the lives of Jesus loyalists would continually overlap with the daily religious and political lives of others. Through activities ranging from sharing accommodations in crowded tenement buildings, to sharing work spaces, to sharing (or refusing to share) in city-wide politico-religious festivals, the lives of Jesus loyalists could not help but be intertwined with the lives of others.[74] Given this context, it may be unrealistic to think that the Pauline faction was able to live as those "set apart" and immersed in their own distinct subculture. Elements of conflict, confrontation, challenge, and resistance would likely have emerged almost immediately in such a context, and one would expect to find something of that reflected in the Pauline letters. Of course, some might respond by saying that this is precisely what one *does* find when the Pauline factions tell Jesus loyalists to try and make a good impression on outsiders, but this seems like rather weak advice and an uncharacteristically poorly thought-out response—as though Paul and his co-authors are saying: "Embody these values in practices that others will find horribly offensive . . . but, oh, try to make a good impression."[75]

Third, we must note that even if the Pauline faction was trying to build a subculture, their work and the assemblies associated with them would be taken as unmistakably political by outsiders in general and by the Roman and civic authorities in particular. This becomes apparent when one

74. The notion that the early assemblies of Jesus loyalists met in crowded tenement buildings is strengthened by Horrell's astute observation that in 1 Cor 10:32, Paul and his coworkers presume that "unbelieving outsiders may well be present during the worship meetings of the congregation, including (most probably) the Lord's supper celebration" (*Solidarity and Difference*, 261).

75. Many scholars emphasize this point about trying to make a good impression on outsiders (see, for example, Sanders, *Paul: The Apostle's Life*, 188; Horrell, *Solidarity and Difference*, 257–61) but they do not resolve how Paul and his coworkers also advise local assemblies to do many things that problematize this approach and that exacerbate conflicts with outsiders.

contextualizes some of their activities. For example, engaging in weekly or daily meetings—outside of the context of groups that were legally permitted to do so—was seen as a political threat to the Roman Empire and was officially illegal.[76] To proclaim a crucified slave as the true Lord of all (as per Phil 2:5–11) was to elevate a person Rome had condemned as a criminal—more specifically, as a terrorist—to a status higher than Caesar. I personally cannot see how any member of Paul's society could have missed the political ramifications of this. Additionally, moving beyond Paul to Acts, we should also note that the very title given to the early members of the movement associated with Jesus—*Christianoi*—is a political title. In all likelihood, this title was given to the Jesus loyalists by the imperial authorities of Antioch in order to mark the emergence of a new political faction. That is, just as the terms "Herodians" and "Caesareans" reflected the political allegiances of those who saw Herod or Caesar as their Lords, the term "Christians" reflected the political allegiance of those who recognized the Anointed as their Lord.[77] As often happens with minority groups that are perceived as—at the very least—potentially deviant, the name was probably coined in a pejorative manner by outsiders and then adopted as an act of defiance by those who refused to be shamed by the label "Christ-partisan."[78]

Given these realities, and given Rome's policy of exterminating alternative political movements that made no room for the ideo-theology of Rome, one must ask whether Paul and his coworkers were doing more than simply focusing on cultural issues and ignoring political matters. Perhaps, instead, they were walking the line between political resistance and survival, finding ways to speak that would allow them to get past the censors and

76. This is why the Judeans needed to get a special legal exemption to observe the Sabbath; it is also, as we will see, one of the reasons the Jesus loyalists had a vested interest in remaining connected to the Judean communities.

77. See Dunn, *Beginning from Jerusalem*, 303–5. However, Dunn is cautious about putting too much political significance into this.

78. See Hurtado, *Destroyer of the Gods*, 94–96. Granted, the term "Christian" does not appear in the Pauline letters. However, the emergence of this term for Jesus loyalists in Antioch (see Acts 11:26) probably occurred at a time when Paul was deeply connected with that community (see Dunn, *Beginning from Jerusalem*, 369–75). The term also reappears in Acts 26:28 in a conversation between Paul and Agrippa. The question, then, is this: does the Pauline faction avoid this term because they reject its political overtones or do they avoid this term because they want the Roman authorities to think of their (fundamentally political) work as apolitical—or what? For other examples of this kind of top-down labeling being appropriated in a defiant bottom-up manner, think of feminist uses of the "B" word or the ways in which some Black people use the "N" word.

spies (and any others who felt they might be able to advance themselves by reporting the assemblies).[79] I believe that it is worth trying to understand Paulinism in this way. Therefore, while a great deal of important work has been done by those who view Paul as the founder of a "Christian" sub-culture, I believe this perspective still presents us with an incomplete and fundamentally flawed understanding of what the Pauline faction and the assemblies associated with them were doing.

Finally, before departing from this perspective, it is worth noting that creating a sharp divide between "culture" and "politics"—and then focusing on the cultural instead of the political—is precisely the sort of practice that favors (and is favored by) those who possess political and economic power. All too often, in our context, we turn to "culture" when we feel politically impotent but still wish to engage in activities that feel significant. In the past, when people have felt politically potent, they have thrown up barricades, marched against the police, driven slave-owners off the land, regained stolen wealth from the powerful, reclaimed factories, beheaded monarchs, bombed tsars, blocked pipelines, and changed societies. However, in our present moment (a moment defined by a general bourgeois sense of political helplessness and hopelessness), people create art, deconstruct literature, analyze films, and engage in a whole host of other cultural activities . . . and by doing so maintain the belief that they are, somehow, making a difference. Not surprisingly, it is in this context that cultural readings of Paul have gained prominence—particularly among scholars who are members of the cultural elite but believe themselves to be largely powerless when it comes to political matters. Such readings have only limited liberating potential. Understood in this way, Paul may offer us a greater sense of personal freedom in this-or-that area of our private lives—but by remaining limited to that small sphere, this Paul also ends up trapping us within broader oppressive political structures. We would do well to recall one of the sayings made famous by Second Wave Feminism: "The personal is political."[80] As I hope to demonstrate, the Pauline faction knew this very well. If we forget it, we may end up being blinded to our own bondage to and complicity within oppressive structures.

79. As Jennings says, the letters written by Paul and his coworkers were "a kind of political dynamite that had to be handled with care" (*Outlaw Justice*, 229).

80. See Hanisch's famous essay: "Personal is Political."

The No-Longer-Directly-Applicable Paul—Summary

The third broad perspective on Paul and politics is held by scholars who—being especially concerned with the ongoing relevance of Paulinism—believe that Paul's reflections on matters related to politics or ethics are no longer directly applicable or relevant. The no-longer-directly-applicable Paul tends to be explained in one of three (not mutually exclusive) ways. First, some scholars assert that Paulinism actually has much deeper political implications than Paul himself realized. Second, some believe that Paul provides us with multiple options of how to act politically, so it is up to us to choose which option is most appropriate for our context. Third, others accept Paul's general principles and their theological underpinnings but argue that his specific political teachings and practices should be questioned or rejected.

Paul Did Not Realize the Implications
of His Own Thinking and Writing

Scholars have found various ways to express this first point. Beker argues that Pauline theology contains a great deal of "catalytic power" that, when followed through to its appropriate conclusions, leads to much more radical or subversive (and apocalyptic) sociopolitical implications.[81] Ernst Käsemann makes a similar but distinct point when he argues that Paul and the Jesus loyalists associated with him may have been aware of these political implications but unable to fully develop them due to their low status and lack of power.[82] Keck makes a related point while stressing the eschatological aspect of Paul's thinking: because we no longer adhere to Paul's understanding of an imminent end, and because Paul never sanctified the status quo but instead rejected it in expectation of this end, the foundation has been laid for future readers to be more politically engaged in their historical moments.[83] E. P. Sanders repeats this point: because Paul believed the end was near, "there was not time to remake society." In our day and

---

81. Beker, *Paul's Apocalyptic Gospel*, 111.

82. Käsemann, *New Testament Questions*, 205. This is another example of how our understanding of the socioeconomic status of Paul and the early Jesus loyalists can impact our understanding of the Pauline letters.

83. Keck, *Paul and His Letters*, 93–94. Once again, we see the importance of eschatology in political readings of Paul.

age, however, Pauline theology is "potentially more revolutionary than [Paul] himself, a social conservative, realized."[84] Finally, Joseph Fitzpatrick argues that Paul's perspective as a member of the Roman Empire in the first century simply did not lead him to think in political terms like we do today. Paul, Fitzpatrick argues, would not naturally have thought in terms of social structures, but was focused upon individuals in their day-to-day lives. Consequently, while Paul has prepared the way, it is up to us to extend Paulinism into the structural and political realms.[85] In one way or another, then, each of these scholars suggests that Pauline theology offers at least the potential for more subversive or confrontational political readings in our current context—even if Paul was unaware of those implications within his own context.

Paul Provides Us with Multiple Political Options

This argument—that the texts in question offer multiple, sometimes contradictory, sociopolitical options—is most often applied to the New Testament generally. It can, however, be applied to Paul more specifically, especially in light of the work of Heikki Räisänen.[86] Thus, while scholars such as Richard Bauckham and Warren Carter argue that the New Testament as a whole acts as a resource that provides various political options, Philip Esler applies this line of thinking to Paul in particular, writing: "With some features of Paul's thought we need to retain our critical faculties and possibly reject features of his message inappropriate for our time."[87] Robin Scroggs presses this point further and argues that Paul may be self-contradictory, thereby

84. Sanders, *Paul*, 12, 106. A point he repeats about Paul in his latest book (*Paul: The Apostle's Life*, 211), although in that book he does not suggest that we may want to move beyond Paul's so-called "social conservatism" in our context.

85. Fitzpatrick, *Paul*, 26–31, 90. Of all those mentioned in this section, I find Fitzpatrick the least convincing. He argues that Paul was focused upon "the individual, while it is up to us to apply this focus to the broader community." To me, this seems to be an odd reversal. Paul, as a first-century diaspora Judean, was surely much more of a community-focused person than most (or all?) of those who have lived in the highly individualized twentieth-century West. To discover an individualism within Paulinism (even if to overcome it) seems to be projecting our own paradigms onto Paulinism, instead of reading it within its own context.

86. See Räisänen, *Paul and the Law*.

87. See Bauckham, *Bible in Politics*; Carter, *Roman Empire*, 143; Esler, *New Testament Theology*, 282.

providing the reader with no clear or obvious way forward.[88] As a result, Paulinists are left making decisions that will sometimes contradict parts of Paulinism itself. One might, for example, wish to reject the sections of Paul that appear more politically conservative while affirming those that seem more politically subversive (or vice versa), without engaging in a (perhaps excessively?) complex hermeneutic that tries to tie everything into a coherent whole.

Scholars holding this view explain the ambiguities or contradictions in Pauline writings by arguing that Paul was ambivalent about the surrounding culture—speaking positively and negatively about it at different times—because, as Charles Cousar puts it, his "churches" were still in the process of moving toward a definable identity.[89] Wayne Meeks develops this point more fully, arguing that Paul and his churches experienced dis/continuity with social standards because they were involved in an ongoing process of resocialization.[90] According to Meeks, Paul spoke polyphonically—with many voices—as this process continued, and it is not for the contemporary reader to filter out all but one voice.[91] One must not look to Paul for a consistent (let alone eternal) social ethic, because doing so "confuses historical constructions with normative judgments."[92] Instead, one learns that the Paulinist pattern of moral discernment is an ongoing interpretive and social process, shaped by an eschatological orientation that is focused on the future and therefore not exhausted by what is immediately at hand.[93]

88. Scroggs, *Text and the Times*, 192, 207–11.

89. Cousar, *Letters of Paul*, 71.

90. Meeks, *Moral World*, 13–15; Meeks, *Origins of Christian Morality*, 48–50.

91. Meeks, *In Search of the Early Christians*, 197, 203, 207.

92. Meeks, *In Search of the Early Christians*, xiv.

93. Meeks, *In Search of the Early Christians*, 208. Hays makes a similar point about the ambiguity found in Pauline ethics and concludes that "[t]o live faithfully in the time between the times is to walk a tightrope of moral discernment, claiming neither too much nor too little for God's transformative power within the community of faith" (*Moral Vision*, 27; see also 21–27).

Accepting Paul's General Principles
While Rejecting the Specific Details

Of the three subcategories within this section, this third option is the most prominent. Essentially, this is the argument that the broader theological underpinnings of Paulinism remain important over the course of history, while the ways in which Paul specifically applied that theology in his day are no longer acceptable or directly applicable. Thus, W. D. Davies emphasizes that there is a large gulf between Paul's time and his time, and that this gulf cannot be directly bridged. He writes:

> The content of Paul's understanding of liberation was defined by his first-century milieu. In its political and economic stance, time has made this not only unacceptable but even barbarous . . . But neither the context nor the political and economic content of Paul's theology should primarily concern us. Rather, we should concentrate on the ground on which it was founded.[94]

Therefore, for Davies, the foundation Paul provides assists subsequent readers in pursuing a new creation existence in their unique historical moments and discerning what God's redemptive purposes were at that time.[95] Davies sees eschatology as an important part of this process, as does Victor Paul Furnish, who also emphasizes the gap that exists between Paul and his present—one aspect of which is that contemporary readers, unlike Paul, are reckoning with a political order of indefinite duration.[96] Thus, while emphasizing the need to avoid treating Paul's letters like a "sacred-cow" and noting that Paul "nowhere lays down a rigid, legalistic code of Christian conduct," Furnish also focuses on Paul's general ethical appeals while avoiding the more concrete points of application.[97] J. Albert Harrill develops similar points, focusing more on the observation that a direct application of Paul's thinking (on slavery in particular) would be immoral. He further argues that Paul himself was "implicated in ancient prejudice,"

94. Davies, *Jewish and Pauline Studies*, 222.

95. Davies, *Jewish and Pauline Studies*, 223–24, 292.

96. Furnish, *Moral Teaching of Paul*, 46. See also, Keck and Furnish, *Pauline Letters*, 94. Francis Fukuyama makes a similar point about the supposed indefinite duration of our contemporary socioeconomic and political order, and the ability of capitalism to not only endure but actually thrive through crises (rather than ultimately collapsing into communism as per the classical Marxist analysis) has become an increasing focus of the post-Marxist Left (see Fukuyama, *End of History*; Klein, *Shock Doctrine*).

97. Furnish, *Moral Teaching of Paul*, 13, 17.

so contemporary discussions of morals should, perhaps, "move beyond the specious biblicism of 'family values,' and create a better moral vision."[98] Calvin J. Roetzel also notes these oppressive elements within Paul (within a nuanced mixture of subversion and reinforcement) and asks: "how much should we worry about Paul's cultural views?" In the end, he argues we should not worry too much about them, for "it is the gospel that Paul preaches rather than Paul's apparent application and witness to it that is definitive for our times."[99]

Shifting to an internal focus, Eduard Lohse argues that Paul places a heavy emphasis on the conscience. While Paul provides us with some "illustrative examples" of how a person is to act with a good conscience, he "offers no legalistic directions that claim to be valid for all time."[100] Consequently, Paul does not offer contemporary readers a specific social ethic, but does help them look at traditional issues through a specific lens (i.e., according to Lohse's Paul, the will of God).[101] Richard Longenecker also reinforces this internal shift when he emphasizes that Paul offers a trajectory to follow, rather than a detailed code of conduct, as the reader is directed internally by the Spirit and shaped by loving relationships with God and with others.[102] Thus, Paul does not give us the "final word" on ethics; instead, we are faced with the task of engaging in the "organic development" of what is written in the epistles. This organic development exhibits continuity with the foundational core of what is written and also exhibits real growth in "conceptualization and expression."[103]

David Horrell negotiates this issue by separating specific injunctions from what he calls Paul's "metanorms" of "corporate solidarity and other-regard" (which are bounded by Paul's christology), while also allowing for

---

98. Harrill, *Slaves in the New Testament*, 196.

99. Roetzel, *Letters of Paul*, 188–89.

100. Lohse, *Theological Ethics*, 89–93. For a time in Pauline scholarship the relatively few references to the conscience within the Pauline letters received an undeserved amount of attention. A point that has now been addressed, largely due to the influence of Krister Stendahl.

101. Lohse, *Theological Ethics*, 93–95.

102. Longenecker, *New Testament Social Ethics*, 14–15. For another scholar who makes a similar argument, although from a more Bultmannian perspective that sees a Christocentric anthropological or existential core as the key to contemporary appropriations of Paul, see Segundo, *Humanist Christology of Paul*, 3:163–65, 173–80.

103. Longenecker, *New Testament Social Ethics*, 21–26.

considerable internal differences.[104] The self-giving love of Anointed Jesus is especially significant as a model for ethical behavior and causes any specific command or injunction to be relativized—as Horrell writes: "right action is not a matter of knowledge but of love . . . the basis for discerning what is good and acceptable is not what one knows to be the case . . . and what is therefore justifiable . . . but rather a generous regard for the other, a self-giving love as embodied by Christ."[105] Consequently,

> the Pauline Christian cannot do ethics monologically, reflecting in isolation on what is right and wrong, but can only make that discernment as a situated participant, in the context of human relationships: What is right or wrong in terms of one's conduct cannot be specified in the abstract, but only in terms of a particular community setting, in relation to the others with whom one is placed.[106]

One strength of Horrell's argument lies in making the case that accepting general principles while being critical of specific points of application is, in fact, the same approach that Paul takes to the ethical material he inherits and values.

In general, the large gap that exists between Paul and contemporary readers is of vital importance here. For some, such as Jerome Neyrey, this makes Paul very different from us and much less modern and relevant than some might wish him to be (though this does not lead Neyrey to dismiss Paul altogether).[107] For others, such as J. Paul Sampley, both "substantial points" of contact and "certain points of distance" arise when we encounter Paul.[108] Different scholars then emphasize both the distance and that which bridges the distance to varying degrees. The point remains: (a) there is a gap between Paul and the contemporary reader; and (b) this gap is not insurmountable but can be negotiated. Therefore, the recognition of this gap need not be an intimidating or negative thing. Rather, by noting these differences readers can recognize themselves as empowered moral agents capable of making their own decisions.[109]

104. Horrell, *Solidarity and Difference*, 274–79.

105. Horrell, *Solidarity and Difference*, 174; see also 177, 181, 187–88.

106. Horrell, *Solidarity and Difference*, 188.

107. Neyrey, *Paul, In Other Words*, 224, and all throughout. Engberg-Pederson takes much the same approach as he tries to negotiate Paul in *Paul and the Stoics*.

108. Sampley, *Walking Between the Times*, 107; see also 111–13.

109. A point made in Marxsen, *New Testament Foundations*, 224.

The No-Longer-Directly-Applicable Paul—
Questions and Criticisms

It is worth highlighting a few things about this perspective before asking some more critical questions. First, I admire both the careful readings proposed by many of these scholars and the way in which they do not rush to impose some sort of (artificial?) coherence or (strained?) points of immediate application to the Pauline corpus. Instead, they attempt to allow the various texts to speak for themselves and only then draw their conclusions, often (but not always) *despite* what they might wish to find in Paul. Second, I admire their willingness to stand firm in their values, particularly in relation to the politics of exploitation and oppression, even when those values are contradicted by the supposed practices of Paul himself. I find this degree of struggle and honesty to be refreshing. Third, we continue to see in these scholars' work the important role that Pauline eschatology and Paul's purported social location play in shaping any understanding of Pauline politics.

Essentially, this position relies on the acceptance of three different divisions within Paul, and it is these divisions which end up complicating or negating the application of Paul's political ethics to our current context. Option A posits a division between Paul's writings and Paul's life, in order to privilege what Paul wrote over what Paul did. Option B posits a division between Paul at one historical moment and Paul at another historical moment, thereby freeing the contemporary reader to choose which model is most appropriate for this historical moment. Option C posits a division between the general in Paul and the specific in Paul, in order to drain a good many specifics of much (or any) ongoing relevance. It is worth examining these divisions in more detail.

Regarding the first division, in which Paul's writings are affirmed over against his lived actions, it is worth highlighting some insights developed by ideological criticisms over the last hundred years. For example, criticisms levied against the streams of Marxism, socialism, or communism came and went over the course of the twentieth century. Initially, defenders of these movements sought to dissociate the theories behind these movements from the way in which these movements played out within actual history (thus, for example, the effort was made to vindicate Marxist theory over against Stalinist practices). However, as this thinking developed, it became apparent, even among those on the Left, that it was not so easy to separate the theoretical from the practical or the written word from the embodied deed. Thus, it is now accepted by representatives of both the Right and the Left that there are fatal and fundamental flaws or blind spots within the theories that led to the disasters that played out in the Soviet Union—not least of which was the final triumph of capitalism over the communism imagined by the Naradnaya Volya, anarchists like Peter Kropotkin or Emma Goldman, and the early Bolsheviks.[110] This is not to say that there is nothing good to be found in the writings of Marx, or Lenin, or Trotsky, but it does mean that the reverence with which some circles have treated these figures has been challenged by a much more critical hermeneutic and a greater awareness of the need to radically rework their theories if they are to speak to our contemporary context.

It seems to me that if we wish to create a similar gap between Paul's writings and Paul's deeds, then we need to practice the same suspicion and exercise the same radical reworking of his writings. True, Paul's writings may be beautiful and inspiring (just like the writings of Marx, Lenin, and Trotsky), but if his practices were as dictatorial and abusive as some in this camp suppose, then the Pauline texts can hardly be treated with the reverence and respect that many grant them. Indeed, as with the more contemporary voices mentioned, this "do as I say, not as I do" Paul is open to being charged with employing a deceptively liberating rhetoric precisely in order to mask and further enforce an oppressive practice. This, then, would make Paul's letters an exercise in ideology—understood in the popular and negative sense of the word—which means that rejecting Paul's practices should also lead us to reject his letters![111]

Of course, this need not be a wholesale rejection. Critical readers may still gain from reading contentious figures, and one need only recall the controversies surrounding Heidegger's complicity with Nazism, or Sartre's sympathy for Stalinism, to see that the thoughts or words of an individual may exceed their personal actions or sociopolitical maneuvering. However, coming to this realization requires us to treat Paul in the same manner as all of these other writers—not as the *Vox Dei* (i.e., the very Voice of God) but as a person who got some things right, other things wrong, and whom

---

110. Of course, similar criticisms have been made of liberal, capitalist democracies.

111. I.e., ideology is popularly understood as a means of deception. More accurately, however, ideology should be understood as the body of beliefs undergirding the manifold practices of our daily lives.

we must engage with a great deal of critical reflection in order to see how he might be applicable to our own day and age.

Finally, it seems to me that this divide between word and deed reflects a certain Western focus upon the *logos*, wherein the written word is privileged over historical action. From this perspective, what matters is not what Paul did but what he said and wrote. However, I wish to argue strongly against this position—what matters is not what we say, nor is it even what we believe, but what we do.[112] If Paul's actions were as far removed from his writings as some in this camp suggest then I, personally, question the value of studying, let alone imitating, Paul. However, as will be argued below, I believe that Pauline praxis and theory were far more consistent than those in this camp allow. In fact, I believe—and hope to show—that prioritizing the deed over the word is a very Pauline thing to do.

The second division, between the Paul of one historical moment and the Paul of another historical moment, is the one that strikes me as the most plausible. To assume that any single person can be completely consistent over a number of years, through various crises, and in very different situations strikes me as both naïve and undesirable: naïve because all people have their foibles and ways in which they can both develop or regress, and undesirable because it seems to me that all of us who strive to engage our contexts in ways that both contribute to that which is Life-giving and resist that which is Death-dealing, inevitably develop our perspectives over time (especially regarding the wide variety of issues addressed in the Pauline letters). Therefore, it seems reasonable to see some change within both Pauline praxis and theory. The question then becomes about the degree of change and about how this change is understood. Regarding the degree of change, we need only recall Paul's experience on the Damascus road to realize that Paul did, at least once, undergo a major shift in his thinking and living. What subsequently changed after that event is hotly debated. Furthermore, how this change is understood frequently depends on the

112. This is a point made repeatedly by Slavoj Žižek. Generally, he has targeted Western appropriations of Buddhism with this criticism. He argues that Westernized Buddhism is the means by which people who engage in the physical, economic, and political oppression of others are able to distance themselves from that oppression. See Žižek, *On Belief*, 12–15; and Žižek, *Puppet and the Dwarf*, 26–33. Thus, the CEO of a company that relies upon slave labor in the two-thirds world may distance herself from her complicity in this abusive practice through her Buddhist spirituality, and so on. Of course, the same criticism can be applied to much of contemporary Western Christianity and we should heed Žižek's conclusion that the stories we tell ourselves about ourselves often "serve to obfuscate the true ethical dimensions of our acts" (Žižek, *First as Tragedy*, 40).

presuppositions of the reader. For example, the argument that Paul became more conservative (or more radical) over the years could be understood as either a positive development or a negative regression, depending on one's own political views. Ultimately, however, the answer to this question regarding changes in Paulinism can only be discovered by a detailed study of that Pauline approach to various issues—something I will attempt to do in this series.

Finally, the division between Pauline "general theology" and particular "moral instructions" is the one that strikes me as most open to abuse. First, it is worth noting that Paul himself likely saw no inconsistency between the generalities of his beliefs and the specifics of his practice. Second, as soon as a person dissociates generalities from specifics in any thinker, those generalities become all too easily manipulated and made to fit into any other form of practice. In this way, a person like Paul can be manipulated into supporting any number of divergent contemporary practices—and, in fact, this is what has been done. Paul's general theology has been used to support whatever moral or political practices are espoused by whoever is exegeting his letters. If we are to attempt to understand Paul for who he was, and on his own terms, we must look more closely at the interconnectedness of general principles and particular ethical instructions.

The Counter-Imperial Paul—Summary

The final major position taken in relation to Paul and politics understands Paul as a proponent of a politically subversive counter-imperial theory and praxis. Given that the following chapters will provide a detailed exploration of this reading of Paul, this section will provide only a brief summary and introduction to this perspective. Essentially, scholars who belong to this camp are attempting to restore Paul not only to his *ethnic* Judean and *cultural* Greco-Roman contexts, but also to his rootedness within the *political and economic* empire that existed under the Julio-Claudian dynasty. Here, it is frequently emphasized that things like "ethnicity" and "culture" were very much socioeconomic and political matters in Paul's day. This point of view restores to the foreground an often neglected but inescapable and ever-present aspect of the day-to-day life of Paul and his coworkers.

This study of the political and economic contexts of Paul's day has led many to conclude that Paul himself was far more political in his life and writings than many have allowed. In part, this conclusion is based on the ways in which religion (imperial cult[s] in particular), politics, and economics were inextricably connected in the first-century Mediterranean world.[113] Indeed, within that world it is almost anachronistic to use multiple terms—"religion," "politics," "culture," and "economics"—to speak of what was really an integrated, albeit multi-faceted, whole. As Simon Price has demonstrated in his ground-breaking study, *Rituals and Power*, this is especially true of the imperial cult(s)—which, when taken as a whole, formed a fundamental and ubiquitous part of the web of power, shaping and sustaining the fabric of the Greco-Roman political economy.[114] Thus, for example, the authority of the emperor was not only material and political but also moral and religious.[115] Similarly, temples were never simply religious institutions—they were simultaneously banks, marketplaces, and trading centers, governed by socio-political elites.[116] I will examine the imperial cult(s) in more detail in volume 2. The point to be grasped here is that in the Julio-Claudian context, the religious *is* political and the political *is* religious.

The same is true of the Judean context in which Paul was raised. As Dieter Georgi has demonstrated, the heritage of the Judean Scriptures is inherently political, and religion and politics are inextricably connected in everything from Israel's historical narratives to her institutions, to her recorded traditions (including the Deuteronomic Law, the exilic and Priestly writings, Wisdom literature, and Apocalyptic literature).[117] The worship of

113. See Carter, *John and Empire*, x, 7; Grant, "Economic Background," 97; Harink, *Paul Among the Postliberals*, 113; Jeffers, *Greco-Roman World*, 89; Malina and Pilch, *Social-Science Commentary*, 392–93; Theissen, *Religion of the Earliest Churches*, 84. This runs counter to an earlier trend in Pauline scholarship, which understood the state religions of the Greco-Roman world as uninvolved with morals or ethics, or as largely artificial. See, respectively, Aune, *Cultic Setting of Realized Eschatology*, 21; and Jeffers, *Greco-Roman World*, 100.

114. Price, *Rituals and Power*, 234–38. Of course, this need not imply that the imperial cult was simply a tool manipulated by the powerful. To see things in this way is to once again import a modern understanding of the divide between "religion" and "politics" into the first century. I use the term "imperial cult(s)" to signify that, while there are consistent overarching ideo-theological beliefs, practices, and objectives to the imperial cult as a whole, there were a number of imperial cults (in that there were shrines dedicated to Augustus, to Nero, to Germanicus, and so on).

115. See "The Gospel of Imperial Salvation: Introduction," in Horsley, *Paul and Empire*, 15–17.

116. See Carter, *John and Empire*, 261–63; Carter, *Roman Empire*, 64; Jeffers, *Greco-Roman World*, 23; Horsley, *Covenant Economics*, 85.

117. Georgi, *Theocracy*, 1–18.

the sole sovereign—God—always contains concomitant political practices. As Horrell notes, using slightly different terminology, "myths are not apolitical. On the contrary, myths are used to construct and legitimate patterns of social organization."[118]

Now, given that imperial Rome and Second Temple Judaism(s) made mutually-exclusive theopolitical claims, resulting in contradictory socioeconomic and political practices, it is not surprising that conflict should occur.[119] Various factions of Second Temple Judaism attempted to negotiate this conflict in different ways: the Herodians and Sadducees, who often benefited from Roman rule, practiced political accommodation (like most other local elites around the Roman Empire); the Pharisees urged for a reform of the system, while also seeking to advance their own party status within traditional, institutional power structures; the more "zealous" Pharisees pursued a political revolt alongside other militant movements; and the Essenes and the members of the Qumran community attempted to withdraw in order to create their own alternative political bodies.[120]

Consequently, scholars in this camp argue that Pauline theory and praxis are as deeply political as they are theological. Further, these scholars tend to argue that Paul is most likely located within the more "zealous" apocalyptic elements of Second Temple Judaism—elements well-known for their anti-imperial outlooks and practices. Therefore, as Richard Horsley and Neil Silberman put it:

> Early Christianity was, in fact, a down-to-earth response to an oppressive ideology of earthly power that had recently leapt across continents, disrupted economics, and overturned ancient traditions . . . The movement that began with Jesus of Nazareth was primarily concerned with the way that people could somehow resist exploitation by the rich and powerful without either surrendering their traditions or resorting to violence. Likewise,

118. Horrell, *Solidarity and Difference*, 90.

119. Note how this occurs even at the most basic level. The affirmation of monotheism—under the reign of emperors who were understood as sons of gods and, as Virgil asserts, descendants of Zeus (who is God the Father) end up being a direct challenge to the theopolitical claims of the empire. Thus, the clash between "Judaism" and "paganism" is as much political as it is religious. See Carter, "Vulnerable Power," 473; Wright, *Paul*, 69; Wright, "Paul's Gospel and Caesar's Empire," 160, 164.

120. For a more detailed exploration of these and other factions, see Horsley and Silberman, *Message and the Kingdom*, Wright, *New Testament and the People of God*, 170–214; Horsley, *Religion and Empire*, 78–85; Horsley, *Liberation of Christmas*, 50–51, 93–96; Horsley, *Jesus and Empire*, 38–53.

> the Apostle Paul . . . engaged in a career of confrontation with the forces of patronage and empire and died in the attempt.[121]

The plausibility of this understanding is only strengthened when one realizes that the death of Jesus—and the cross of the Anointed, which plays such a prominent role in the Pauline letters—was a "nakedly political" event in which the imperial authorities assigned to Jesus the form of death reserved for slaves, rebels, and terrorists.[122] Thus, according to this camp, solidarity with the Anointed who had been crucified by Rome led Paul and his coworkers to engage in active resistance against the empire and solidarity with all the others who are crucified by the empire.[123] Consequently, when the Pauline faction speaks so negatively about "this present evil age" (Gal 1:4) or against "the pattern of this world" (Rom 12:2), they are not simply talking about historical or material existence as opposed to a supposed future, spiritual existence in heaven; rather, they are referring to the present age and world of the Roman imperial order—an order that God has condemned due to its evil and unjust practices.[124]

From this perspective, after his encounter with the resurrected Anointed Jesus, Paul engaged in a "radical rethinking of Judaism" and a "renewal of the Covenant of Israel" in order to establish alternative communities of subversion and liberation at core locations within the Roman Empire.[125] In essence, the Pauline faction engaged in an effort to find a third way of pursuing, and participating in, the in-breaking of God's rule into the day-to-day mess and oppression of Roman conquest and imperialism—one that avoids the equally fatal extremes of passive acceptance of the way things are, and violent total revolt against the powers that be.[126] This

---

121. Horsley and Silberman, *Message and the Kingdom*, 10, 231.

122. The quotation is from Elliott, *Liberating Paul*, 227.

123. Elliott, *Liberating Paul*, 228–30.

124. See Carter, *Roman Empire*, 18–19, 120–24; "Building an Alternative Society," in Horsley, *Paul and Empire*, 210. For an alternative take on the earthiness of Pauline notions of salvation, over against some contemporary Christians views about the destruction of the world and the flight of the soul to heaven, see Wright, *Surprised by Hope*. The problem with the view of Wright, and those like him, is that it still essentially defers salvation to the "afterlife"—even if it changes the location of that afterlife—and it does not do justice to the notion of salvation assembled by Paul and other early Jesus loyalists.

125. See, Georgi, *Theocracy*, 21–22; Horsley and Silberman, *Message and the Kingdom*, 91, 104–6.

126. In this regard, those who have written against more explicitly political or subversive readings of Paul have tended to operate with rather limited imaginations. The

is why the Pauline faction described the members of the assemblies associated with them as citizens of a different empire (Phil 3:20)—the empire of God—who should both express and embody alternative values.[127]

Scholars in this camp note, however, that Paul—like members of every other resistance movement in history—was constantly negotiating the space between opposition and accommodation.[128] Despite his best efforts to be a part of communities embodying God's new-creation reality within the present moment, Paul was still a product of his age and could never completely break from some of its practices and ideological constraints.[129] Consequently, one can and probably should expect to find some tensions in Paulinism: while the Pauline faction may proclaim a forthright message of liberation in one area of life, they may be blind to other areas where they are perpetuating some of the oppressive practices or ideologies of their time.

One of the particular strengths of this position is the way in which it takes seriously the force of the arguments proposed by the other three perspectives we have examined. It extends the insights of those who argue for a subcultural Paul, it nuances the insights gained by those who no longer see Paul as entirely consistent, relevant, or applicable, and it substantively engages the arguments made by those who argue for a conservative Paul.[130] Like these other views on Pauline politics, this analysis relies heavily on

---

assertion is commonly made that, because Paul did not engage in a violent revolt, he must have been a political conservative. The truth is that there we are always confronted with more than these two options, and it is possible to be subversive in the political realm without engaging in violence. See "Introduction," in Horsley, *Hidden Transcripts*, 7. That said, I will return to the theme of Pauline violence at the end of volume 3.

127. Wright, "Paul's Gospel and Caesar's Empire," 173–81; Carter, *Roman Empiret*, 20–21, 85–86, 92; Carter, "Vulnerable Power," 454–55.

128. See Carter, *Roman Empire*, 25–26; Carter, *John and Empire*, 13–14.

129. See Elliott, *Arrogance of Nations*, 15; Carter, "Vulnerable Power," 477; Strom, *Reframing Paul*, 169–70. As Warren Carter reminds us, no group can live an unqualified existence of opposition to its dominant society without some degree of participation and accommodation (*John and Empire*, 13). This is an increasingly prominent theme among readers of Paul who have been informed by postcolonial themes like "hybridity" and "making do" and I will return to it in volume 3 of this series.

130. Given that this counter-imperial Paulinism has been a minority position since it was resurrected near the end of the twentieth century, it must reckon with conservative readings of Paulinism in order to attempt to create a recognized space for itself within scholarship and the broader community of people interested in Paulinism. Unfortunately, the hegemony of the conservative position in the English-speaking world means that it tends to do what people in dominant positions do—simply refuse to engage or acknowledge in any depth the arguments that rise up against it.

both eschatological and social elements. First, the language of "new creation" is eschatological language, and it speaks of the Pauline belief that the assemblies of Jesus loyalists would be able to live a resurrection existence, even in the context of oppression (i.e., cruciformity). The new age has dawned in the raising of Jesus, and the outpouring of the eschatological Spirit of Life has taken place. As a result, Paul, his companions, and the great host of those left for dead within the borders of an ever-expanding empire, are empowered and commissioned to seek God's justice and liberation for people from all the nations vanquished and colonized by Rome. Yet socioeconomic experiences of powerlessness persist as key factors in how this unfolds. Given the powerlessness and vulnerability of Paul and the other members of the early Jesus movement, total, armed opposition to the old age—that is, the age of the Roman Empire—would have been completely unsustainable. As Ramsay MacMullen states: "No challenge on all fronts could have prevailed."[131] Thus, in this negotiation of the space between opposition and accommodation, survival is an important factor.

However, despite this tension between opposition and accommodation, the primary Pauline emphasis was on embodying God's new creation in opposition to Sin and Death as they were expressed through the regnant socioeconomic and political structures.[132] Despite their blind spots, Paul and others who were loyal to Jesus begin a movement that increasingly led away from accommodation and ever deeper into active resistance and the formation of an alternative *polis*.[133] In fact, as we will see, they often did so in a foolhardy, life-jeopardizing manner, so we should be cautious about overstating the importance of survival (and the necessity of accommodation that surviving often brings with it) to Paul and other members of the early assemblies of Jesus loyalists.

The implication of this, for many in this camp, is that anyone who claims to follow Jesus and imitate Paul should pursue the same trajectory today. Even beyond those circles, any person or group desiring to move beyond the death-dealing structures of our contemporary status quo would

131. MacMullen, *Changes in the Roman Empire*, 130.

132. See Wink's trilogy on the powers—Wink, *Naming the Powers*; *Unmasking the Powers*; *Engaging the Powers*. Contra Wink, I personally do not believe a good many of these Powers are redeemable. (Is Boeing redeemable? Is Coca-Cola? Or are the colonial States of Canada and the US any more redeemable than Rhodesia and the Belgian Congo? Or are they only, ultimately, extinguishable?) This will be explored in more detail in volume 3 of this series.

133. See Tellbe, *Paul Between Synagogue and State*, 291–94.

do well to pay attention to movements like those assisted by the Pauline faction. Applying Paul today means moving out of places of oppressive privilege and into places of solidarity with the crucified, colonized, oppressed, enslaved, and dispossessed people of today in order to participate in the eschatological new creation of all things as it bursts forth within our present evil age.

The Counter-Imperial Paul—Questions and Criticisms

Although most of the objections to the counter-imperial Paul will be individually addressed in what follows, it is worth emphasizing two significant obstacles at this point. The first and most important obstacle is that this understanding of Paulinism, unlike the positions discussed above, lacks a body of passages within the non-contested letters that immediately strike the contemporary reader as advocating this type of political economy. In fact, there are other passages—notably Rom 13:1–7—that appear to straightforwardly advocate the opposite. This is why a more detailed analysis of Paul's language, including the overtones of the words he employed, becomes so important to scholars who hold to this view. In performing this analysis, some scholars have utilized James C. Scott's notion of "hidden transcripts" to explore how Paul and his co-authors might be finding more subtle ways to speak against the power structures of Rome. Some conservative scholars, including Seyoon Kim, have treated this idea dismissively, as if it is little more than an eisegetical conspiracy theory, but it is worth taking the time to see if this claim holds any weight. One need not be a conspiracy theorist to understand that people who are oppressed may desire to avoid suffering and persecution or total annihilation by looking for ambiguous ways to speak about things that may draw unwanted attention. Consequently, what strikes the twentieth- or twenty-first-century reader as obvious or subtle may well be very different from what struck the first-century listener as obvious or subtle. Further, it seems to me that the social location of the reader will impact the reader's sympathies in this regard. For those who are primarily accustomed to speaking the dominant discourse of society or the elitist discourse of the academy, the notion of "hidden transcripts" may seem far-fetched. However, for those who are accustomed to encountering ambiguously coded language (as I have, for example, in my interactions with members of communities targeted by legally justified, state-based violence) this notion is entirely plausible—it just remains to be seen if it is true of Paul.

This points to the second obstacle. Bluntly stated, it seems to me that many who claim to be inspired by Paul today, scholarly and otherwise, simply do not *want* Paul to have written or acted in this way. Not only does this understanding go against many of the cultural values that members of dominant populations have been taught to internalize from a young age (serve your family, work hard, be responsible citizens, respect the order of things, develop a good credit rating, and so on), it also calls every area of upper- and middle-class living into question. Imitating Paul suddenly becomes a great deal costlier, and it seems only natural to resist this and favor a Paul who allows us to have our cake and eat it too (private property now and the kingdom of heaven later!). Indeed, having studied all of these various positions on Paul, I cannot help but wonder if this obstacle is the main reason why counter-imperial readings of Paul have been so often ignored or dismissed out of hand.

Conclusion

In this chapter I have surveyed four significant scholarly positions on Paul and politics. While I have been honest about which position I find most compelling, I have tried to present all options sympathetically and ask critical questions of each position. Furthermore, it should be noted that each of these positions on Paul has some plausibility—which is why I opened this chapter with a quotation from Jacob Taubes.[134] We are too far away from Paul, and possess too little knowledge about him, to ever possess full certainty about our own reading of him. Therefore, as much as we should strive to understand Paul accurately, we should also recognize that Paul will forever be contested.

In such a contested situation, we should always ask ourselves questions. Why is it that this particular reading of Paul strikes me as convincing? Why is it that I want to understand Paul in this way? Am I simply drawn to this reading of Paul because it fits with my previously established faith tradition? Am I drawn to this reading of Paul because it fits rather seamlessly with my own socioeconomic status? Or am I drawn to this reading of Paul

---

134. In this regard, I appreciate Engberg-Pedersen's remark about his own work: "There is no suggestion that the perspective to be developed here is the only one that may be adopted for a 'good' interpretation of Paul. Of course not" (*Paul and the Stoics*, 4).

because it meshes with values and commitments I have developed for other reasons? Answering "yes" to any of these last three questions does not immediately invalidate our understandings of Paulinism, but it should serve as a reminder that, as much as we are questioning Paul, we must also question ourselves. In particular, we must question our own political and economic commitments, for the fact is that *all* of these positions on Paul end up assisting and affirming certain political and economic agendas.

All that said, although one may affirm all of these positions on Paul as containing at least some degree or appearance of plausibility, some may be more plausible than others. In what follows I will attempt to demonstrate why I think a particular counter-imperial understanding of Paulinism is the most plausible—and, in fact, desirable—position to take. In the next chapters, I will explore two of the key issues that play a prominent role in each political reading of Paul: the socioeconomic location of Paul and other early Jesus loyalists and matters related to Pauline eschatology.

3

THE SOCIOECONOMIC STATUS
OF PAUL AND THE EARLY JESUS
LOYALISTS

Introduction

I WILL NOW EXAMINE the elements that contribute to competing socioeconomic understandings of the Pauline faction and the assemblies of Jesus loyalists associated with them. As any exegete knows—and as Wayne Meeks emphasized in his ground-breaking study of *The First Urban Christians*—knowledge of the context in which a person or faction is situated is crucial to understanding the words and reported actions of that person or faction.[1] In this chapter, I will begin by looking at Paul himself and the elements of his reconstructed biography that have been highlighted as scholars have attempted to understand his socioeconomic status. I will then take a step back and look at broader studies of the socioeconomic status of the general population in the eastern portion of the Roman Empire during the Julio-Claudian period, before looking in detail at the models related to the proposed socioeconomic status levels of members within the assemblies

1. Meeks, *First Urban Christians*. Meeks's thesis is that knowledge of "early Christianity" is dependent upon knowledge of the social world of the early Christians. Thus, as he writes elsewhere, it is no longer possible to "conceive of early Christianity's environment as *background* divided into two neatly separated worlds" but, instead, everything must be understood in a much more integrated and porous manner" (*In Search of the Early Christians*, xxv). Halvor Moxnes also develops this idea (Moxnes, "Introduction," 2).

Paul helped to establish. Finally, I will highlight Paul's repeated reflections upon his and others' experiences of suffering and persecution—a crucial but often neglected element of this broader discussion—before concluding with some remarks about the ways in which the presentation of Paul provided in Acts challenges the reading of socioeconomic matters offered here.

Paul: Initial Points of Contact

To understand a man [*sic*] we need to know the class out of which he sprang and with which he associated himself. [2]

—Adolf Deissmann, *Paul*

At the same time, the course of Paul's life prior to his emergence as a Pharisee zealous for the ancestral traditions lies more or less in the dark.[3]

—Udo Schnelle, *Apostle Paul: His Life and Theology*

For the twenty-first-century reader who valorizes Paul and goes to him seeking to find the kind of rugged individual they have been taught to admire (whether that be "Paul the Theological Genius," or "Paul the Revolutionary"), Paul is frustratingly circumspect. Despite his influence and the controversies in which he became embroiled (see Gal 2:1–14; 2 Pet 3:14–16; much of Acts)—controversies that only gained in importance as the grassroots Jesus movement turned into institutional Christianity—Paul does not seem inclined to speak about himself more than he and his coauthors deem necessary. It is quite possible that this is a deliberate, strategic choice on their part. Perhaps, as we will see, this is a fundamental part of the Pauline embrace of cruciformity, of shame, and of dying so that the Anointed may, through the power of the Spirit of *anastasis* life, live through them. One hint of this may be in Paul's name. If Acts is correct, Paul was once named Saul, but chose to change his name to Paul. Older scholars sometimes hypothesized that this was the case because Paul had a Roman patron or an imperial Roman authority who favored him and from whom Saul derived the name Paul. There is no evidence for this, and others

2. Deissmann, *Light from the Ancient East*, 47.
3. Schnelle, *Apostle Paul*, 32.

highlight that it was actually fairly common practice for Greek speaking Judeans to use both Aramaic and Latin names.[4] This may be the case but, in the non-contested letters, Paul is never named anything but Paul. The name Paul—*Paulus*—means "small" or "of little significance."[5] As Giorgio Agamben highlights, this contrasts quite remarkably with the regal history associated with the name Saul—Saul was the first Israelite king and was taller, larger, and more significant in the eyes of a people longing for a leader and a king. Thus, Agamben argues, "[t]he substitution of *sigma* by *pi* therefore signifies no less than the passage from the regal to the insignificant, from grandeur to smallness."[6] This, too, fits in with Paul ever only using a single name (and never providing any evidence of possessing any other names, as citizens normally would have). Paul, the small and insignificant one, is a slave of the Anointed (Rom 1:1) and slaves ever only received a single name from their masters.[7] I find this reading quite appealing but it is all conjecture. It makes good sense to me to accept it as a reasonable, perhaps even likely, possibility—but where one falls on this understanding of Paul's name will depend a great deal on what one makes of the material presented in this and subsequent chapters.

Because the Pauline faction is so circumspect about Paul's background, arguments related to Paul's socioeconomic location tend to rely heavily on the account of Paul provided in Acts. However, there are at least three points of hesitation that we should reiterate regarding Acts. First, we must recognize that Luke has his own agenda when it comes to his presentation of Paul, and this may cause him to be more than a little dishonest at times. Second, a focus upon Acts can lead scholars to neglect relevant material from the non-contested Pauline Epistles—notably the material related to suffering and persecution that will be explored below. Finally, as we will see momentarily, even the standard markers of status that have been studied in Luke's account may be more ambiguous than many have previously assumed. With these provisos in mind, we may examine the key relevant points scholars have highlighted in their reconstructions of

4. So Jeffers, *Greco-Roman World*, 205. However, Jeffers's subsequent discussion, in which he assumes *Paulus* was the *cognomen* of Paul's citizen name, which would also have a *praenomen* and *nomen,* assumes rather a lot.

5. I believe it was Giorgio Agamben who first started capturing interest with this point. See Agamben, *Time That Remains*, 9–11, for this and what follows. Ted Jennings follows Agamben in *Outlaw Justice*, 15–17.

6. Agamben, *Time That Remains*, 9.

7. Agamben, *Time That Remains*, 11.

a Pauline biography in order to evaluate his likely socioeconomic status. Here, we will look at questions related to Paul's (1) citizenships; (2) education; (3) supposed class-based sensitivities; and (4) his chosen profession.

Questions of Citizenship

Luke asserts that Paul's city of origin was Tarsus, the Roman capital of the province of Cilicia (see Acts 9:11, 30; 11:25; 21:39; 22:3; 24:34).[8] Scholars estimate that Paul was born there somewhere between 5 BCE and 11 CE.[9] At that time, Tarsus was a thriving town of approximately 75,000 people. Located at a significant juncture of major trade routes, bordering Greek and Semitic cultures, it was noted for its university which, according to Strabo, surpassed those of Athens and Alexandria.[10] Even the governor of Tarsus was a Stoic philosopher named Athenodorus, a former tutor of Caesar Augustus, and another famous Stoic philosopher, Cicero, was a former governor.[11]

However, as with all the major cities in Asia Minor, Tarsus paid a high price for the Roman civil wars that occurred for much of the first century BCE (including an especially devastating and nearly unbroken period spanning from Julius Caesar crossing the Rubicon in 49 BCE to Octavian's final victory at Actium in 31 BCE, when the civil wars were finally ended). Not too long before the birth of Paul, Tarsus had faced heavy taxes and, after the death of Julius Caesar, all public money was confiscated, private citizens were ordered to surrender all their gold and silver, landed estates and other properties were confiscated, and a large part of the non-elite population

8. It was Pompey who made Tarsus the provincial capital after he defeated the "pirates" in 67 BCE.

9. See, for example, Dunn, *Beginning from Jerusalem*, 323–24; Gorman, *Apostle of the Crucified Lord*, 50; Crossan and Borg, *First Paul*, 60.

10. Gorman, *Apostle of the Crucified Lord*, 51; Wrede, *Paul*, 2; Crossan and Borg, *First Paul*, 60–62. Strabo, *Geography* 14.5.13. Tarsus was also known for producing high grade linens, which brought local weavers a steady income, but at such a low level of profit, that most producers would not be able to afford the 500 drachmae Tarsian citizenship fee (see Finley, *Ancient Economy*, 137). Finley cites Dio Chrysostom on this point, but Justin J. Meggitt problematizes a straightforward reading of Dio Chrysostom by observing that many artisans and other long-term residents of Tarsus had become enfranchised and behaved as citizens, even though they had not and often could not pay official citizenship fees (Meggitt, *Paul, Poverty and Survival*, 83).

11. Bruce, *Apostle of the Heart*, 33–34; Schnelle, *Apostle Paul*, 58–59.

was sold into slavery.[12] As at most times of crisis, many members of the elite lost possessions and several members would have fallen out of the ranks of the elite altogether, but some of them would have survived, others would have been able to rebuild, and a very few of them would have been able to exploit the crisis to increase their fortunes. The non-elite paid a much higher price—more than losing wealth, they lost their freedom and often their lives. It could take the non-elites generations to recover, if they even had the opportunity to do so. However, as the civil wars wound down, and as Roman power sought to not completely alienate its eastern provinces, after winning the war with Brutus and Cassius, Antony restored freedom to the Tarsians sold into slavery (at least to those who had survived and who were able to maintain and demonstrate their connection to Tarsus), and, after Antony's defeat at Actium, Augustus made Tarsus a free city, exempting it from imperial taxes.[13] Thus, despite the civil wars, Tarsus had somewhat recovered by Paul's day. Certainly, the elite were once again well-connected with Roman imperial power and its philosophical rulers, but the recent history of the city suggests that a good many from the general population would have had fewer positive feelings about Rome, Romanic influence, and the devastation recently wrought among the provinces.

This history of mass enslavement and subsequent emancipation provides a tantalizing connection to the discussion regarding Paul's family of origin and his possible possession of Tarsian and Roman citizenships—the first key marker that may reveal something of Paul's inherited socioeconomic status. We learn of these citizenships only through Luke's account of Paul in Acts (Paul is referred to as a Roman citizen in Acts 16:37–38; 22:25–29; and 23:27; and as a citizen of Tarsus in Acts 21:39). Noting that citizenship was often costly (for example, it cost a minimum of 500 drachmae to enroll as a citizen in Tarsus), the argument has often been made that Paul's citizenships reveal him to be a person of privilege from a well-to-do family.[14]

---

12. See Rostovtzeff, *Social and Economic History*, 2:1003–7.

13. See Rostovtzeff, *Social and Economic History*, 2:1005; Bruce, *Apostle of the Heart*, 33–34. I will discuss these civil wars in more detail in volume 2 when I explore their relevance for the imperial ideology—which I refer to as "ideo-theology" in order to highlight the blend of religion and politics it contains—that arose after Augustus became the sole ruler.

14. See Bruce, *Apostle of the Heart*, 33–34; Dahl and Donahue, *Studies in Paul*, 35–36; Lietzmann, *Beginnings of the Christian Church*, 104; Schüssler-Fiorenza, *In Memory of Her*, 169; Weiss, *Earliest Christianity*, 1:182; Malherbe, *Social Aspects of Early Christianity*, 47; Dibelius, *Paul*, 15; Judge, *Social Distinctives of the Christians*, 41–42.

This experience of high status through citizenship-which-implies-wealth then tends to be used to favor a more conservative reading of Paul. For example, Johannes Weiss argues that the general population may have been inclined to "despise" Rome and exhibit "revolutionary tendencies" but Paul does not share these feelings because "he was not a Rome-hating Jewish fanatic, but a Hellenist and a Roman citizen. Up to a certain degree he shares the thankful feeling of the provinces which saw in the empire the refuge of peace."[15] Thus, it immediately becomes apparent that considerable issues of interpretation (relating to the degrees of plausibility associated with various renderings of Paulinism), are at stake when we consider these socioeconomic factors. Not only this, but we see how some markers, like citizenship, are granted greater significance than other markers, like being a member of vanquished and colonized people.

However, it is now more frequently noted that wealth was not necessarily tied to citizenship—a person could also be made a citizen through the performance of a deed that served the public good or a person could gain citizenship if manumitted from slavery in the right circumstances.[16] Indeed, in the absence of any strong evidence one way or another, it is the status given to a freed slave, and then to the children of that slave—by far the most common route to citizenship—that provides the most historically plausible explanation of Luke's claim that Paul was a citizen of Tarsus and Rome. Interestingly, this fits with the oldest known commentary on this matter, that produced by Jerome. According to Jerome, Paul's grandfather was brought to Tarsus from Gishala in northern Galilee and forced into slavery there as a part of the Roman suppression of a Judean uprising. Jerome then claims that Paul's father was manumitted.[17] This would, then, be one way of explaining the exchange that occurs between Paul and the

15. Weiss, *Earliest Christianity*, 2:591. Of course, this notion of the empire as a "refuge of peace" will be considerably problematized in the subsequent volumes of this series.

16. See Gorman, *Apostle of the Crucified Lord*, 50–51; Dunn, *Beginning from Jerusalem*, 325; Bruce, *Apostle of the Heart*, 37. Osiek notes some of the conditions relevant to attaining citizenship through manumission ("Family Matters," 213). Bruce W. Longenecker thinks citizenship demonstrates "middling status" (*Remember the Poor*, 304). I will examine his work in more detail later in this chapter and in volume 3.

17. Jerome, *St. Jerome's Commentary on Galatians*, 23; Jerome, *De virus illustibus*, 5; Lietzmann, *Beginnings of the Christian Church*, 104; Schnabel, *Early Christian Mission*, 2:924–26; Meggitt, *Paul, Poverty and Survival*, 82–83. Callahan doubts the veracity of this story (see Callahan, "Paul, Ekklesia, and Emancipation," 223), although large numbers of Judean slaves were removed from Judea in Roman conquests in both 63 BCE and 37 BCE.

Roman tribune in Acts 22:25–29. The Roman is amazed that Paul is a citizen, given the amount of money that it cost the tribune to purchase his citizenship. Paul replies that he did not purchase his citizenship but was born a citizen.[18] This could be the case if he were the child of a freed slave. Paul could possess a citizenship, but this would be a citizenship not necessarily associated with things like wealth.

At this point, we begin to see how this possible status marker is not unambiguously connected to other markers of high status, like wealth. Furthermore, after Augustus, a general drift was occurring in relation to citizenship in Asia Minor. In order to court allies and alleviate some of the tensions that resulted from the civil war, Julius Caesar, followed by Augustus, and then Claudius, began to loosen the connections between Roman citizenship and Latin birth, culture, and power.[19] Thus, something of a hierarchy was created within the notion of citizenship itself. Full Roman citizens were on one end of the spectrum, and those like manumitted slaves (called "Junian Latins") were on the other end. The key point is that these Junian Latins lacked many legal rights granted to those with full citizenship. For example, they were not able to make a will and, although their children were freed, those children were unable to inherit anything from their parents.[20] Thus, different forms of citizenship develop reflecting very different degrees of status, wealth, and privilege. Therefore, if Paul possessed a citizenship, it is most likely that he was Junian Latin.

However, this discussion reflects the scholarly preoccupation with Luke's claims about Paul's Roman citizenship. What of the claim that Paul is also a citizen of Tarsus? This is much less discussed because it does not play nearly the same function in the narrative trajectory of Acts as the claim about Roman citizenship. Furthermore, the term employed by Luke in Acts 21:39 is ambiguous. The Greek word "citizen" (*polites*) can refer to an official citizenship or simply be a term referring to one's place of origin.[21] Therefore, given the high cost of citizenship already mentioned (and given the observation that only a tiny minority of the population would be able

18. It is worth noting that the tribune's amazement may imply something about Paul's possible social status—i.e., the tribune is amazed because Paul does not appear to be the sort of person who could afford to purchase a citizenship.

19. See Sherwin-White, *Roman Citizenship*, 222, 225–30, 237–41, 244–49, 309. Also Judge, *Social Distinctives of the Christians*, 82; Jeffers, *Greco-Roman World*, 208; Meggitt, *Paul, Poverty and Survival*, 81; Garnsey and Saller, *Roman Empire*, 115.

20. See Osiek, "Family Matters," 213.

21. Schnelle, *Apostle Paul*, 59; see also Meggitt, *Paul, Poverty and Survival*, 83.

to afford that fee—although some in Tarsus seem to have acted like citizens without being formally recognized as such), the most historically plausible conjecture would be to assume that Paul was only referring to his city of origin (but perhaps doing so with deliberately ambiguous language as he engages with Roman officials and faces the threat of corporal punishment?).[22]

Some make the counterclaim that Paul was not a Roman (or Tarsian) citizen.[23] Citizenship is taken to be a Lukan fabrication that contradicts evidence in the non-contested Pauline Epistles. Thus, for example, not only is it historically unlikely that Paul would possess these citizenships, but the Pauline faction describes Paul being beaten with rods on three occasions by civic authorities (2 Cor 11:25). This is problematical because it was illegal to punish Roman citizens this way. Already in the late Republic, Roman citizens were legally protected against floggings, torture, and any arbitrary use of force by magistrates (as Cicero says, "It is an outrage to shackle a Roman citizen, an abomination to flog him, and all but parricide to kill him"[24]) and this carried through until Paul's day. From this perspective, Paul never writes about his citizenships because he did not possess them!

However, as James Dunn notes, the reference to 2 Cor 11:25 is not as convincing as it might appear to be. In all likelihood, there were times when local officials would not believe claims of citizenship or would ignore those claims in order to assert their will or power.[25] Furthermore, as Dunn also observes, Paul's citizenship is the most plausible explanation of his appeal

22. A third possible issue with Luke's presentation of Paul as possessing both Roman and Tarsian citizenships is that Rome, historically, did not permit people to be citizens of Rome and of another city out of a fear of the divided loyalties this might create (see Cicero, *Balb.* 30). However, as Sean A. Adams observes, this approach was well on the wane by Paul's day because citizenships were being distributed more broadly, citizens were living in more places in the empire, and preventing them from holding dual citizenship would cause considerable hardship for the cities in which they lived. See Adams, "Paul the Roman Citizen," 321–23.

23. See, for example, Crossan and Borg, *First Paul*, 67–68.

24. For this quotation see Cicero, *In Verrem* 2.5.170. Cicero even goes so far as to say that if foreign nationals treated Roman citizens in this way, such actions would be tantamount to a declaration of war (*In Verrem* 2.5.149). See also Garnsey and Saller, *Roman Empire*, 117.

25. Dunn, *Beginning from Jerusalem*, 325–27. See also Longenecker, *Remember the Poor*, 302–3. Schnelle agrees and provides helpful references to classical sources that demonstrate this (*Apostle Paul*, 61n22). Cicero himself, who was adamant that the Law protected Roman citizens from such abuses, also expresses outrage about situations where Romans were, in fact, flogged, whipped, beaten with rods, and even crucified (Cicero, *In Verrem* 2.5.72, 139–71; see also Cicero, *De imperio Cn. Pompei* 11).

to Caesar (as non-citizens would almost universally be denied this option) and so it becomes the best explanation of Luke's account of Paul's sustained imprisonment and transportation to Rome.[26] A good many scholars find this reason to be the most convincing one—the narrative trajectory of Acts simply does not work if Paul is not a citizen. However, the circular nature of the argument should be noted. It is Acts that tells us Paul was a Roman (and Tarsian) citizen, and then it is Acts that makes this citizenship essential to the story. Outside of Acts, we know that Paul wanted to go to Rome (see Rom 1:8–15 and the rest of that epistle) but we do not know how he actually got there. Therefore, the power of Dunn's observation depends on how credible one finds Acts to be and, while most people are willing to say that Acts plays a bit fast-and-loose with the facts here and there (or in relation to certain favorite Lukan themes), most are skeptical that Acts could be fabricating such a critical point so soon after the time of Paul. I am not so sure about this.

Even if Luke is honestly communicating Paul's *claims*, it is quite plausible to imagine Paul lying in order to use the tools of the empire against the empire itself. Such a tactic, although bold, sits well within the range of the "weapons of the weak," and is the kind of thing that tricksters, holy fools, and revolutionaries have long been doing in relation to dominant powers.[27] Perhaps this is why Paul never mentions his citizenship(s) in the epistles he co-authored—it is not necessary to lie about such things within the intimate assemblies of Jesus loyalists.[28] As a result, I am not sure if the argument based upon the narrative trajectory of Acts is as persuasive as many make it out to be. More compelling, to me, is the observation that Cicero makes in relation to how a good many people of low status could travel and be unknown to the elites and civic authorities at various locales, thereby making it difficult to ascertain their true status. In a passage highly relevant to the question of Paul's Roman citizenship, and it's possible

26. Dunn, *Beginning from Jerusalem*, 325–27. In my opinion, this is the strongest point made by those who argue that Paul was a Roman citizen. See also Schnelle, *Apostle Paul*, 60–61.

27. See Scott, *Weapons of the Weak*.

28. Alternatively, Bruce W. Longenecker argues that Paul mentioning his citizenship(s) would not have advanced any of the arguments he makes in all of his letters, and then quickly appeals to Rom 13:1–7, wherein Paul "talks like a citizen would talk" (*Remember the Poor*, 302). I disagree with Longenecker, and believe that mentioning citizenship(s) would add to the sections when the Pauline faction engages in a "foolish" form of boasting and describes Paul with status markers valued by the status quo (for example, 2 Cor 11:22 and Phil 3:4–6).

ramifications for our understanding of Paul's socioeconomic status, Cicero writes:

> Humble men of obscure birth sail the seas and travel to places they have never seen before. They are unknown there, and often do not have the people with them who can vouch that they are who they say they are. Nevertheless, they have complete confidence in their status as Roman citizens, and they count on being safe not only in the presence of our magistrates, who are restrained by fear of the law and of public opinion, nor only in the presence of other Roman citizens, with whom they have language, rights, and a thousand other things in common: no, where they go, they believe that this status they enjoy will protect them. Remove this belief, remove this protection from Roman citizens . . . and anyone else may inflict whatever punishments they like on those who state that they are Roman citizens and get away with it, simply because they do not know who they are.[29]

In light of these things, I find it difficult to fully resolve the question of Paul's possible citizenships. I am inclined to view it as a Lukan fabrication, especially since the Pauline faction never mentions them (not even in passages when Paul's credentials are being used to mock the notion of boasting about traditional status markers). However, the key point that should be realized by now, is that *if* Paul possessed these citizenships (particularly the Roman citizenship), they cannot be understood to be immediately correlated with other markers of high status like wealth. Granted, citizenship, even that of Junian Latins, does present a *relatively* higher status than non-citizenship, but there is nothing about citizenship itself that prevents it from being present among all but the most abjectly poor and oppressed members of society. Thus, if Paul, for example, was a citizen because he was the child of a manumitted slave, that would give him a higher status than some (slaves and sex workers, for example), but we cannot extrapolate much more about Paul's social status from this. He could well have been a citizen who was simultaneously poor or homeless and marginalized. In such a situation, Paul would be a person with overall low status, but with relatively higher status than those at the very lowest level.[30]

---

29. Cicero, *In Verrem* 2.5.167–68.

30. Once again, I believe comparisons to contemporary communities of people experiencing poverty are instructive here. When those communities are viewed from outside, and compared with very wealthy communities—they appear to be monolithic, undifferentiated wholes. However, when experienced internally, remarkable differences

Questions of Education

The second significant item that is explored as a potential marker of status for Paul are the claims made around his education or lack thereof. The primary claim for this is made in Acts 22:3 (when Luke's Paul claims to have been brought up at the feet of Gamaliel and educated strictly according to the Judean law), but many have also studied Paul's rhetoric in order to try and assess this claim and determine Paul's level of literacy and what this implies about his education.

In many ways, this discussion was stimulated by Adolf Deissmann. Challenging previously dominant assumptions about Paul's high level of education and status, Deissmann engaged in a sustained study of Pauline rhetoric, compared it to other writings contemporary to Paul, and concluded that the Pauline letters do not demonstrate the style of rhetoric prevalent among those who had received a significant level of education. Instead, Deissmann argued, the letters reflect the Greek of simple, unlearned people—the non-literary lower classes.[31] Thus, Deissmann notes how later pagan critics mock the language of the New Testament as "boatman's idiom."[32]

However, Deissmann's argument has been strongly challenged. Edwin Judge, Howard Clark Kee, and Charles Cousar criticize its reliance upon literary sources too far removed from Paul (notably Egyptian papyri), and challenge the distinction Deissmann wants to make between literary

---

in wealth, status, and socioeconomic stratification appear. Imagine, for example, an heterosexual couple who habitually use large amounts of crystal meth. In order to support this habit, the couple agrees that the cis-man will pimp out the cis-woman (the cis-man partner agrees to play the role of the pimp so that they do not lose any of their profits to a third party and to help prevent the cis-woman from being exploited by violent men). Although outsiders may quickly gloss over them as "drug addicts living in poverty and engaging in high risk activities" (or some such thing), internally there are significant differences between the status, wealth, and power of the man and the status, wealth, and power of the woman. No one, however, would mistake the man for a person of high status and wealth because he sells the body of another person for profit. I stress this point because I think that these are the kinds of differences in wealth and status that we see in the assemblies of early Jesus loyalists but we, as distant outsiders, have tended to play them up as if the differences are those between the very rich and the very poor.

31. See Deissmann, *Light from the Ancient East*, 68, 70, 149, 230–39; Deissmann, *New Testament*, 75–77; Deissmann, *Paul*, 8–13, 47–48, 74–75.

32. Deissmann, *Light from the Ancient East*, 71. According to Judge, this opinion was also shared by early church leaders (*Social Distinctives of the Christians*, 61–62).

epistles and non-literary letters.[33] Likewise, Abraham Malherbe challenges Deissmann's connection between Paul's rhetoric and the lower classes, arguing that the New Testament Greek is simply a reflection of the Judean variant of common Greek—the ordinary koine of people with some education.[34] Malherbe also goes on to argue that Paul's (admittedly sporadic) use of literary allusions and philosophical quotations suggest that Paul received an upper level Greco-Roman education.[35]

Once again, the careful scholarship of James Dunn can help us negotiate this terrain. Dunn argues that Paul likely did not receive a Greco-Roman form of higher education. The letters do not share high Greek values, Paul shows no knowledge of classical Greek literature (the few allusions and quotations can be treated as "commonplace philosophical maxims") and his rhetorical ability could easily have been learned through experience.[36] Therefore, as is now widely noted, it is difficult to form any opinion on Paul's level of education or status based upon the rhetoric we find in the letters ascribed to him. The evidence is inconclusive and we simply do not know enough about what was circulated in popular rhetorical handbooks or what access Paul might have had to those handbooks (especially in a city like Tarsus) to come to any firm conclusions.[37] That co-authors or scribes are involved in writing all of the non-contested Pauline letters only further complicates the possibility of drawing any conclusions here—especially when we recall that the use of scribes was also an option for poor and low

33. Judge, *Social Distinctives of the Christians,* 90, 137; Kee, *Beginnings of Christianity,* 234; Cousar, *Letters of Paul,* 25–26.

34. Malherbe, *Social Aspects of Early Christianity,* 32–39.

35. Malherbe, *Social Aspects of Early Christianity,* 43–45. Malherbe recognizes that the sole allusion we see in the non-contested Pauline letters is found in 1 Cor 15:33 but he also highlights allusions made in Titus 1:12 and Acts 17:28. Betz's commentary on Galatians is probably the finest example of the effort to relate Paul's letters to the rhetoric of the educated (see Betz, *Galatians*).

36. Dunn, *Beginning from Jerusalem,* 329–30.

37. See Cousar, *Letters of Paul,* 37; Judge, *Social Distinctives of the Christians,* 60–61; "Introduction: Unearthing a People's History," in Horsley, *Christian Origins,* 17; Roetzel, *Letters of Paul,* 17. Nowhere does this ambiguity present itself more clearly than in 2 Cor 11:6 (a much-debated passage in this context). Here, Paul admits that he "may be untrained in speech" but that he is still knowledgeable. Taken at face value, this would seem to confirm the assertion that Paul was uneducated. However, to claim to be a layman in rhetoric was, itself, a rhetorical *tropoi* known as *asteismos* or *prospoiesis*, wherein a skilled speaker pretends to be otherwise. Despite the (possibly endless) debate about what is actually going on here, the fact is we simply lack the evidence to know if Paul is being straightforward or if he is being sneaky.

status illiterate people.[38] However, one thing we do observe from the non-contested letters is that Paul himself does not seem to be able to write well. This is demonstrated in his postscript to the Galatians which he must write with "such large letters" (Gal 6:11). This point certainly suggests that Paul was not well-educated.

What then of the assertions made in Acts regarding Paul's education? Although he denies a classical Greco-Roman education to Paul, Dunn argues that Paul did receive primary and secondary levels of education in Jerusalem.[39] This could then be seen as a sign that Paul was situated among the privileged.[40] However, as Justin Meggitt argues, the reception of this education is not necessarily connected to a high level of wealth or status—while higher levels of Greco-Roman education were costly, the education Paul received at Jerusalem could very well have come at little or no financial cost.[41] Therefore, even if we accept the premise that Paul was educated in Jerusalem, we are left with the same ambiguity that we discovered in our study of Paul's purported citizenships.

All of this is only further problematized when we factor in E. P. Sanders's argument that Paul was not educated in Jerusalem at all.[42] By examining key themes of "Palestinian Judaism," and key ways in which Judeans presented their arguments, and contrasting these with Pauline themes and modes of argumentation, Sanders argues that "[w]hen we study the letters we shall not find a man highly educated in the Hebrew Bible and in Pharisaic Law and traditions, but one completely at home among the Greek-speaking Jews of the western Diaspora."[43] Sanders's expertise in this area gives his argument special weight. He concludes that Paul may have received some schooling at a Greek-speaking school in Tarsus but suggests that it is likely that Paul had to quit school at a young age in order to support his family by engaging in manual labor of the sort described elsewhere in the Pauline Epistles.[44]

---

38. See Meggitt, *Paul, Poverty and Survival*, 96, who also notes that Paul's reference to writing with large letters in Gal 6:11 suggests that Paul wasn't very literate.

39. Meggitt, *Paul, Poverty and Survival*, 330–33.

40. As asserted, for example, by Schnabel, *Early Christian Mission*, 926.

41. Meggitt, *Paul, Poverty and Survival*, 83–87.

42. Sanders, *Paul: The Apostle's Life*, 20–81.

43. Sanders, *Paul: The Apostle's Life*, 20.

44. Sanders, *Paul: The Apostle's Life*, 70–71, 76.

Therefore, it seems likely that the claims made in Acts are unreliable and that evidence of Paul having received a high level of education—which could then be correlated with wealth and other markers of high status—is not nearly so firm as some scholars have suggested. Based on claims related to Pauline rhetoric in relation to Paul's level of education, we cannot draw any firm or reliable conclusions. However, based on the observation that the overwhelming majority of people were not well-educated, the odds are strongly against Paul having received much formal education. Again, what we see is something that affords Paul a relatively higher status than some (those who were totally illiterate, for example, and who could not even sloppily write their own names) but nothing that would make us conclude that Paul possessed anything that would take him out of the lower levels of society and situate him among the small minority of people who held a high degree of status, wealth, and power.[45]

Questions of Class Sensitivities

In a more creative move, Edwin Judge argues that Paul's high-status background is revealed not by his education but by the sensitivity he demonstrates in relation to suffering humiliations. He writes: "There was no point in a lowly man's [*sic*] complaining of what he had to put up with. But for a man of St Paul's rank, the formal recital of affronts is itself . . . a mark of his own sensitivity to questions of status."[46] Paul's sensitivity reveals that he experiences these humiliations as "indignities he ought not to have been subjected to" due to his placement among those of higher status.[47] A number of scholars comfortably situated in high-status institutions find this argument compelling. Thus, for example, Sanders comments on the way in which Paul highlights the shame associated with his manual labor and says: "the poor do not find working with their hands to be worthy of special remark."[48]

45. Further, Paul's literacy—his writing with large letters—may simply be the case of Paul copying letters that others put before him, or an example of a person attaining basic literacy by teaching himself how to read and write—something that happens more frequently than folks of higher wealth and status like to imagine due to class- and race-based biases. See, for example, Rancière, *Ignorant Schoolmaster*.

46. Judge, *Social Distinctives of the Christians*, 100.

47. Judge, *Social Distinctives of the Christians*, 42; see also 86.

48. Sanders, *Paul: The Apostle's Life*, 144. Bruce W. Longenecker also thinks Paul's sensitivity to matters related to manual labor and shame are rooted in him having a

However, as Meggitt points out, feelings of pride and shame are not the exclusive territory of the elite.[49] There is no reason to think that a person of low status would not be painfully aware of the shame that brings upon him or her. In fact, there is nothing to suggest that shame does not operate just as much in dispossessed populations as in other socioeconomic groups. Despite what elite members of society may think, they are no more sensitive to sufferings, losses, and humiliations than other groups of people. Having personally spent more than twenty years journeying alongside of people experiencing poverty, housing deprivation, oppression, colonization, and humiliation in Canadian-occupied territories, I can attest to this. At minimum, the oppressed (or, if you prefer, "the poor") are just as human and just as full of feeling as the oppressors ("the rich"). More frequently, however, I find that the oppressed are the clearest voices speaking out against humiliating structures which the oppressors—despite their supposed sensitivity—continually overlook. It seems that the class allegiances of Judge et al. have made it difficult for them to imagine the human experiences of those suffering poverty and humiliation while living in close proximity to those who are wealthy and honored. Given the condescending snobbery of this argument and its lack of awareness of how people who experience poverty and hard labor experience those things, I see little reason to give it much weight.

Questions of Labor

In what I consider to be a more fruitful move—given that it relies more heavily upon the non-contested Pauline writings and not upon secondary literature or hypotheses sustained by inconclusive evidence—a more careful examination of Paul's profession as a leather-worker, and his reflections upon labor in general, could function as markers of his status.[50] The Pauline

---

relatively higher ("middling") status (*Remember the Poor*, 305).

49. See Meggitt, *Paul, Poverty and Survival*, 87–88.

50. Based upon a more careful lexical study of the word *skenopoios* (which has traditionally been translated as "tentmaker" or "leather-worker"), Larry Welborn argues that Paul actually identifies as a "maker of stage props" (Welborn, *Paul*, 11–12, 111). Welborn is interested in the closeness of Paul's connection to the theater due to the importance he gives to theatrical themes and types in his work on 1 Cor 1–4. Sean A. Adams questions this translation by noting the weakness of the lexical case, which makes it rather inconclusive (Adams, "Crucifixion in the Ancient World," 123–24). Curiously, to the best of my knowledge other scholars have not tried to explore this idea further. I am unsure

faction frequently mentions this subject in their letters. In 1 Thess 2:9 they write: "You remember our labour and toil, [siblings], we worked night and day, so that we might not burden any of you." In 1 Cor 4:12, they speak of Paul growing weary because of the hard work he does, and in 2 Cor 11:27, they repeat the assertion of Paul experiencing work as "toil" and "hardship." Further, as they specify in 1 Cor 9:6, these long hard days (and nights?) of work are the means by which Paul financially supports himself.[51] Not only that, but he also expects others to live in this way. In 1 Thess 4:11–12, the Pauline faction tells the Thessalonians to "work with your hands, as we directed you, so that you may behave properly and be dependent on no one." Paul, then, likely spent the bulk of his time engaging in laborious work. Much of his so-called "ministry" probably took place in whatever space he could use as a workshop.[52] What comes to mind here, if one is to search for parallels from recent history, are not elite members of society, but factory workers, laboring under appalling conditions, and then organizing late into the night, during meals, and in the early hours of the morning in order to improve their conditions.[53]

This approach to work—both Paul's commitment to manual labor and the Pauline call for others to engage in it—is supported by the evidence in Acts and the deutero-Pauline epistles. Thus, Luke portrays Paul as a leather-worker earning his living by his profession and encouraging others to work hard in order to support the less fortunate members of the community (Acts 18:2–3 and 20:33–35). This call for others to imitate Paul through work is made even more forcefully in 2 Thess 3:7–12, which bears quoting in full:

---

what to make of it, or how it might change much about our understanding of Paul's socioeconomic status, so I prefer to remain with the general term "leather-worker" (in the theater? making tents?), as I think that sufficiently captures relevant points.

51. Here I should emphasize that, although Paul may be classified as an "artisan," we should not understand that term as denoting something distinct from very hard work. In fact, leather-working was very physically demanding, and Paul would have had to work long hours in order to earn a living—something only aggravated by the fact that he was also using time to develop assemblies of Jesus loyalists around the empire. See Fitzpatrick, *Paul*, 33; Jeffers, *Greco-Roman World*, 27–29; von Campenhausen, *Ecclesiastical Authority*, 65; Meggitt, *Paul, Poverty and Survival*, 75–76; Dunn, *Beginning from Jerusalem*, 565. Crossan and Borg suggest that Paul developed this appreciation for hard work due to his origins in Tarsus—which was known to be a city that had worked hard to build and establish itself (*First Paul*, 61).

52. See Sanders, *Paul: The Apostle's Life*, 112–13.

53. Novels such as Zola's *Germinal* and Sinclair's *The Jungle* come to mind.

> For you yourselves know how you ought to imitate us; we were not idle when we were with you, and we did not eat anyone's bread without paying for it; but with toil and labour we worked night and day so that we might not burden you. This was not because we do not have that right, but in order to give you an example to imitate. For even when we were with you, we gave you this command: Anyone unwilling to work should not eat. For we hear that some of you are living in idleness, mere busybodies, not doing any work. Now such persons we command and exhort in the Lord Jesus [Anointed] to do their work quietly and to earn their own living.

Whereas contemporary middle-class Christians tend to be conditioned to hear this as a Pauline verification of the "Protestant work ethic" (frequently employed in order to create a divide between the "deserving" and the "undeserving" poor in order to justify the accumulation of property and wealth in the company of others experiencing deprivation), a contextual reading of this theme leads to some very different conclusions—as the call to work hard in order to care for "the weak" already suggests.

The first thing to remember is that physical labor was a marker of low status.[54] The hard work Paul did, and that is remembered by the authors of 2 Thess, was shameful. It would be avoided if at all possible by any self-respecting person of status. Therefore, regardless of the status Paul was born into or developed, it is clear that, by the time he is functioning as a divinely appointed ambassador to the nations, he is remembered as fully embracing a profession that marked him as a person who would be despised by the reputable members of society. This is true even if Paul's motivation was to simply follow a rabbinic practice by adopting a trade.[55] Regardless of what inspires a person to work a manual job (physical need or religious or philosophical commitments), the fact that a person worked manually and worked hard was a marker of shame.

---

54. On this point in general see Grant, *Early Christianity and Society*, 80–81; Jeffers, *Greco-Roman World*, 22–24; Gorman, *Apostle of the Crucified Lord*, 68–69; Carter, "Vulnerable Power," 459; Judge, *Social Distinctives of the Christians*, 132; Boff and Pixley, *Bible, the Church, and the Poor*, 88; Dunn, *Beginning from Jerusalem*, 565.

55. As Dunn and others believe. See, for example, Dunn, *Beginning from Jerusalem*, 334. Meggitt notes, a number of those rabbis were driven to adopt this practice out of sheer need and in order to avoid starvation but he argues against this as a standard rabbinic practice in Paul's day arguing, instead, that this custom does not develop until the second century after the "economic trauma that followed the Jewish wars" (*Paul, Poverty and Survival*, 88; see also 87–88).

This, then, leads to a second realization. When 2 Thess says that Paul calls others to imitate him and work hard, he is not perpetuating some sort of "Protestant work ethic" but is, instead, urging others to embrace a way of living that was considered the humiliating lot of those with low status.[56] This is important because, as the early Jesus movement spread, it likely attracted members of *relatively* higher status and wealth categories (who might want to bring the number of people in the local assemblies into their personal sphere of patronage, thereby boosting their status). Or perhaps it attracted charismatic figures who sought to exploit their ability to influence others in order to achieve a relative idleness. I will explore these points in more detail in volume 3 when I examine Pauline approaches to both patronage and slavery. For now, it is worth highlighting that the main group of people who would fall under the Paul-inspired criticisms of those who do not work, would likely be people with relatively greater wealth and status who did not work and who considered it shameful to do so. It is worth emphasizing, then, that the authors of 2 Thess are not targeting the undeserving (purportedly lazy) poor members of society, but are instead targeting the more parasitical relatively wealthier members who have begun to infiltrate and co-opt the early assemblies of Jesus loyalists.

One thing is quite clear in all of this: the non-contested Pauline letters, as well as Acts and the Deutero-Pauline letters, all exhibit Paul as engaging in a difficult, shameful, and low-paying form of daily labor. Here, rather than possessing a marker of high status and wealth, Paul is marked as a person with very little of either of those things. Although not utterly destitute, he appears to be one small step above the very poorest of the poor.

Paul's Status: High, Low, or High moving to Low?

At this point, I have reviewed most of the markers that scholars study in order to try and determine Paul's socioeconomic status (a few markers, like the extent and nature of his contact with social elites, will be discussed when we turn to the socioeconomic status of the members of the assemblies of Jesus loyalists). What has become apparent is that the previously dominant view of Paul as a person of high status lacks any firm foundation.

---

56. Here I am siding with Robert M. Grant and Peter Oakes over against the older "Protestant work ethic" perspective, represented by scholars such as Dibelius. See Grant, *Early Christianity and Society*, 67–73; Oakes, *Reading Romans in Pompeii*, 112–13, 121–23; Dibelius, *Paul*, 37; also Schrage, *Ethics of the New Testament*, 229–31.

We have good reason to question whether or not Paul possessed Roman or Tarsian citizenships and, even if such citizenships were in his possession (or even if Paul claimed them but did not possess them), their relation to other markers of status are ambiguous due to the absence of other evidence. Similarly, the claim that Paul was highly educated has been shown to be unlikely and the hard evidence we have suggests only a small amount of education—although here again the overall lack of evidence makes it difficult for us to draw anything close to certain conclusions. Paul's apparent sensitivity to the shame associated with the manual labor he performed reveals nothing of his class background—and to suggest that it does reveals much more of the class (and classism) of those suggesting that it does. The only firm marker we have of Paul's socioeconomic status is not related to his past, but is related to his work as a manual laborer. This was clearly the mark of a person with low status and even if Acts is constantly trying to nudge Paul up into a higher category of status, we should conjecture that as a slave of the Anointed, he was still very much counted among the lowly.

As far as I can tell, this leaves us with two possible options: Paul was either a person of low status from start to finish, or he was a person born into *relatively* higher status but who ended up embracing low status as a part of his understanding of what it meant to follow the crucified Anointed Jesus. A number of prominent scholars have embraced the second possibility. Noted counter-imperial interpreters, Neil Elliott and Richard Horsley, both see Paul as a person of high status who embraced "downward mobility" in order to faithfully follow Jesus.[57] Calvin Roetzel makes this point even more thoroughly. He argues that Paul was a "marginal Jew" who was forced to the margins by both Judaism and the Jerusalem church, but who embraced the margins as a place of radical openness where God's new creation could bear the most fruit.[58] Thus, for Paul, the embrace of marginality and downward mobility is a part of his embrace of the sort of cruciformity that is praised in Phil 2:5–11.

Given the examination of the evidence above, I am not convinced by Roetzel. The unambiguous evidence points to Paul being a person of low

57. Elliott, *Liberating Paul*, 61–63; "Introduction: A People's History," in Horsley, *Christian Origins*, 17. Boff and Pixley, in their Marxist exegesis, agree (see *The Bible, the Church, and the Poor*, 87). Bruce W. Longenecker, in a manner similar to conservatives like Theissen, also makes this argument (*Remember the Poor*, 306–7). Edwin Judge was the first to gain widespread attention for arguing this point (see Judge, *Social Distinctives of the Christians*, 74, 97–100, 132). See also Schottroff, "'Not Many Powerful,'" 281.

58. Roetzel, *Paul*, ix–x, 1–4, 88.

status, devoid of wealth, and the ambiguous evidence also leans in this direction (although with less certainty). The most likely and plausible conclusion, in light of what we know about both Paul and his context, is that he was a person with almost no status, living at or near the subsistence level. What is certain is that the least plausible position, based upon that which we have examined so far, is the one taken by those who assert that Paul was a person of high status and remained that way. Consequently, any political position attributed to Paul due to his purported high status is lacking a solid foundation. However, there are several other elements to this discussion—especially when sociological studies are made of the assemblies of Jesus loyalists mentioned in the epistles. In order to explore those elements, it is necessary to provide a broader sketch of the socioeconomic world in which Paul lived.

Day-to-Day Life in the Early Empire

> With money you've got a yacht with a following breeze;
> With money you've got Lady Luck on her knees.
>
> —Petronius, *Satyricon*

Exploring this broader context helps us to evaluate the plausibility of various hypotheses about Paul and other Jesus loyalists in the first century CE. In later sections, I will address other relevant factors like Pauline approaches to honor, shame, and patronage. For now, I will focus upon economic models, how they have been created, and how they relate to a person's social status in the Pauline context. While doing this, it is important to remember that a person's level of income or accumulated capital was only one element in determining a person's status. Other factors, like access to power, rank or title, gender, able-bodiedness, occupational prestige, education, religious or social purity, family of origin, and ethnic group (and one's position therein), are also important and multilayered, in terms of local, provincial, and imperial contexts.[59] However, the importance of economic models should not be lost or neglected within this confluence of factors. As Steven Friesen has noted, while financial resources were not the only measure for determining a person's place in society, in day-to-day life, they

---

59. See Meeks, *First Urban Christians*, 54; Malina, "Social Levels, Morals and Daily Life," 369–70.

frequently were the most important one.[60] Thus, for example, one could be wealthy without being a member of the higher orders of Roman society (the decurions, equestrians, and senators), but one could not be a member of those higher orders without wealth (senators were required to prove that they had property valued at a minimum of 1,000,000 sesterces, and equestrians were required to hold property valued at a minimum of 400,000 sesterces).

The Economics of Empire: The Great Unbridgeable Divide

Prior to the development of more nuanced sociological exegesis over the last century, it was not uncommon for scholars on all sides to impose modern class divisions onto Greco-Roman society. Thus, the imperial elites and their local allies were seen as the upper-classes, the urban tradespeople (who were considered the most likely candidates for membership within the early assemblies of Jesus loyalists) were seen as the middle-class, and the rural peasant populations along with the urban homeless were the lower-classes. Here, one posits a smooth and well-demarcated continuum from the aristocracy down to the lumpenproletariat. For the most part, this understanding was conducive to White, middle-class, Christian readings of the texts. Paul and the early Christians were taken to be representatives of the middle-class, and they reinforced the middle-class values already affirmed by these readers. However, some left-leaning scholars argued against this—they used this class-based analysis to posit a Marxist and revolutionary Paul—but the fundamental post-industrial, European-class structure of their understanding of Paul and his context remained.

It has now become apparent that this is a false projection of modern socioeconomic structures and values onto Greco-Roman society. In actuality, during Paul's life, there was no such thing as a middle-class—instead, there was a massive gap that existed between the clearly demarcated high status and wealthy few and the low status and almost universally poor masses.[61] Between 2 and 5 percent of the population, located in the urban centers or

60. Friesen, "Injustice or God's Will," 242. See also Oakes, "Methodological Issues," 11–12.

61. See Jeffers, *Greco-Roman World*, 48–49, 180–96; Garnsey and Saller, *Roman Empire*, 116; Meggitt, *Paul, Poverty and Survival*, 7, 41–42, 46, 49–50; Esler, *Early Christian World*, 12; Esler, *Conflict and Identity in Romans*, 78; Holmberg, *Sociology and the New Testament*, 22–23.

on country estates, monopolized almost all of the wealth, land, property, education, and capital, and consumed around 65 percent of that which was produced by the empire.[62] It was this tiny minority that also shaped the culture, faith, loyalties, and values of the rest of the population—they were the bearers of society's "Great Traditions"—and this is one of the crucial ways in which they retained their monopoly.[63] As the wealthy and powerful are want to do at any time in history, they claimed a monopoly on both goods and goodness. Thus, Moses Finley observes: "The judgment of antiquity about wealth was fundamentally unequivocal and uncomplicated. Wealth was necessary and it was good; it was an absolute requisite for the good life; and on the whole that was all there was to it."[64] Therefore, one of the central ways in which one's wealth and goodness was demonstrated was through acts of conspicuous consumption.[65]

It is also this massive monopoly of wealth and consumption that created the rise of the urban populations of artisans, tradespeople, and retainers who existed in order to serve the elite. Yet most members of the urban populations lived lives deeply marked by low status, poverty, and suffering. Most people hovered around the subsistence level. For roughly 90 percent of the people in the empire, simply earning enough in order to buy food to eat was the challenge of every single day (hence, around Paul's time, Cicero

62. See Esler, *Early Christian World*, 11–12; Esler, *Conflict and Identity in Romans*, 79; Malina, "Social Levels, Morals and Daily Life," 83–84; Carter, "Matthew Negotiates the Roman Empire," 120.

63. See Malina, "Social Levels, Morals and Daily Life," 87; Esler, *Conflict and Identity in Romans*, 81. This would be an example of what Foucault refers to as the exercise of biopower, whereby people are made into self-disciplining subjects who meet the needs of those in power without those in power needing to employ brute force in order to attain the outcomes they desire (see Foucault, *Discipline and Punish*).

64. Finley, *Ancient Economy*, 35–36.

65. Garnsey and Saller, *Roman Empire*, 74, 121–22. As Garnsey and Saller explain, valuing conspicuous consumption helps to show why it persisted, even when laws were passed to try and limit it, and why productive investment was not widely practiced in the Greco-Roman period. Conspicuous consumption, along with the devastating impact of disasters (a sunken ship, a lost crop, a war or rebellion in one's territory, or simply falling out of favor in the court), and short life expectancies also help to explain the high turnover Garnsey and Saller observe in senatorial families (they argue ~75 percent were disappearing per generation) (Garnsey and Saller, *Roman Empire*, 123). This should not be taken as a marker of the possibility of socioeconomic or political mobility under the principate but, rather, shows that internal conflict and jockeying for position within the top 2 to 5 percent of the population could led to remarkable shifts of power between aristocratic families.

depicts the common folk of the city, as "wretched and starving" and Lucan depicts them as "barefoot and half naked").[66] Of course, due to the rise of *latifundia* during the early imperial period (when the wealthy few gradually purchased vast amounts of the arable land in Italy and in the provinces, in a trend comparable to the ways in which corporate mega-farms have devastated rural populations in the two-thirds world today), rural populations as a whole often suffered more than urban populations. In many areas in Paul's day (including Palestine), wealth disparity was growing—the rich were getting richer, the poor were getting poorer, the indebted were getting ever more deeply into debt, and more and more people were dispossessed as the wealthy ate up the land and lives and families of those who fell into their ever expanding territories.[67] Half-starved and driven into debt, the rural poor frequently ended up as slaves or bandits, or they moved to the cities to swell the ranks of the beggars and the homeless poor who slept in tombs, under stairs, or in cellars, taverns, and shanties.[68]

For all but the elite minority, life in the city was very difficult.[69] Child mortality was high, disease was rampant, quarters were cramped, dark, and unsanitary, physical and sexual violence were ever-present threats (not to mention the ever-present threat that one may be forced to choose between starvation, migration, or slavery—or requiring one's families members to undergo those things) in order to survive.[70] Here, even the most dedicated and skilled workers most likely did not escape the threat of poverty but only lived somewhat above the subsistence level. As Meggitt notes: "Evidence for

66. See Meggitt, *Paul, Poverty and Survival*, 59–61; Horsley, "Introduction: A People's History," 9; Maier, *Picturing Paul in Empire*, 13; Malina, "Social Levels, Morals and Daily Life," 89; Elliott, "Strategies of Resistance," 98–99; Horsley and Silberman, *Message and the Kingdom*, 154–55; Kim, *Christ's Body in Corinth*, 81; Wrede, *Paul*, 52; Carter, *Roman Empire and the New Testament*, 46.

67. Wright, *New Testament and the People of God*, 168–69; Horsley, *Liberation of Christmas*, 68–70; Horsley, *Covenant Economics*, 89–91; Horsley and Silberman, *Message and the Kingdom*, 25–29; Bruce W. Longenecker highlights how the ongoing acquisitive nature of wealth in advanced agrarian culture create a situation where the wealthy and powerful continually acquire the resources of others (*Remember the Poor*, 27).

68. See Malina, "Social Levels, Morals and Daily Life," 85–89; Holmberg, *Sociology and the New Testament*, 24–25; Esler, "Mediterranean Context of Early Christianity," 13; Meggitt, *Paul, Poverty and Survival*, 62–64.

69. See Malina, "Social Levels, Morals and Daily Life," 86.

70. See Countryman, *Rich Christians in the Church*, 24–25; Howard-Brook and Gwyther, *Unveiling Empire*, 99–101; Crossan and Borg, *First Paul*, 83; Osiek, "Family Matters," 203–6; Malina, "Social Levels, Morals and Daily Life," 394–95; Meggitt, *Paul, Poverty and Survival*, 59–73.

skilled workers lifting themselves out of their subsistence existence is scant . . . thrift and hard work did not lead to a life of affluence."[71] Even those who worked closely with the elites and in their direct personal employ had little security. Thus, in his work *De Mercede Conductis*, Lucian describes the situation of a slave with a wealthy master in this way:

> after garnering all that was most profitable in you, after consuming the most fruitful years of your life and the great vigour of your body, after reducing you to a thing of rags and tatters, he (the master) is looking about for a rubbish heap on which to cast you aside unceremoniously, and for another man to engage who can stand the work.[72]

Thus, while a great deal of attention has been given to a select few slaves who were emancipated and named in the wills of their masters, and who then became quite wealthy (Trimalchio from the *Satyricon* being an obvious example), it bears remembering that such cases were few and far between and, for most, slavery was a dehumanizing experience of shame, physical and sexual violence, loss of agency and identity, separation from one's family members and loved ones, hard labor, servitude, and early death. To be a slave is to see loved ones bound, torn away from you, and crucified. And it is to live knowing you could well be the next one up on a cross.

It is also worth emphasizing the cramped and unsanitary living quarters of most urban dwellers. Prior conversations about "Christian house churches" have focused upon villas or entire floors within buildings owned by wealthy individuals, and have provided misleading assumptions about the living conditions of the vast majority of people who lived in cities (almost as though the "first urban Christians" were the "first suburban Christians" or the "first condo-dwelling Christians"). In actuality, most urban dwellers lived in multi-story tenement buildings (*insulae*), which contained no plumbing or cooking spaces, with entire families crammed into a single small room, and multiple families sharing a single common space.[73] These buildings were poorly made and were prone to collapsing or catching fire, harming or killing a good many of the people living therein—a point mocked by Juvenal in his *Satires*:

---

71. Meggitt, *Paul, Poverty and Survival*, 55–56.

72. Quoted in Meggitt, *Paul, Poverty and Survival*, 59.

73. See Crossan and Borg, *First Paul*, 83–85; Meggitt, *Paul, Poverty and Survival*, 62–66; Dunn, *Beginning from Jerusalem*, 606–7.

We live in a city shored up, for the most part, with gimcrack

Stays and props: that's how our landlords arrest

The collapse of their property, papering over the cracks

In the ramshackle fabric, reassuring the tenants

They can sleep secure, when all the time the building

Is poised like a house of cards

I prefer to live where

Fires and midnight panics are not quite such common events.[74]

Thus, if we are looking for a contemporary parallel to the experiences of the urban populations at the time of Paul, closer matches are found in the slums of Mumbai, Rio de Janeiro, or Gaza than are found in the suburbs and condos of Europe or European colonized territories on Turtle Island.

Not only was there a massive gap between the wealthy and high status few and the poor and low status many, but Greco-Roman society was also structured so as to make social mobility nearly impossible. As Wayne Meeks notes, this society was "rigidly stratified" and there could be little expectation of change.[75] Indeed, any who tried to climb the social ladder were frowned upon, and any who tried to disrupt the social order were mocked or attacked. This, in fact, is one of the central themes of Juvenal's writing. Juvenal, despite his biting wit, is a staunch protector of Roman values, and he most viciously and consistently attacks those exhibiting some sort of status dissonance—notably freed slaves, like Trimalchio, who have inherited vast amounts of money from their former owners and who then go on to mimic the dress and actions of members of superior orders.[76] The mere existence of such people, who are little more than "silt washed down by the Nile," are all the justification Juvenal thinks he needs for his satires.[77]

Therefore, a more detailed socioeconomic exploration of the societies in which Paul lived should alter the assumptions we bring to our readings of the Pauline letters and significantly impact the plausibility of historical hypotheses about the socioeconomic status of the early Jesus loyalists. As Richard Horsley writes, "claims that the participants in Pauline churches represented a cross section of urban society simply do not fit the sharp

74. Juvenal, *Satires* 3.194–200.

75. Meeks, *Moral World of the First Christians*, 32, 34; see also Meeks, *First Urban Christians*, 20.

76. Juvenal, *Satires* 1.23–26.

77. See Juvenal, *Satires* 1.27–32.

divide in ancient Roman urban society known from evidence outside the New Testament and other Christian sources."[78] Simply put, unless there is stark evidence to the contrary, we should assume that Paul and all of the other participants in the early Jesus movement were members of the 90 percent of the empire's population who hovered around the subsistence level.[79]

There is nothing new about this conclusion—Adolf Deissmann already came to it one hundred years ago. Yet Deissmann did not set the trajectory for scholarship. Although a consensus had begun to form around his writings, this consensus was replaced by a "new consensus" which made the argument that there was, after all, a great deal of social diversity in the early assemblies of Jesus loyalists. In fact, the assemblies were said to be dominated by a wealthy and high-status minority. Therefore, I will turn to examining the evidence offered by this "new consensus" and the counter-arguments that have been raised against it in more recent years, before drawing my own conclusions on these matters.

The Case for a Dominant Wealthy and High-Status Minority within the Assemblies

> If the Corinthians are at all typical, the early Christians were dominated by a socially pretentious section of the population of the big cities. Beyond that they seem to have drawn on a broad constituency, probably representing the household dependents of the leading members.[80]
>
> —Edwin A. Judge, *Social Distinctives of the Christians in the First Century*

The strongest voices challenging Deissmann's view and the "old consensus" on the socioeconomic status of the early Jesus loyalists, are those of Edwin Judge, Wayne Meeks, Gerd Theissen, and Abraham Malherbe (with Meeks

78. Horsley, *Christian Origins*, 10.

79. As claimed by the likes of Horsley, "Introduction: A People's History," 20; Meggitt, *Paul, Poverty and Survival*, 75, 97–99; Deissmann, *Light from the Ancient East*, 9. Other scholars who claim that we lack the evidence needed to draw any firm conclusions about the social status of the early Jesus loyalists implicitly strengthen the case for this (see, for example, Holmberg, *Sociology and the New Testament*, 67–69; Meeks, *First Urban Christians*, 72).

80. Judge, *Social Distinctives of the Christians*, 43.

and Theissen being the most influential, Judge being an often-neglected precursor, and Malherbe being a prominent follower). Simply stated, "new consensus" proponents do not deny the strength of much of Deissmann's analysis. Instead, they incorporate a lot of it, while also challenging crucial elements of it, in order to significantly modify the emphases and outcomes.

Initially, the concession is made that the early Jesus movement was strongly rooted among "the lowly" and "the poor" and that most of the members of the early assemblies of Jesus loyalists in Paul's day would be lowly and poor members of society. However, an important proviso is then made: not *all* of the early members of the assemblies of Jesus were lowly and poor. In fact, it is argued, there was a small minority of members who possessed both high status and wealth and it was this minority who played the most prominent role in sustaining, leading, and developing the local assemblies.[81] Thus, concluding a significant amount of study on this issue, Theissen writes: "it can be said that Hellenistic primitive Christianity was neither a proletarian movement among the lower classes nor an affair of the upper classes. On the contrary, what was characteristic of its social structure is that it encompassed various strata."[82] Indeed, it is precisely this existence as a "cross section of society" that is said to make early Christianity unique, as other cultic movements were much more homogeneous.[83]

The strongest case is made for this position on the basis of Paul's first epistle to the Corinthians, which is taken—even by some of the staunchest anti-imperial readers of Paul—to reveal assemblies of Jesus loyalists that contain both high status and wealthy members and low status and poor members.[84] As Dunn argues, 1 Corinthians "'takes the lid off' a first-century church as no other Christian literature of the first two or three

81. On this concession and its critical modification, see Holmberg, *Sociology and the New Testament*, 36–60, 64; Judge, *Social Distinctives of the Christians*, 43–44; Theissen, *Social Reality and the Early Christians*, 270–71; Dunn, *Beginning from Jerusalem*, 622–37, 710; Carter, *Roman Empire*, 56–57; Malherbe, *Social Aspects of Early Christianity*, 31; Sampley, *Walking Between the Times*, 37–39; Winter, *See the Welfare of the City*, 203; Sanders, *Paul*, 10–11; Winter, *Divine Honours for the Caesars*, 142–43; Strom, *Reframing Paul*, 10; Harland, "Connections with Elites," 393–94; Welborn, *Paul, the Fool of Christ*, 102, 125–28.

82. Theissen, *Social Setting of Pauline Christianity*, 106.

83. See Malherbe, *Social Aspects of Early Christianity*, 87.

84. See Dunn, *Beginning from Jerusalem*, 799; Crossan and Borg, *First Paul*, 197–200; Carter, *Roman Empire and the New Testament*, 56–57; Horrell, *Social Ethos*, 94–119; Malherbe, *Social Aspects of Early Christianity*, 84; Theissen, *Social Setting of Pauline Christianity*.

centuries does."[85] Thus, premised upon readings of 1 Corinthians, the "new consensus" tries to demonstrate that there is sufficient evidence in the Pauline material to lead us to the conclusion that the existence of wealthy and high status members in the early assemblies of Jesus is not only historically plausible but actually probable. In what follows, I will summarize six issues raised in 1 Corinthians that may suggest the presence of wealthy and high-status Jesus loyalists.

Factions in 1 Cor 1–4

1 Cor 1:26 is a critical passage in the shift from the old to the new consensus. It is located within the context of 1 Cor 1–4, wherein Paul and his coworkers address various factions that have arisen in Corinth after their departure from the city. They write: "Consider your own call, [siblings]: not many of you were wise by human standards, not many were powerful, not many were of noble birth." The point is this: if *not many* were wise, powerful or of noble birth, the implication is that *at least a few were* (otherwise, Paul should have said, *not any* were wise, powerful, or of noble birth).[86] Therefore, a possible explanation of the various factions that have broken out at Corinth is that people with different degrees of status and wealth were not able to remain united.[87] Those who are "wise" ended up feuding with those who were "foolish" (the "powerful" with the "weak," the "noble" with the "lowly"), and these divisions were just as deeply economic as they were theological. Hence, the Pauline faction's letter is a sustained call for the various economically-rooted factions to be united in the Anointed, as Paul makes clear very early on: "I appeal to you, [siblings], by the name of our Lord Jesus [Anointed], that all of you be in agreement and that there be no divisions among you, but that you be united in the same mind and the same purpose" (1 Cor 1:10). Significantly, as we will see, those who favor this reading see the Pauline call to unity as one that favors the position taken by those with high status and wealth.

85. Dunn, *Beginning from Jerusalem*, 785.

86. In light of this, the statements in 1 Cor 4:8, 10 ("Already you have all you want! Already you have become rich! Quite apart from us you have become kings! Indeed, I wish that you had become kings . . . you are strong, you are held in honor") may not be entirely hyperbolic.

87. See Horrell, *Social Ethos*, 112–17. A trend that certainly seems to be pretty constant across different cultures and different historical moments.

Sexual Immorality in 1 Cor 5:1–13 and 6:15–17

Continuing through the letter, we arrive at a case that would be considered incestuous (a man having sex with his father's wife) in 1 Cor 5. The pertinent question is this: why would the Corinthians have permitted this relationship to continue unhindered, given that incest was widely and strongly condemned in Greco-Roman society and in Second Temple Judaism(s)? The proposed solution is that the man responsible for the incestuous actions was a person with high status and wealth and probably a patron of the assembly or assemblies of Jesus loyalists at Corinth. Given that the vast majority of the Jesus loyalists at Corinth would be lowly and poor, they would have relied upon the ongoing financial (and other) support of this patron and would be hesitant to call him to account for his sexual activity.[88] As James Dunn writes: "To offend such a one could have entailed serious social consequences for livelihood and social acceptability. The very viability of the church itself may have been at stake if its existence depended on the protection and benefaction of such a powerful figure."[89]

A similar case is made in relation to those who need to be warned not to be "united to a prostitute" in 1 Cor 6:12–20. At dinner parties among the wealthy members of society, it was standard practice for sex workers or sexually exploited slaves to be employed as companions for the dinner guests, and sexual activities regularly occurred over the course of the evening.[90] This was a fully legal practice ("all things are lawful for me," goes the saying the Pauline faction quotes from some at Corinth), as young men with status who had reached the age of adulthood were able "by choice and convention" to engage in sexually promiscuous acts whilst reclining at dinner.[91] However, to others for whom this was not a regular unquestioned event, such as those who were lowly and poor (who might even be employed as slaves who had almost certainly been targets of sexual violence and exploitation) this would be a very offensive practice. Thus, on sexual matters, Paul is also said to be negotiating a divide between those with high and low status and wealth.

88. See Elliott, *Liberating Paul*, 212–13; Winter, *After Paul Left Corinth*, 44–57; Dunn, *Beginning from Jerusalem*, 796–97.

89. Dunn, *Beginning from Jerusalem*, 797.

90. See Dunn, *Beginning from Jerusalem*, 787; Elliott, *Liberating Paul*, 212–13.

91. Winter, *After Paul Left Corinth*, 89–91.

Litigation in 1 Cor 6:1–11

The next matter raised is the issue of some members engaging in lawsuits against other members and taking them before the civic courts. The courts, along with the rule of law, were domains shaped by the interests of the socioeconomic and political elites.[92] Not all members of society are said to have the right to prosecute others and so the observation that some at Corinth were engaging in this practice (a common means of pursuing a social rival or of exploiting a social inferior) suggests that these people had the level of status and wealth required to both access the courts and expect positive outcomes.[93] Therefore, the argument is made that Paul is either addressing (and condemning) rivalries among elite factions in the assemblies of Jesus at Corinth or he is condemning elites who are exploiting the lowly through judiciary avenues.

Issues Related to Food in 1 Cor 8:1–13; 10:1–31; 11:17–34

Matters related to food, established patterns of eating, and table fellowship, take up a great deal of space in the Pauline letters. In much of this discussion the Pauline faction speaks of two conflicting parties, "the strong" and "the weak," and the majority of scholars have taken these as references to those with high and low status.[94] Two primary points of contention emerge: first, eating meat sacrificed to idols at dinner parties (1 Cor 8 and 10); and second, the way in which the community was gathering to celebrate the Lord's Supper (1 Cor 11:17–34).

In terms of eating meat offered to idols at dinner parties, two main points merit attention. First, some argue that eating meat was generally the prerogative of the elites who could afford this more expensive type of food

92. Cicero, for example, comments on the financial corruption of the courts with some concern in *In Verrem* 1.1: "a belief, disastrous for the state and dangerous for you, has become widespread, and has been increasingly talked about not only among ourselves but among foreign peoples as well—the belief that, in these courts as they are currently constituted, it is impossible for a man with money, no matter how guilty he may be, to be convicted" (see also, 1.47).

93. See Dunn, *Beginning from Jerusalem*, 797; Horrell, *Social Ethos*, 109–12; Malherbe, *Social Aspects of Early Christianity*, 76; Theissen, *Social Setting of Pauline Christianity*, 97; Winter, *Seek the Welfare of the City*, 106–8, 120; Winter, *After Paul Left Corinth*, 58–75.

94. See Dunn, *Beginning from Jerusalem*, 701–2; Winter, *After Paul Left Corinth*, 4; Elliott, *Liberating Paul*, 204; Meeks, *First Urban Christians*, 98.

as an unexceptional part of their daily meals. However, for those who were poor, meat tended to have religious or sacred connotations because the primary venue wherein poor people could eat meat was in cultic settings or celebrations. As the Pauline faction writes: "Since some have become so accustomed to idols until now, they still think of the food they eat as food offered to an idol; and their conscience, being weak, is defiled" (1 Cor 8:7).[95] Therefore, from this perspective, Paul and his coworkers counsel those with high status to relinquish the "right" they have to eat meat (even though they essentially agree with the elite position described in 1 Cor 8:4–6, 8–9, and 10:23–30) because the need for unity among Jesus loyalists, and the state of the consciences of the "weak" members, are more important than exercising the rights granted to the wealthy.[96]

Second, some also highlight how those with high status were more likely to receive invitations to dinner parties like those mentioned in 1 Cor 10:27. In fact, this was one of the important means by which wealthy and high status people maintained their social ties.[97] Therefore, the Pauline faction tries to offer advice that permits those with high status and wealth to maintain their connections, while also urging them to exercise caution and, at times, actually jeopardize their status due to prioritizing the unity that is required among Jesus loyalists.

Paul and his coworkers further jeopardize the position of the wealthy in the context of 1 Cor 10 when they shift from affirming that "idols are nothing" (1 Cor 8:4) to referring to idols as *daimonion* ("demons") and asserting that the Corinthians "cannot drink the cup of the Lord and the cup of [*daimonion*]" (1 Cor 10:21). What has prompted this shift? Without overly anticipating the content of volume 2 (wherein festivals and the calendar of the imperial cult are examined in detail), it is worth pausing on this point. Bruce Winter has built a strong argument that this shift in focus is explained by the difference between attending meals that were held at private homes and meals that were held at cultic celebrations of the imperial

95. See Elliott, *Liberating Paul*, 205–6; Horrell, *Social Ethos*, 105–9; Meeks, *First Urban Christians*, 98; Theissen, *Fortress Introduction*, 75; Theissen, *Social Setting of Pauline Christianity*, 124–30; Dunn, *Beginning from Jerusalem*, 802–4.

96. See Theissen, *Fortress Introduction*, 75; Theissen, *Social Setting of Pauline Christianity*, 137–39; Wright, *Climax of the Covenant*, 134–36; Dunn, *Beginning from Jerusalem*, 804–5; Winter, *After Paul Left Corinth*, 280–83.

97. See Theissen, *Social Setting of Pauline Christianity*, 30; Winter, *Divine Honours for the Caesars*, 223–25.

cult—another important gathering place for those with status and wealth.[98] Winter notes that from early on, Corinth was a leading center of imperial cultic activity and Romanization in Achaea.[99] Even before the Roman senate affirmed the perpetual divinity of Julius Caesar in 42 BCE, Corinth recognized him as divine in this way (Caesar had re-founded Corinth as a colony in 44 BCE), and statues to imperial divinities were prominent both in imperial cultic temples in Corinth but also in other public places like the theater, marketplace, and the Julian Basilica where court cases were heard.[100] Corinth was quick to recognize other imperial figures—from Augustus to Claudius to Livia to Octavia (and even Gaius)—in this way.[101] Thus, the imperial cult was very well established in Corinth prior to Paul's arrival there in the mid-50s CE.[102] The prominent presence of this cult only increased after Paul left Corinth. Cultic festivities expanded greatly after the ascension of Nero (in 54 CE) and the Isthmian Games became an important celebration associated with that cult.[103] The Games were a time when all Corinthians were expected to participate in imperial cultic meals, prayers, sacrifices, and celebrations.[104] The president of the Games hosted a meal that all Corinthian citizens had the right to attend (once again calling to mind the Corinthian aphorism that "all things are lawful to me" in 1 Cor 10:23).[105] In light of this, Winter argues that the *daimonion* the Pauline faction mentions are the imperial *genii*—the guiding spirits of the emperors, who gave emperors their faculties of reason and acted as intermediaries between them and the gods.[106] Here, the term *daimonion* lacks the negative associations it carries in later traditions—it is not an oxymoron to speak of the "good demon" (a term applied to Nero on Alexandrian coinage) or to

---

98. Winter, *Divine Honours for the Caesars*, 191, 223–25.

99. Winter, *Divine Honours for the Caesars*, 184.

100. Winter, *Divine Honours for the Caesars*, 65, 184–85.

101. Winter, *Divine Honours for the Caesars*, 65, 185, 189.

102. Winter says the cult was already in Corinth half a century before Paul (*Divine Honours for the Caesars*, 167), but worship of the divinized Caesars in Corinth actually preceded Paul's arrival by about ninety years.

103. See Winter, *After Paul Left Corinth*, 4–6, 169–86; 271–78; Dunn follows Winter, as do many others (see, for example, Dunn, *Beginning from Jerusalem*, 781–82); also Winter, *Divine Honours for the Caesars*, 209.

104. Winter, *Divine Honours for the Caesars*, 178, 191–92.

105. See Winter, *Seek the Welfare of the City*, 166–74; Winter, *After Paul Left Corinth*, 93–95.

106. Winter, *Divine Honours for the Caesars*, 214–15.

praise the "good genius" of Nero, as is found in an inscription in Corinth.[107] Indeed, from the reign of Claudius onwards, cultic centers were established around devotion to the genius of the living emperor.[108] Winter's argument, that the issue faced by the Corinthians is participation in imperial cultic meals, is strengthened when attention is paid to the mention of "so-called gods in heaven or on earth" in 1 Cor 8:5. Winter demonstrates that the term "in heaven or on earth" was "the official Roman convention for referring to present and deceased Emperors."[109] Gods are mentioned in the plural due to the veneration of several members of the imperial household, but they are only "so-called gods" because the Pauline faction refuses to recognize their divinity and, in fact, desires that those in the assemblies of Jesus loyalists refrain from participating in communion with such gods (or *daimonion*) at cultic meals both for their own sake and in order to prevent "the weak" from stumbling. In terms of socioeconomic matters, Winter's emphasis is that it was wealthy and high-status people who had the opportunity to participate in such meals—and who also stood to gain more from participation therein.

A similar division between the wealthy and the poor is posited in the discussion of the Lord's supper in 2 Cor 11:17–34. Here, it is claimed that the wealthy members of the assemblies have fallen into treating the poor members shamefully during the meal, because they (the wealthy) are acting out standard social conventions rather than treating others (the poor) with the mutuality demanded by the equal status afforded to all those who are in the Anointed.[110] At Greco-Roman dinner parties, those with high status (like a patron and his close friends) ate better quality food and more courses than those with lower status who might be in attendance (like the clients of that patron). Thus, as the Pauline faction notes, "when the time comes to eat . . . one goes hungry and another becomes drunk" (1 Cor 11:21).[111] Those who could afford a lifestyle of leisure could begin eating and drinking early, while those who were forced to work long hard hours would have to come later and perhaps end up going hungry. Therefore, in a manner that again subtly favors the position of the wealthier members,

107. Winter, *Divine Honours for the Caesars*, 217–18.

108. Winter, *Divine Honours for the Caesars*, 219.

109. Winter, *Divine Honours for the Caesars*, 210–11.

110. See Winter, *After Paul Left Corinth*, 142–58; Theissen, *Social Setting of Pauline Christianity*, 96, 150–62; Horrell, *Social Ethos*, 102–5.

111. This status divide at dinners is well illustrated by a lengthy dinner party described in the *Satyricon*.

Paul encourages them to first "eat at home" (1 Cor 11:34) so as not to offend the lower members.[112]

Possession of Homes and Slaves: The Status of the Named People in the Pauline Letters

Mention of eating "at home" leads to the next point employed to suggest a mixture of those with high status and wealth at Corinth and beyond. Possessing homes or other forms of property is taken to be a marker of high status. Thus, in 1 Cor 4:8, the Pauline faction mentions the wealth of some of the Corinthians: "Already you have all you want! Already you have become rich!" Throughout the Pauline Epistles, we see references to others in various cities who appear to have the means to possess enough resources and a large enough home to host assemblies of Jesus loyalists or to host Paul as a guest—Philemon at Colossae, who is also wealthy enough to own at least one slave (Phlm), Crispus, Gaius, Stephanas, and maybe also Chloe at Corinth (1 Cor 1:1, 11, 14, 16; 16:15; Rom 16:23), Aristobulus and Narcissus at Rome (Rom 16:10–11) and so on. Add to that the reference to Phoebe as a "patron" in Rom 16:23 and the mention of Erastus in the same verse—whom many have taken to be the *aedile* and city treasurer of Corinth mentioned on an inscription that is dated to Paul's time—and the possibility that Prisca and Aquila as well as Lydia are successful and wealthy business people (1 Cor 16:19; Acts 16:11–40), and the case is made that the wealthy and high-status minority dominates those who are named by Paul and make up his most intimate circle of coworkers and companions.[113]

Mobility

Finally, it is also worth briefly noting that the ability to travel is frequently interpreted as a marker of wealth and privilege, as those who were poor

---

112. Theissen, *Social Setting of Pauline Christianity*, 164.

113. See Dunn, *Beginning from Jerusalem*, 626–29, 696, 671; Theissen, *Social Setting of Pauline Christianity*, 95; Winter, *Seek the Welfare of the City*, 180, 192–95; Malherbe, *Social Aspects of Early Christianity*, 77. On Erastus as an *aedile* see Winter, *Seek the Welfare of the City*, 180, 193–95. Judge notes that of the ninety-one people named in the New Testament in relation to Paul, one-third have Latin names which could be markers of Roman citizenship (Judge, *Social Distinctives*, 142–43). However, what is more likely, as we will see below, is that these were slave names.

could not afford to travel. Travel was time-consuming, dangerous, costly, and not to be taken lightly. That Paul and at least seventeen of his peers were able to travel is taken as a sign of wealth and status.[114]

Locality and Status Dissonance

Therefore, with the single exception of Erastus (who, in this reading, is an *aedile* and so would be among the most elite 2–3 or 2–5 percent of the empire), this perspective argues that a dominant minority of Jesus loyalists held a significant degree of status and wealth in their own civic contexts, even if they were still minor characters in light of the great power-players of the empire. Here, the importance of studying local details, instead of dealing with overarching empire-wide generalizations comes to the fore. As Judge notes: "If the common assertion that the Christian groups were constituted from the lower order of the society is meant to imply that they did not draw upon the upper orders of the Roman ranking system, this observation is correct, and pointless."[115] Instead, Judge locates the early Jesus loyalists among those who experienced "status dissonance" and who knew "the discord between relatively high status in the home town and low rank in Roman eyes."[116] Meeks arrives at a similar conclusion. He argues that the key members of the assemblies associated with the Pauline faction are among a minority of the Greco-Roman population who have experienced some upward mobility (perhaps through emancipation or obtaining a significant amount of wealth) and who therefore are experiencing "status inconsistency."[117]

Therefore, the six factors explored in this section are taken as sufficient evidence that, despite the odds, the early assemblies of Jesus loyalists

114. Malherbe, *Social Aspects of Early Christianity*, 75. There is one last argument that is sometimes made regarding the possible wealth of folks at Corinth and elsewhere— namely that the Pauline Collection for the poor in Jerusalem is only possible if some in the assemblies are fairly wealthy. See Sanders, *Paul: The Apostle's Life*, 143; Welborn, "That There May Be Equality," 76–80. This will be addressed in more detail when the topic of the Collection is examined in volume 3.

115. Judge, *Social Distinctives of the Christians*, 37; also 37–39. See also Jennings, *Outlaw Justice*, 228; and the examination of the economic models that follow below.

116. Judge, *Social Distinctives of the Christians*, 140–44, although Judge makes this conclusion cautiously given the lack of available evidence.

117. See Meeks, *First Urban Christians*, 72–73, and throughout. Many have followed Meeks (see, for example, Holmberg, *Sociology and the New Testament*, 73–76; Jeffers, *Greco-Roman World*, 194).

reflected a cross-section of society, with the individual assemblies being composed of a majority of people who possess little status and wealth but who were organized and lead by a dominant minority of people who, within their own civic environments, possessed relatively high status and wealth.

Outworkings of High Status and Wealth: Love-Patriarchalism

Conclusions drawn from these studies tend to affirm a mostly conservative understanding of the socioeconomic and political ethics of the Pauline faction and the early assemblies of Jesus loyalists. Especially influential in this regard has been Gerd Theissen's restatement of Ernst Troeltsch's argument that the ethics of the early Jesus loyalists can be described as a form of "love-patriarchalism." Troeltsch, in his noted history of Christianity, argued strenuously against Karl Kautsky and other Marxist scholars. Kautsky et al., drawing especially upon Acts 2:44 and 4:32, argued that nascent Christianity was defined by the practice and ideology of a "love communism." Against this, Troeltsch asserted that Paul and others did not remove daily inequalities from the lives of Jesus loyalists but instead focused upon their *spiritual* status, and an ethics of love and charitable service.[118] Thus, Theissen argues that the early Christians are marked by a tension between a "'democratization' of an ancient aristocratic ethic" that comes from the top downwards and an "'aristocratization' of a popular mentality" that comes from the bottom upwards.[119] Social stratifications were maintained, but new forms of generosity and solidarity were created as a "realistic" solution to the challenges faced by the Pauline communities in an ethics of "familial love-patriarchalism."[120] According to Theissen, this produces a "moderate social conservatism" that ends up making "a lasting impact upon Christianity" as members of different socioeconomic strata learn to respect

---

118. See Troeltsch, *Social Teachings of the Christian Churches*, 1:76–80. Weiss makes a similar argument around the same time and Lietzmann follows this trajectory prior to Theissen (see Weiss, *Earliest Christianity*, 1:74–75; Lietzmann, *Beginnings of the Christian Church*, 134). Schüssler-Fiorenza offers some criticisms of the ways in which this justifies patriarchalism and makes it essential to the development of Christianity (*In Memory of Her*, 83).

119. Theissen, *Religion of the Earliest Churches*, 82.

120. See Theissen, *Religion of the Earliest Churches*, 81; Theissen, *Social Setting of Pauline Christianity*, 37, 69, 107–9.

each other, even as those strata continue to exist without being seriously challenged.[121]

The Case for the Absence of High Status and Wealthy Members in the Early Assemblies

An increasing number of scholars are uncomfortable with the analysis and conclusions of Theissen and the "new consensus," along with their concomitant implications for Pauline ethics. In this section, I will explore ways in which the six issues described above have been reexamined. I will then turn to the economic models offered by Steven Friesen, Peter Oakes, and Bruce W. Longenecker, and will conclude by briefly mentioning three further points that support an understanding of the early Jesus loyalists as both "lowly" and "poor."

Reexamining Socioeconomic Issues at Corinth

Justin Meggitt has engaged in the most sustained analysis of the issues raised above in order to posit a compelling alternative to the "new consensus."[122] I will quickly run through his counterpoints. Beginning with the factions mentioned in the rather hyperbolic passage of 1 Cor 1–4 (and addressed continually throughout that letter), Meggitt argues that the terms employed in 1 Cor 1:26 are more elusive and were employed with a broader variety of meanings—some more literal and some more metaphorical—than those suggested by Theissen et al. Thus, the divide suggested between various groups could simply be a small but significant gap distinguishing those who were slightly more fortunate (but still lowly and poor) from those who were less fortunate.[123] Similarly, the reference to honor in 1 Cor 4:10 could just as easily refer to some who were laying claim to greater *spiritual* honor—through the manifestation of various gifts, like tongues—and is not an unambiguous reference to *social* honor.[124] Finally, given the charismatic nature of the early assemblies, and given that they still lacked an established hierarchy in Paul's day (a point I will explore in more detail below), such factions could simply reflect the not-yet-centralized and not-yet-organized

121. Theissen, *Social Setting of Pauline Christianity*, 108.
122. See Meggitt, *Paul, Poverty and Survival*.
123. Meggitt, *Paul, Poverty and Survival*, 101–6.
124. Meggitt, *Paul, Poverty and Survival*, 106–7.

nature of these communities and need not be rooted in clearly delineated economic stratifications.

Second, Meggitt notes that the case of incest mentioned in 1 Cor 5:1–13 need not be class-specific and he observes how there is actually evidence that clients could and did sometimes charge their patrons with this offense ("popular justice" was often dispensed in these cases, regardless of the status of the accused), thereby countering proponents of the "new consensus" when they claim that this could not happen.[125]

Third, looking at the ligation in 1 Cor 6:1–11, Meggitt agrees that the legal system was heavily biased towards the elite members of society. However, he also notes multiple examples of social equals among the lower classes taking each other to court. Although the poor could not prosecute the rich, they could and did prosecute each other. Therefore, using the courts to further one's interests was not the exclusive territory of the elite.[126]

Fourth, turning to matters of food, Meggitt builds a strong case that the eating of meat, mentioned in 1 Cor 8 and 10, was actually far more common among non-elites than scholars previously assumed. Meat was available at lower-class cookhouses and wineshops, from street vendors, and at baths. Therefore, the argument that meat was a more regular, secular item for the elites, but was considered more sacred and associated with the gods by the non-elites, simply does not hold up in light of the historical evidence.[127] Additionally, Winter's division between private meals and public meals associated with the imperial cult(s) blurs in actual practice. Often, in private homes, prayers were said to the emperor or the imperial family as a part of the celebration of the meal. Winter's association of participation in public cultic meals with higher status and wealth is also problematized by the increasing recognition that entire civic populations were not only invited but expected to participate in these festivities (a point Winter observes but then neglects). Given the ubiquity of such festivities, and the universal attendance they demanded, caution should be exercised about concluding that Winter's otherwise strong argument about imperial cultic meals at Corinth points to members of high status within the assemblies of Jesus loyalists there.

Turning to the divisions mentioned around the Lord's Supper in 1 Cor 11:17–34, it should be observed that nothing requires these to be division

125. Meggitt, *Paul, Poverty and Survival*, 150–53.
126. Meggitt, *Paul, Poverty and Survival*, 122–25.
127. Meggitt, *Paul, Poverty and Survival*, 107–12.

between those with high and low status. Rather, there could be a few who were devouring the little bread and wine that were to be shared among all.[128] Further, as Deissmann notes, this could be occurring not out of greed but out of sheer hunger.[129] Thus, for example, those who were poor and jobless may have shown up early and starving, and eaten the meal before the working poor had time to arrive.

Fifth, on matters of property—notably homes and slaves—Meggitt observes that the mention of homes need not imply ownership of those homes. It was far more likely that people were simply tenants renting homes that were small and cramped.[130] That Paul expects outsiders to be able to witness events in the assemblies of Jesus loyalists in 1 Cor 14:20–25, only adds to this conclusion. If Jesus loyalists were meeting in properly private homes, such intrusions would not be likely. Further, it has now become clear that slavery extended far deeper into Greco-Roman society than previously imagined. Slaves could be owned in great numbers by the elites, but struggling artisans, peasants, and even others slaves sometimes owned slaves.[131] Therefore, the mere mention of a person owning a slave cannot be taken as an unambiguous marker of high status and wealth. It does show that the owner has a higher status than the slave that is owned but, again, this need not be correlated with other markers of high status or wealth. There are many degrees of status that exist between being a slave and being anything close to well-to-do.

The same caution also applies to studies of those who are named in the Pauline letters. Against previously confident assertions, James Dunn notes how many of those named in Rom 16 actually possess common slave names—thus, Andronicus, Junia, Ampliatus, Herodion, Tryphaena, Tryphosa, Persis, Asyncritus, Hermes, Patrobas, Philologus, Julia, and Nereus—which, coupled with the observation that about one-third of people in urban centers were slaves, leads to the conclusion that a good many of those previously taken to be high status—as well as a good many of the other members of the assemblies of Jesus—were more probably slaves.[132]

128. Meggitt, *Paul, Poverty and Survival*, 118–22.

129. Deissmann, *Paul*, 242.

130. Meggitt, *Paul Poverty and Survival*, 120–21, 129; Pickett, "Conflicts at Corinth," 123–24.

131. Meggitt, *Paul, Poverty and Survival*, 129–32.

132. Dunn, *Beginning from Jerusalem*, 632; see also Martin, "Eyes Have It," 221; Osiek, "Family Matters," 209; Deissmann, *Paul*, 243; Clarke, "Jew and Greek," 113–14. Here it is worth anticipating some of our subsequent discussion by asking why it might

Further, other Latin names that had been taken as status markers were common slave names—a point that comes through in translation. Fortunatus means "Lucky" (1 Cor 16:17), Achaias means "the Greek" (1 Cor 16:17) and Onesimus means "Useful" (Phlm 8, 10).[133] The same insight applies to the members of "Caesar's house" mentioned in Phil 4:22. In all likelihood, these were slaves who had some relation to the governor's household in Philippi.[134] Thus, all these people are more plausibly of much lower status than many assumed previously.

Caution is also needed when looking at other named members of the assemblies of Jesus. Meggitt notes how the title applies to Erastus in Rom 16:23, "the *oikonomos* of the city," is somewhat ambiguous and could be used as a reference for anybody from a high-ranking municipal officer to a public slave. Further, despite the tantalizing suggestions offered by the inscription found at Corinth that mentions an *aedile* named Erastus, Meggitt demonstrates that the name Erastus was more common than previously assumed.[135] Not only that but, as Bruce W. Longenecker notes, the famous *aedile* inscription breaks off at the first "E," meaning that the name might be different than Erastus (Eperastus being another relatively common name). Longenecker also observes that the inscription likely dates to the late first century or early second century CE.[136] Similarly, mention of Crispus in 1 Cor 1:14 relies entirely upon the identification of this Crispus with the synagogue official of the same name mentioned in Acts 18:17. It is tempting to bring the texts together this way but we have seen that Acts is somewhat unreliable and Crispus (which means "curly-haired") could just as easily be a nickname for any curly-haired person (or slave) as it could be a proper name. However, hedging his bets, Meggitt notes that, in Paul's day, a synagogue official need not be a person with a great deal of wealth, but could

---

be that the early Jesus movement attracted slaves in this way.

133. Pickett, "Conflicts at Corinth," 124.

134. See Meggitt, *Paul, Poverty and Survival*, 126–27; also Harland, "Connections with Elites," 395–96, who also includes freedpersons as possible members of this group, as they would still be legally bonded to their former masters. Sanders notes that "Caesar's house" would likely be the name for the house of Caesar's representative, the governor, in Philippi (*Paul: The Apostle's Life*, 585). This name came about, in part, because in the early days of the principate the imperial bureaucracy grew out of freedmen and slaves attached to the emperor's household (see Saller, *Personal Patronage*, 66–67).

135. Meggitt, *Paul, Poverty and Survival*, 135–40; see also Harland, "Connections with Elites," 394–95.

136. Longenecker, *Remember the Poor*, 237–39.

simply be a person who managed the funds of others.[137] Finally, turning to Phoebe (Rom 16:1–2), Meggitt notes how her independence need not be a mark of status (as she could be a widow from any social stratum). That she is referred to as a "patron" is likely an example of the Pauline faction manipulating socially emotive language in order to compliment her and in order to encourage the Romans to accept her.[138]

Sixth, the argument for high status and wealth, based on the ability of Paul and some of his coworkers to travel, is also ambiguous. Despite assertions to the contrary, a wide variety of people traveled in Paul's day and various means of transportation—from the expensive to the inexpensive—were available.[139] In fact, there was a great deal of migration occurring during the early imperial period. Peasant populations who were forced off their lands were driven to the city to work, artisans unable to find work in the overpopulated urban centers would move to other cities, and so on. Many people were forced to travel, whether they could afford it or not. Paul, Prisca, and Aquilla, as leather-workers, may have been able to do so slightly more easily than some others, like some displaced rural populations. Their labor, although poorly paid, would be in demand in various cities, and the lightness of their tools (rather than their purported high status or wealth) made travel relatively easier for them than it would have been for others.[140] In fact, the Pauline faction's reference to the great dangers and suffering involved with Paul's travels (e.g., 2 Cor 11:25–27), suggests that he was not traveling as the elite traveled. Granted, the wealthy could also face dangers while traveling but, for them, such dangers were not paired with "toil and hardship, through many a sleepless night, hungry and thirsty, often without food, cold and naked." This is not the kind of travel that one experienced because one was rich enough to pick up and go wherever one wanted to go. It is, yet again, one step above the experiences of those so abjectly poor, sick, or enslaved, that they cannot go anywhere.

137. Meggitt, *Paul, Poverty and Survival*, 141–43.

138. Meggitt, *Paul, Poverty and Survival*, 141–49. That this is the only Pauline use of the term "patron" strengthens the plausibility of this conclusion. Also, as Meggitt notes, if Phoebe was a genuine patron, it would be entirely backwards for Paul, as her client, to write a reference letter for her. The Roman patronage system will be explored in volume 2. Volume 3 will present a sibling-based economic mutuality as the Pauline alternative to this system.

139. Meggitt, *Paul, Poverty and Survival*, 133–34.

140. See Crossan and Borg, *First Paul*, 85.

Finally, the financial support offered to Paul and his coworkers who needed assistance traveling is a sign of the low status and lack of wealth they experienced (given their need for support), but it has also been taken by some as a marker of the high status and wealth enjoyed by other members in the early assemblies of Jesus. I will explore this in more detail when I discuss Pauline economics and the Collection in volume 3. For now, it is worth noting that sharing finances need not be a marker of high status and wealth.[141] Often, in fact, some form of economic mutuality or communalism is more common (frequently as a necessary survival strategy) among people experiencing poverty and deprivation. Thus, in the case of Paul and his coworkers, it could be that those who lived slightly above the subsistence level were able to gather their small surplus in order to care for others and fund projects that they cared about deeply.[142]

Therefore, given the overwhelming historical odds that the early Jesus loyalists were situated among the lowly and poor, and given the counter-evidence to the points raised by the "new consensus" (which makes each case more questionable and seriously undermines the cumulative persuasiveness of the whole argument), Meggitt concludes that the most realistic proposal is to view Paul and the other members of the assemblies

141. See Meggitt, *Paul, Poverty and Survival*, 77, 117, 132–33; Oakes, *Reading Romans in Pompeii*, 78.

142. There is nothing inherently implausible about this suggestion. History shows this kind of action taking place frequently (one is tempted to say all the time) among people experiencing poverty and oppression. See, for example, James C. Scott's *The Art of Not Being Governed*; or the history of the Wobblies or that of the United Farm Workers (see, for example, Renshaw, *Wobblies*; and Bardacke, *Tramping Out the Vintage*). Bourgois and Schonberg draw attention to some of this in what they refer to as the "moral economy of sharing" among people who use intravenous drugs in San Francisco (*Righteous Dopefiend*). Revolutionary movements often pool resources deliberately to fund projects that assist a community to break free from financial reliance upon colonizing powers—from the Black Panther's breakfast program for school children (Bloom and Martin Jr., *Black Against Empire*) to Hamas's funding of all kinds of necessary civic infrastructures (Malka, *Gaza's Health Sector Under Hamas*). These become both means of resistance and the embodiment of liberation, and are generally accomplished by many very poor people contributing what they can for the greater good. In this regard, I think Peter Oakes makes an excellent point when he asks how the letter to the Philippians sounds when read to people from very different backgrounds. When heard by a low-level slave, themes of justice and a new status jump out, to a poor tradesperson, themes of survival, endurance, and eternal life might jump out, to a sexually exploited female bar worker, themes of the redemption of the body and living in the midst of tensions might jump out, and to a relatively wealthier homeowner, themes of the Judean nature of salvation for the nations might be striking (Oakes, *Reading Romans in Pompeii*, 127–74).

of Jesus as lowly and poor. However, Meggitt's argument is open to some criticisms. Despite some of the remarks he makes about the possible gaps that may have existed among various members of the non-elite populations of the Roman Empire, he never develops the grounds or significance of these differences. It is here that Steven Friesen, Peter Oakes, and Bruce W. Longenecker develop Meggitt's insights in a critical manner in order to provide a more nuanced picture of the socioeconomic status of the early Jesus loyalists.

The Models of Friesen, Oakes, and Longenecker

I will examine these models in chronological order, beginning with Friesen before turning to Oakes, and concluding with Longenecker. Friesen starts by looking at general ways of measuring poverty. He highlights indicators like income, mortality, undernourishment, gender discrimination, health care, unemployment, and education, while also looking at structural factors that are maintained in order to ensure that the poor remain poor.[143] Reflecting upon these things within the Greco-Roman context of the first century CE, Friesen arrives at the following "Poverty Scale" (PS), which he uses in order to construct the following seven-tiered model of society in Paul's day:[144]

TABLE 1

Level (Poverty Scale)	Constituents	Percentage of Population (in a city of 10,000+)
1	Imperial elites	0.04
2	Regional or municipal elites	1
3	Municipal elites	1.76
4	Moderate surplus resources	7 (?)
5	Stable near subsistence level	22 (?)
6	At Subsistence	40
7	Below Subsistence	28

Based upon this, his study of prior models, and the research of those like Theissen and Meggitt, Friesen then relates this scale to the people named

143. Friesen, "Paul and Economics," 33. Friesen is drawing on the work of Amartya Sen here.

144. Friesen, "Paul and Economics," 36–37.

in the Pauline Epistles, in order to try and construct a historically plausible socioeconomic model for the early Jesus loyalists:[145]

TABLE 2

Person Named	Poverty Scale (PS) Level
Chloe (?)	4
Gaius	4
Erastus	4–5
Philemon	4–5
Phoebe	4–5
Aquila	4–5
Prisca	4–5
Chloe's people	4–5
Those with food for the Lord's Supper	4–6
Onesimus	4–7
Stephanas	5–6
The household of Stephanas	5–6
The Saints in Corinth	6
The assemblies of Macedonia	6
Paul	6–7
Those with no food for the Lord's Supper	6–7

There are a few important observations to make here. First, all of the elite members of society (PS1–3) are missing from the assemblies of Jesus loyalists. Friesen charges those like Theissen with not developing a properly full set of criteria to evaluate whether or not a person is a member of the elite. For example, if elite people (those at PS1–3) were present, one would also expect mention of things like imperial, provincial, or municipal offices, high-ranking military service, major religious titles, decrees in their honor, large benefactions, major business interests, households with many slaves, wealthy family members, hosting and attending lavish banquets, and an elite education in relation to this population—but none of these things characterize those mentioned in Paul's letters.[146] Instead, what Friesen finds is one or two, with a maximum of seven people who have a moderate surplus and all the rest are hovering just above, at, or below the subsistence

145. Friesen, "Paul and Economics," 40.
146. Friesen, "Paul and Economics," 41.

level.[147] He then fills out the numbers, making some estimates about the sizes of the assemblies of Jesus loyalists throughout Asia Minor and arrives at these figures regarding the socioeconomic status of those in Paul's sphere of influence: 9.58 members with a moderate surplus, 50.41 members stable near the subsistence level, 121.91 unstable at the same level, and 9.08 living below subsistence.[148] Thus, Friesen affirms Meggitt's argument that, unless we have strong evidence to the contrary, we should assume that people lived at the subsistence level, while also developing Meggitt's argument and demonstrating some of the diversity that existed among the non-elite.[149]

However, Friesen's model remains somewhat vague and hypothetical. Peter Oakes in his study *Reading Romans in Pompeii: Paul's Letter at Ground Level*, provides a more grounded approach that parallels Friesen's work.[150] Noting the ways in which previous models did not sufficiently differentiate between the non-elite of the Roman empire, Oakes emphasizes that there was "a diversity that involved social stratification" within that population.[151] The lived experiences of many were neither that of abject poverty (understood as low-level slavery or the experience of homelessness) nor privileged abundance of the top 2–3 percent or 2–5 percent, and so there is a need to move beyond the "scholarly dichotomy between the rich and the abjectly poor."[152] In order to arrive at these conclusions, Oakes employs a "space distribution model" in relation to wealth distribution at Pompeii (a site chosen due to the richness of archaeological evidence it provides), before exploring what this might mean for the composition of assemblies of early Jesus loyalists. In exploring Pompeii, a city comparable to Philippi, Oakes observes the following:

147. Friesen, "Paul and Economics," 40–41.

148. Friesen, "Paul and Economics," 42.

149. On this point see also Friesen, "Injustice or God's Will," 243. Friesen has been the key influence in regards to several others. See, for example, Pickett, "Conflicts at Corinth," 115; Carter, *John and Empire*, 52–58.

150. Oakes, *Reading Romans in Pompeii*.

151. Oakes, *Reading Romans in Pompeii*, xi; for his criticism of previous models see 62–67; and also Oakes, "Methodological Issues," 27–30. Here Oakes defines the economic élite as "a wealthy group that monopolizes an undue proportion of scarce resources" (*Reading Romans in Pompeii*, 32).

152. Oakes, *Reading Romans in Pompeii*, 32. Here, both Friesen and Oakes are responding to the challenge of Judge quoted above.

- the largest group of households occupies less than 100m² (34.72 percent of the houses examined);

- at least 50 percent of the households occupy less than 200m²;

- a significant minority of non-elite households occupy between 200 and 800m² (35.28 percent of the homes examined);

- as many households occupy 400–500m² as occupy 300–400m²;

- the distribution of space does not fade off at the upper end but a small group (around 5 percent) occupies far more space (1000+m²) than they would in a random distribution.[153]

This then leads Oakes to create a tentative model comparing urban space occupied to income distribution as a percentage of the population:[154]

TABLE 3

Urban Space Occupied in Square Meters	Income Distribution as a Percentage of the Population
1000+	2.5
900–999	0.2
800–899	0.3
700–799	0.5
600–699	1
500–599	2.5
400–499	4
300–399	4
200–299	7
100–199	11
0–99	67

Thus, over against those like Theissen who posit "house churches" in the homes of the elites, and those like Jewett who posit gatherings in crowded tenement buildings (*insulae*), Oakes argues for the use of the more modest homes of the non-elite craftworkers who, nonetheless, did have enough space to host a small group of people (although at some points, Oakes notes, the distinction between a rented house and a small apartment

153. Oakes, *Reading Romans in Pompeii*, 47–51.
154. Oakes, *Reading Romans in Pompeii*, 61.

starts to blur).[155] In Pompeii, based upon this "space distribution model," a sample craftworker "house church" would likely have the following amount of space represented by its membership:[156]

Table 4

Space Represented in Square Meters	Number of People Occupying this amount of Space
400+	1 (person wealthier than the host)
300–399	5 (the host and his family)
200–299	4 (close peers of the host)
100–199	5
0–99	10
No space	15 (9 slaves and 6 people with no homes)

Therefore, once again, we see a marked absence of any elite members, but we also see considerably more diversity of both status and wealth among the non-elite.[157] Translating this to the city of Rome, and taking into account local differences, Oakes imagines a craftworker "house church" composed of thirty people and comprising:

- a craftworker who rents a fairly large workshop (around 45m²) and some separate living accommodations for his wife, children, a couple of (male) craftworking slaves, a (female) domestic slave, and a dependent relative;
- a few other householders (mainly, but not necessarily, all male) who rent less space than the first householder and some (but not all) of their spouses, children, slaves, and dependents;
- A couple of members of families whose householder was not a part of the church;
- a couple of slaves whose owners were not a part of the church;
- a couple of free or freed dependents of people who are not a part of the church;

155. Oakes, *Reading Romans in Pompeii*, 69–97.

156. Oakes, *Reading Romans in Pompeii*, 85. Oakes notes how the presence of the family of the host creates a disproportionate bulge at the upper end (*Reading Romans in Pompeii*, 86).

157. Oakes observes how this complicates prior definitions of poverty (*Reading Romans in Pompeii*, 55–57).

- a couple of people experiencing homelessness;
- a few people who are renting space in shared rooms (like migrant workers).[158]

Thus, all are poor and of low status, but there is still a significant gap between the host of the "church" and slaves, migrant workers, or people entirely deprived of housing. As Oakes concludes: "The key impression is of social diversity and social hierarchy, even when the wealthiest member is only a craftworker with a modest household."[159] Thus, in Oakes's model, the early Jesus loyalists did represent a cross-section of much of society, but those with high status and wealth were not present in Paul's day.[160]

Bruce W. Longenecker offers a slightly modified version of these models. He argues that the binary between an extremely small group of elite people and a huge, undifferentiated mass of non-elites living at subsistence level (as per Meggitt, in Longenecker's estimation) is unhelpful and needs to be further differentiated.[161] He approvingly cites Friesen's work with Poverty Scales, although Longenecker prefers to deploy an "Economy Scale" (ES) given that not everybody mentioned lives in poverty.[162] In light of some other work in this field (notably Walter Schiedel's "The Distribution of Income in the Roman Empire"), Longenecker modifies Friesen's numbers and arrives at the following distribution of the population within his Economy Scale:[163]

TABLE 5

Economy Scale (ES) Level	Percentage of the Population (in a city with 10,000+ members)
1–3	3 (Friesen: 2.8)
4	15 (Friesen 7 [?])
5	27 (Friesen: 22 [?])
6	30 (Friesen: 40)

158. Oakes, *Reading Romans in Pompeii*, 96.

159. Oakes, *Reading Romans in Pompeii*, 98. The irony here, as Oakes observes, is that Friesen—and those who follow Meggitt against Theissen—posit more social diversity among the non-elite thereby making Theissen's original solution far more workable, albeit in a revised form (Oakes, *Reading Romans in Pompeii*, 67).

160. A conclusion Warren Carter already reaches in 2002 ("Vulnerable Power," 453).

161. Longenecker, *Remember the Poor*, 40–44.

162. Longenecker, *Remember the Poor*, 44–46.

163. Longenecker, *Remember the Poor*, 46–53.

7	25 (Friesen: 28)

As can be seen, the major difference here is that Longenecker puts sub-stantially more people at ES4 and somewhat more people at ES5, creating a considerably lower percentage of people at ES6 and only slightly less people at ES7 (ES6–7 thus moves from being 68 percent of the population to being 55 percent, and ES4–5 move from being 29[?]percent of the population to being 42 percent). Longenecker notes that, arguing for this shift he is being "optimistic" and countering what he sees as Friesen's pessimism.[164] Remain-ing optimistic, Longenecker highlights that, although 55 percent of people were at ES6–7, a good many of them belonged to households wherein their needs could and would be met.[165] That said, noting the substantial increase in the percentage of people at ES4, Longenecker asserts that he has no wish to retroject or resurrect a "middle class" within Paul's context. But this is not due to economic considerations. Rather, it is because *class consciousness* was absent at that time. Thus, Longenecker writes, "[t]here may have been no middle class, but there were *middling groups*."[166]

Turning, then, to an examination of some of the named members of the assemblies associated with Paul (Onesimus is markedly absent), Longenecker proposes the following distribution:[167]

TABLE 6

Person Named	Level
Gaius	ES4 (Friesen: PS4)
Erastus	ES4 (Friesen PS4–5)
Phoebe	ES4 (Friesen PS 4–5)
Philemon	ES4–5 (Friesen PS4–5)
Stephanas	ES4–5 (Friesen PS5–6)
Crispus	ES4–5 (Friesen PS?)
Aquila	ES5–6 (Friesen PS4–5)
Prisca	ES 5–6 (Friesen PS4–5)

164. Longenecker, *Remember the Poor*, 52.

165. Longenecker, *Remember the Poor*, 54.

166. Longenecker, *Remember the Poor*, 56; emphasis added. See also 55–56.

167. Longenecker, *Remember the Poor*, 236–53.

In justifying this distribution, Longenecker makes the following points. First, although he does not believe that Erastus was an *aedile* in Corinth, he does believe that the mention of civic service of some kind places Erastus at ES4, if not in the upper echelons of ES4.[168] In placing Gaius at ES4, Longenecker notes how common the name Gaius was but, because Gaius is said to be able to host all the Jesus loyalists in Corinth at his home (and Longenecker imagines there being three communities at Corinth with fifteen members each), Longenecker believes Gaius is well within ES4, far from the bottom layer of that group.[169] Turning to Phoebe, Longenecker draws upon Paul's references to Phoebe as a "patroness" (*prostasis*) and notes the following: (1) while *prostasis* is not generally a term used for a benefactor in Paul's context; and (2) while it was also unusual for clients to refer their patrons to others, such referrals were not unheard of; and (3) given that Paul says Phoebe was a "patroness" to many, Longenecker concludes that she belongs to ES4.[170] Moving down the scale, Longenecker recognizes that the evidence for Stephanas being at ES4–5 is slim—but because Stephanas is the head of a household and is able to travel to meet Paul, he concludes that this places Stephanas above ES6 and at least in ES5, if not in the lower end of ES4.[171] Philemon is also said to be ES4–5 because he is able to provide Paul with a place to stay and owns at least one slave (although, again, Longenecker recognizes how tenuous this evidence is).[172] Crispus, due to his association with Gaius and the possibility that he may be the synagogue leader mentioned in Acts 18:8, is also placed at ES4–5.[173] Longenecker then places Prisca and Aquila further down at ES5–6 because, although they had a dwelling place, we do not know how many gathered there, but we do know that Paul suffered want while in their company in Corinth. In their case, mobility is said to be related to economic vulnerability—thus, they are placed at ES5 at best.[174]

I find the placement of Prisca and Aquila particularly interesting because Longenecker uses the same data to draw different conclusions about different people. The mobility of Stephanas is used to bump him up the

168. Longenecker, *Remember the Poor*, 237–39.
169. Longenecker, *Remember the Poor*, 239.
170. Longenecker, *Remember the Poor*, 240–42.
171. Longenecker, *Remember the Poor*, 244–45.
172. Longenecker, *Remember the Poor*, 145.
173. Longenecker, *Remember the Poor*, 245–46.
174. Longenecker, *Remember the Poor*, 246–49.

Economy Scale. The mobility of Prisca and Aquila bumps them down. We also do not know how large the home of Prisca and Aquila was, or how many people could meet there, and so they are bumped down; yet the same lack of evidence about Philemon or Gaius bumps them up the Economy Scale. Now, granted, Longenecker openly admits that any study of the named individuals is bound to be fraught with conjectures (he begins his foray into the matter by saying that looking at names is "tentative but beneficial" and concludes by saying that "[w]ith regard to prosopographic reconstruction, it needs to be restated that the useable data are partial and, therefore, inherently unstable . . . prosopographic profiles are never to be held tenaciously").[175] Nevertheless, the conclusions he draws appear to be a re-assertion of the "new consensus" associated with Theissen et al. As such, they are vulnerable to much of the evidence that has been raised against that consensus and explored above—simply put, the reasons Longenecker provides for locating named Jesus loyalists in higher economic status brackets seem to require more than "optimism."

Longenecker continues to follow Theissen's lead when he turns to looking at the assemblies of Jesus loyalists more generally and concludes that, although named members tended towards ES4–5 (although, again, Onesimus is notably absent), the general membership tended to be in ES5 and leaned in the direction of ES6.[176] Longenecker believes that these economic status brackets best explain things like the call to put a little aside each week (1 Cor 16:1–2) and the mentions of working with one's hands (1 Cor 4:11–13; 1 Thess 4:11–12; also Eph 4:28 and Acts 20:34–35).[177] As 1 Cor 11:22 and 2 Cor 8:1–6 make clear, there were likely some ES7 people also involved in the assemblies, but Longenecker still finds ES5 to be the most likely general category.[178] This then leads to an implicit reaffirmation of the "love-patriarchalism" that Theissen and Troeltsch see guiding the assemblies—those at ES4 (and high up ES5) were expected to give charitably to other members, although they are certainly not expected to give up their higher status, or relinquish their hold on wealth while doing so—it is enough that only the most basic needs of the poorest members are met.[179]

175. Longenecker, *Remember the Poor*, 235, 251.

176. Longenecker, *Remember the Poor*, 253.

177. Longenecker, *Remember the Poor*, 253–55.

178. Longenecker, *Remember the Poor*, 256–58.

179. Longenecker, *Remember the Poor*, 279–88. Longenecker argues that those at ES4 who joined the movement were probably already predisposed to charitable giving

In conclusion, in an admittedly "highly speculative exercise," Longenecker proposes the following breakdown of a "typical urban group of Jesus-followers" (although this typical group does not actually refer to any of the groups mentioned in the Pauline letters):[180]

TABLE 7

ES Level	Number of Members
1–3	0
4	4
5	12
6–7	33

Running ES1–3 together makes sense, given the absence of any people from those categories in the assemblies of early Jesus loyalists, but it is interesting that Longenecker blurs ES6 and ES7 together. It shows a curious lack of care for the poor in a book dedicated to the theme of such care. Indeed, rather than remembering the poor, Longenecker seems to prefer to remember the early Jesus loyalists as dominated by a "middling" minority, who are particularly charitable, albeit in a way that seems remarkably similar to contemporary bourgeois Christian morals. The only way this sort of remembrance becomes possible is by forgetting key aspects of the arguments of Meggitt, Friesen, and even Oakes (who leans more in Longenecker's direction than Meggitt's), while also giving far too much influence to historically unlikely conjectures that are based not on evidence but on the lack thereof.

In light of these models, and of the other themes explored earlier in this chapter, I suggest the following conclusions: Paul, along with the vast majority of those involved in the early Jesus movement, was located at ES6—at the subsistence level.[181] Given the ways in which factors that influence one's economic status were prone to fluctuate (for example: the outbreak of a famine, the collapse of the building where one lived, the outbreak of a rebellion, the devastation of a family unit or community through the outbreak of disease, the raising of taxes to sponsor an imperial visit, being forced to migrate to another location, and so on), these people

(*Remember the Poor*, 272–76).

180. Longenecker, *Remember the Poor*, 294–96.

181. Here, I prefer Longenecker's language of an "Economy Scale" to Friesen's language of a "Poverty Scale."

could, and likely would, at times fall into ES7 (below subsistence) or rise into ES5 (stable near subsistence level—wherein this stability can, at times, permit a very small surplus, but not enough of a surplus to be considered "moderate," or bump people up into ES4). I find it too conjectural, and therefore implausible given wealth distribution in eastern territories colonized by Rome in the first century, to posit that any members of the assemblies of Jesus loyalists were in ES4 (moderate surplus resources) let alone ES1–3 (municipal, regional or provincial, and imperial elites).

Here, it seems to me that the socioeconomic status of most New Testament scholars severely limits their ability to imagine what is plausible or possible among communities of people experiencing poverty. I believe that my own experiences living and working in assemblies of people experiencing poverty, oppression, colonization, criminalization, and housing deprivation today (paired with studying other movements of solidarity, resistance, and liberation among oppressed, marginalized, and dispossessed populations) is a significant factor in making this reading of Paul et al. not only plausible but probable. As I have frequently witnessed, people who seem to have nothing regularly find ways not only to survive but to also fund projects about which they are passionate.[182] One need not posit that Paul or any others are in ES4 (as some seem to assume) in order to explain the activities undertaken by Paul and his coworkers. In fact, the Collection seems to well illustrate that the early Jesus loyalists were rooted at ES6 but could and would sometimes move towards ES5 or ES7. The saints in Jerusalem had fallen to ES7. The Jesus loyalists at Corinth may have been experiencing a bump to ES5 (see 2 Cor 8:14, with the emphasis being on the *temporary* present abundance of the Corinthians) and so they are asked to support the saints in Jerusalem, knowing full well that perhaps one day soon the tables will be turned (and also knowing that Macedonian Jesus loyalists have contributed even though they are no higher than ES6 and may well also be in ES7, as per 2 Cor 8:1–6). In all of this, as with the other themes examined, there is no need to posit members in ES1–4, there is no firm evidence to suggest that any members were in ES1–4, and it is statistically unlikely that people in ES1–4 were present. Therefore, I believe that the reading I am offering is the most probable based upon the evidence we have.

182. The Downtown Eastside Power of Women Group, the Alliance Against Displacement, the Carnegie Community Action Project, the Volcano, and the Vancouver Area Network of Drug Users are all striking contemporary examples of this in Vancouver (unceded Coast Salish territories).

Further Evidence of the Lowly
and Poor Status of the Early Jesus Loyalists

Before moving on to an examination of Pauline reflections on suffering and their implications for studies of socioeconomic status, it is worth raising three final points. First, moving away from Corinth to the study of the assemblies of Jesus loyalists at other urban centers strengthens the position I have developed thus far. Second, this thesis accounts for the contempt for those with high status exhibited in Pauline letters. Finally, it also provides a strong historical explanation for the rapid spread of the Jesus movement.

Beginning with the first point, the near exclusive focus on content in 1 Corinthians should not cause us to forget that all of the other assemblies corresponding with the Pauline faction are almost universally taken to be populated by people who are "lowly" and "poor." Take the examples of Rome and Philippi. I have already noted how a number of the people named in the letter to the Romans were likely (at least at one point, if not currently) slaves. This also fits with the historical and archaeological evidence we have of the Judean and early Jesus loyalist communities at Rome. The Judean community came into being in 64 BCE when Magnus Pompey brought thousands of Judean slaves back from his conquest of Judea. Some later became freed citizens, but the Judean community at Rome remained relatively uneducated and impoverished.[183] It is from this community that the early Jesus loyalists originated and the archaeological evidence demonstrates that their assemblies were located in the very poorest neighborhoods of the city—Trastevere and Porta Capena—among the people who possessed the lowest social status.[184] In Rome, it is highly implausible that the mixed membership of the assembly or assemblies of Jesus loyalists would contain any elite members—or anyone with any proximity to the elite.

The same holds true for the assembly or assemblies of Jesus loyalists at Philippi. In his careful study of that city, Peter Oakes arrives at the following breakdown of the population: 37 percent working in the service sector as artisans or craftspeople, 20 percent of the population living as slaves, 20 percent being colonist farmers, 20 percent being abjectly poor, and 3

---

183. See Jewett, *Romans*, 55.

184. Jewett, *Romans*, 62–63; see also Crossan and Reed, *In Search of Paul*, 367–76; and Tellbe, *Paul Between Synagogue and State*, 164–65. Tellbe is a little more cautious in his conclusions.

percent composing the elite.[185] Looking at the groups that were accessible to Paul, as a non-elite urban craftsperson, Oakes arrives at the following composition of the Philippian assemblies of Jesus loyalists: 43 percent of the members would be craftspeople, 16 percent would be slaves, 15 percent would be colonist farmers, 25 percent would be poor, and perhaps 1 percent would be among the elite.[186] Oakes doubts the presence of the 1 percent elite but, at this earlier stage of his research (prior to developing the model described above), he was hesitant to exclude them altogether, even if (as he argues) the letter to the Philippians provides us with no hint of their presence. Incorporating his later insights, however, gives us good grounds to reject their presence as historically plausible. Thus, we also see diversity at Philippi, but a cross-section of society that lacks the presence of any with high status or wealth.

This fits with 2 Cor 8:2's reference to the "extreme poverty" of the Jesus loyalists in Macedonia. I believe that this was also the case in Galatia and Thessalonika (and will discuss them in more detail momentarily) and so discussions of Corinth should not distract us from this bulk of evidence about the social composition of the early Jesus movement. Taking all of the above factors into consideration, we should also conclude that the relatively higher status and wealth enjoyed by some at Corinth was only slightly higher than the total lack of status and abject poverty experienced by others.[187] No wonder, then, that the Pauline faction notes that the Corinthians may very well find themselves in need of financial support in the future (2 Cor 8:13–15). Granted, elite members of society could sometimes very rapidly descend into poverty due to sudden catastrophes, conflicts, or shifts in power, but it strikes me as more probable that the Pauline faction writes this because the Corinthians were only slightly better off than the "extremely poor" Jesus loyalists elsewhere.

Turning briefly to the second point, the location of the assemblies of Jesus loyalists among the lowly and poor also helps to account for the Pauline rejection of elite values and for its focus upon an eschatological reversal

---

185. Oakes, *Philippians*, 50; cf. 1–54.

186. Oakes, *Philippians*, 61; cf. 55–76.

187. We should recall Garnsey and Saller's observation that although Roman society was structured around large-scale status hierarchies, each group contained fine gradations of status and even those at the very bottom experienced a wide range of conditions (Garnsey and Saller, *Roman Empire*, 118–19).

that lifts up the lowly and humiliates the mighty.[188] I will explore all of this in considerable detail in volume 3, but it should at least be mentioned here.

Finally, this ties to the third point. The early Jesus movement was able to spread rapidly across international and other boundaries precisely because of the appeal it held to the lower members of society. This is a point already made a century ago by the Marxist scholar Karl Kautsky and, although Marxist readings of the New Testament fell out of favor, it seems to me that it is the most plausible explanation for the rapid spread of the Jesus movement. Essentially, Kautsky argues that "early Christianity" arose as a movement whose "socialist tendencies" were able to satisfy the "urban-based proletariat" in ways that prior movements (like the Essenes and Zealots) were not.[189] Thus, despite hostility from the wealthy and powerful, early Christianity spreads rapidly within the lower classes. Although Kautsky's language is problematical (he is importing class orders associated with post-industrial Europe into the Pauline context), his central insight is a good one, and it is supported by the charismatic nature of the movement. As Howard Clark Kee observes, charismatic movements were most influential, not among the higher orders, but among the non-privileged and those who experienced marginality—wherein charismata often disrupted prevailing hierarchies and introduced a certain lack of control into social life.[190] This is why the officials of the empire tended to see charismatic leaders as enemies of Roman Law and order.[191] This point will also be developed in more detail in what follows, but here it suffices to say that establishing an economy of sharing so that there is enough for all, among people who have been oppressed and colonized and who are accustomed to not having nearly enough, is a very compelling historical explanation for the spread of the Jesus movement.

188. See Deissmann, *Light from the Ancient East*, 246–47; Schottroff, "Not Many Powerful," 275–87.

189. See Kautsky, *Foundations of Christianity*, 272–74; Bruce W. Longenecker points out that already as far back as Tertullian, concern for the poor was being posited as that which drew the gentile nations to Christianity (*Remember the Poor*, 162). See also Henry Chadwick's argument that the charitable practices of the early church are the best explanation of the spread of the early Jesus movement (Chadwick, *Early Church*). In my opinion, he is on the right track but, as will be shown, there is a very significant difference between charity and the sibling-based economic mutuality that I believe defines the movement.

190. See Kee, *Christian Origins in Sociological Perspective*, 55, 67, 74–75.

191 Kee, *Christian Origins in Sociological Perspective*, 72, here Kee is interacting with the work of Ramsey MacMullen.

Suffering in Relation to Socioeconomic Status
and Pauline Politics

I will now turn to examining a theme that is often neglected in studies of the socioeconomic status of Paul and his companions—their many and often lengthy reflections upon personal and collective suffering. I will begin by studying the significance and nature of the suffering the Pauline faction mentions before exploring sufferings that Paul and others experience as *persecution* from Judean officials or from Greco-Roman civic authorities and others who held socioeconomic power in the cities that Paul visited.

The Significance and Nature of Suffering

Suffering is a prominent overarching theme that the reader encounters in all seven of the non-contested Pauline letters. However, in comparison to the attention given to other subjects that scholars understand to be major themes in Paul's life and writings, significantly less attention has been given to the theme of suffering. What appears to have been of great importance to the Pauline faction has not always been as important to later scholars. It is worth asking ourselves why this disconnect occurs. I suspect it may be because most Pauline scholars are much more comfortably situated than the Pauline faction was. As we see over and over again, suffering tends to be of considerable importance to those who experience it directly but of considerably less importance to those who do not.[192]

Be that as it may, what becomes apparent from the Pauline letters is that suffering is a crucial element of the identity of those who are in the Anointed. It is a badge of membership for those who belong to the assemblies of Jesus loyalists.[193] The Pauline faction offers Paul as an example of

192. See Rom 12:17–21 where the exposure to violence experienced by those in poor neighborhoods in Rome could very well end up costing the Roman Jesus loyalists their lives (a point explored in Oakes, *Reading Romans in Pompeii*, 123–26). As far as I can tell, this possibility is a bit of a different daily reality than the experiences of most Pauline scholars.

193. See Remus, "Persecution," 431; Deissmann, *Religion of Jesus*, 234–35, 40; Gorman, *Reading Paul*, 25–26; Jennings, *Outlaw Justice*, 137, 142–43; Roetzel, *Paul*, 30–33; Sampley, *Walking Between the Times*, 30–31; Walsh and Keesmaat, *Colossians Remixed*, 220–33; Crossan and Reed, *In Search of Paul*, 278–80. Further, as Sanders notes, it may actually increase in importance as Paul's work progresses as Paul moves from speaking of suffering *for* the Anointed in Thess, to suffering *in imitation of* the Anointed in Phil, to suffering *with* the Anointed in Rom (*Paul: The Apostle's Life*, 664).

what it means to suffer in loyal imitation of Jesus. Thus, in passages like Phil 3:1–11 or 1 Cor 11:23–28, Paul's cruciformity is upheld as exemplary. His very real participation in the sufferings of the Anointed is offered as a model to be emulated by others.[194]

A number of those who have picked up on the importance of suffering to Paulinism have taken this to be a reference to the general sufferings one experiences in life. Numerous passages appear to support this conclusion. Rom 8:17–23 mentions the groaning of creation and 2 Cor 4:7, 16–18, reinforces this. Therefore, suffering is understood to be a part of the "now and not yet" of life in a world that is passing away but still dominated by the powers of Sin and Death. From this perspective, the experiences of things like political persecutions, oppression, enslavement, military occupations and colonization, and poverty-by-dispossession, if they are mentioned at all, are only considered here to the extent that they are symptoms of a cosmology shaped by "the fall" and the persistence of "original sin."[195] It is all decidedly apolitical.[196] Sometimes, an even greater spiritual focus has been proposed wherein suffering is seen as the internal conflict between "the Flesh" and "the Spirit."[197] Here, too, the emphasis is on the decidedly apolitical nature of Pauline sufferings. Thus, even when the more material side of Pauline sufferings is emphasized (as in the writings of Thomas Schreiner), this tends to be seen as a "side-effect" of Paul's strictly religious missionary work, related to his "integrity" as a "missionary," and has nothing to do with politics or socioeconomic issues as such.[198]

In response to these readings, I wish to emphasize two interrelated things. First, I will argue that the sufferings experienced by Paul and his companions teach us something about their socioeconomic status. Second, I wish to highlight the political nature of these sufferings as this factor also has socioeconomic implications and, ultimately, is one important basis for counter-imperial understanding of Paulinism. Reading the relevant passages more carefully helps to expose the socioeconomic implications

194. See Elias, *Remember the Future*, 77–79; Gorman, *Cruciformity*, 199–209.

195. For some who hold this view, see Bultmann, *Theology of the New Testament*, 1:349; Dunn, *Theology of Paul*, 482–87; Dunn, *Beginning from Jerusalem*, 848–49; MacDonald, *Pauline Churches*, 79;

196. Although, as we saw above in our survey of conservative readings of Paul, apolitical readings always favor a certain kind of politics.

197. See Cerfaux, "La Propagande," 36–37; Dunn, *Theology of Paul*, 496; Keck, *Paul and His Letters*, 109, 121.

198. See Schreiner, *Paul*, 87, 102.

contained therein. Beginning with 1 Cor 4:10–13, note how the Pauline faction describes the status of the apostles (Paul included):

> We are fools for the sake of [the Anointed] . . . We are weak . . . we [are held] in disrepute. To the present hour we are hungry and thirsty, we are poorly clothed and beaten and homeless, and we grow weary from the work of our own hands. [We are] reviled . . . [we are] persecuted . . . We have become like the rubbish of the world, the dregs of all things, to this very day.

In this passage, it is very clear that the Pauline faction is not simply describing the general sufferings of life. Rather, they are describing the type of sufferings experienced by those who were oppressed, colonized, impoverished, and had little or no status in society.[199] Those with wealth and status could not be described in these terms. They would not be hungry, thirsty, poorly clothed and homeless, nor would they work with their own hands, nor could they be described as rubbish. Yet this is the state of the ambassadors of the Anointed, those recognized as central voices within the early Jesus movement, and most especially of Paul "the least of the ambassadors" (1 Cor 15:9).

The Pauline faction then repeats these assertions in the second letter to the Corinthians. In 2 Cor 6:5–10, they speak of Paul experiencing "labors, sleepless nights, [and] hunger" and being treated with "dishonor," "ill repute," "as poor," and "as having nothing." Again, these are labels that can only be applied to those who are lowly and poor. This is further confirmed in the great list of sufferings mentioned in 2 Cor 11. Here Paul is said to experience "toil and hardship, through many a sleepless night, hungry and thirsty, often without food, cold and naked" (2 Cor 11:27). This is strong evidence that Paul possessed little status or wealth. The sufferings experienced by Paul and those who are called to imitate Paul (1 Cor 11:1) are the sufferings experienced by those who are lowly and the poor.[200]

199. Larry Welborn spends considerable time with this passage (*Paul, the Fool of Christ*, 50–86). His reading is rigorous but the most obvious conclusion to draw from his work is not that Paul is establishing himself within the mimic role of the fool (that may be a secondary conclusion, although it is the one Welborn is highlighting), but that Paul was, in fact, literally, extremely poor, oppressed, and often suffered a great deal of material want and pain at the hands of others.

200. See Gorman, *Cruciformity*, 178–213; Wright, *Climax of the Covenant*, 256; Wright, *New Tasks For a Renewed Church*, 129–30. In these passages Wright records some of his most stirring words about the church seeking out the pain of the world in order to share it and bear it, or coming alongside of those in pain and sharing their sorrow

This conclusion is strengthened when we turn to consider the political nature of the sufferings experienced by Paul and the assemblies of Jesus loyalists. When we look at the bulk of Pauline references to this subject, it becomes clear that suffering is most often related to social, economic, and political conflicts.[201] In 1 Cor 4:12, the passage just quoted by those who prefer apolitical readings of Paulinism, the Pauline faction does not just speak about general suffering, they speak about being "persecuted." Similarly, in the other chapter quoted, the Pauline faction concludes by speaking about Paul being "persecuted" and being threatened by "the sword" of the rulers, who actually seem to be "slaughtering" some of those who follow Jesus (Rom 8:35–39). Similar references to persecution are made in 1 Thess 1:6 and 2:2. Other passages then expand on this. 1 Cor 4:9–13 adds the comments that Paul was also "beaten" and living "as though sentenced to death." In 2 Cor 1:8–10, he writes about being "utterly, unbearably crushed" in Asia by a "deadly peril" that also threatened him with the sentence of death. These are ominous references, especially when we remember that Paul was probably executed by the imperial authorities a few years later. On his way to that fate, he also suffered imprisonments, where he was guarded by Roman soldiers, as he mentions in Phil 1:13–14 and Phlm 9–10. Finally, turning again to 2 Cor 11:21–28, the Pauline faction also observes the following about Paul:

> Are they [Paul's opponents at Corinth] ministers of [the Anointed]? I am talking like a madman—I am a better one: with far greater labors, far more imprisonments, with countless floggings, and often near death. Five times I have received from the [Judeans] the forty lashes minus one. Three times I was beaten with rods. Once I received a stoning . . . [in danger] from my own people, danger from [foreign nationals], danger in the city, danger in the wilderness, danger at sea, danger from false [siblings] . . .
>
> In Damascus, the governor under King Aretas set a guard on the city of Damascus in order to seize me, but I was let down in a basket through a window in the wall, and escaped from his hands.

It is worth noting that the forty lashes minus one Paul received five times was a punishment delivered based upon rulings made by Judean synagogue

---

in a completely uncalculated manner. Unfortunately, for Wright—recently a member of the House of Lords and a member of prestigious academic institutions—this language never leads him into the sort of solidarity it seems to espouse.

201. See Gorman, *Cruciformity*, 146–52; Cousar, *Letters of Paul*, 140; Perrin, *New Testament*, 94–96.

officials.[202] These officials were equal parts social, political, economic, and religious authorities in Judean communities throughout the diaspora. Furthermore, being beaten with rods was a punishment dispensed by Greco-Roman civic officials. The same applies to the imprisonments mentioned, and the other floggings, and it is from the rulers in Damascus that Paul is fleeing. In light of these things, it is also reasonable to wonder if the danger Paul faces from "false siblings" (*pseudodelphois*) is the danger any prominent member of a (potentially) treasonous movement faces from uncommitted or compromised members who are willing to rat out others for personal gain. Subsequent volumes will make this proposal more plausible. For now, we see Paul persecuted by people with high status and wealth within socioeconomic and theopolitical positions of institutional authority, both within diasporic Judean communities and within Greco-Roman society.

Consequently, while I do not wish to deny that the Pauline faction sometimes does talk about the general sufferings of life, it is clear that the place they give to the persecutions they faced from local rulers is much more prominent. This socioeconomic and political root of Pauline suffering is further verified by the account Luke provides in Acts where Paul is charged with: (a) spreading an illegal and un-Roman religion in Philippi; (b) damaging civic pride and the local economy in Ephesus; (c) acting in ways contrary to the decrees of Caesar in Thessalonika; (d) spreading a form of worship that is contrary to the law in Corinth; and, finally, (e) creating strife in Judean communities all throughout the empire when he is brought before Felix in Caesarea.[203] In all likelihood then, the brand marks of the Anointed that Paul carries on his body (Gal 6:12) are the marks and debilitating injuries that resulted from punishments inflected by the juridico-political (but no less religious) authorities. The Anointed was scarred by Rome and Jerusalem—by the socioeconomic and theopolitical Powers—and so was Paul (and many other early members of the movement). It is worth further exploring the extent and nature of these persecutions and how they came about in relation to Paul and the early assemblies of Jesus loyalists.

202. See Sanders, *Paul: The Apostle's Life*, 77.

203. See Jeffers, *Greco-Roman World*, 161–67; Dunn, *Beginning from Jerusalem*, 677–80. Thiselton notes that most scholars think the sufferings mentioned in 2 Cor 11:23–33 belong to the "hidden years" prior to Paul's work as an apostle as it is described in Acts. If this is the case, Paul's work was defined by persecution from the very beginning to the very end (Thiselton, *Living Paul*, 22).

Persecutions Arising from Judean Officials

The persecutions that Paul and others experienced from "the Jews" is often taken to be the primary conflict related to Paul's work.[204] I believe this reading is tainted by a long history of Christian supersessionism that posits "Jewish jealousy" as the major problem encountered by the Pauline mission.[205] This language originates in Luke's narrative. In Acts 13:45, Luke says that the Judeans in Pisidian Antioch become jealous of the large crowds that gathered around Paul and so they start to abuse him. Likewise, in Acts 17:5, some of the Judeans in Thessalonika are said to have grown jealous of Paul and so they incite a mob against him. However, it is likely that Luke has somewhat altered circumstances to fit his own agenda—something that seems to come up fairly often in Luke's presentation of potentially more controversial elements of Paul's life (thus, to pick a widely-noted example, despite its obvious importance to the Pauline faction, and the way Luke uses it to advance his narrative, the fate of the Collection the Pauline faction gathered for the poor in Jerusalem falls completely out of the picture in Acts). I think a similar move is being made when Luke refers to Judean "jealousy" in relation to the persecutions Paul experiences. When conflicts arise in relation to Paul, Luke tends to blame the Judeans and make Paul innocent in the eyes of the Greco-Roman authorities. Of course, this is not to say that members of Judean communities had no conflicts with the Pauline faction. It is simply to suggest that there may have been other more significant political motivation for the persecutions.

Before exploring that in more detail, however, it is worth noting the context in which Paul received the forty lashes minus one on five different occasions. Julius Caesar and Caesar Augustus had both granted diasporic Judean communities the right to assemble weekly, to live by their own laws, to keep the Sabbath and have access to ancestral foods in the marketplace, to contribute money to the temple in Jerusalem, and to have a legal court of their own to decide their own affairs. Subsequent Caesars upheld these legal exemptions and made sure that governors and citizens in cities throughout the eastern provinces were aware of it.[206] Out of gratitude for these excep-

---

204. See, for example, the lengthy passage wherein Schnabel talks about Jewish/Christian conflicts but makes no reference to any conflicts Paul may or may not have had with Greco-Roman authorities (*Early Christian Mission*, 2:983–1030).

205. See, for example, Keresztes, *Imperial Rome and the Christians*, 74–77.

206. Sanders, *Paul: The Apostle's Life*, 63–65; Winter, *Divine Honours for the Caesars*, 105–6.

tional rights, Judean places of assembly were often marked with tokens of gratitude to the emperor (commemorative pillars, inscriptions, slabs, and so on) and prayers on behalf of the emperor were regularly said.[207] Diasporic Judeans also swore a regular oath of loyalty to the emperor and daily sacrifices were made on behalf of the emperor at the Jerusalem temple (the temple tax sent from the diaspora helped to fund this), and this was part of the reason why Judeans were exempted from participating in other sacrifices to the emperor within their cities of residence.[208] In this way, Judeans were able to counter accusations made against them that they were atheists and, therefore, a threat to the peace and security of those around them.[209]

It is in the legal courts of these assemblies, at the ruling of the local Judean leaders (who, again, were not only religious leaders but also legal and socioeconomic leaders), that Paul received the thirty-nine lashes, not once but five times. In a moment, I will explore why this might have happened so frequently. For now, however, we must note how Paul's apparently regular vulnerability to this form of punishment, suggests that he held a weak socioeconomic position in the communities he visited. As John Barclay argues, "[Paul] was a newcomer, of low social status, with no economic or political power base on which to build his defense, and power struggles in the synagogue almost inevitably turned to his disadvantage."[210] That Paul and the other movement members could be defined as "deviant" and prosecuted as such—in diasporic Judean communities that were otherwise quite tolerant—suggests that they were socially and economically vulnerable to being attacked in this way.[211]

To more fully understand the political nature of the persecutions Paul and others faced from Judean officials, it is necessary to comment further on the status of the diasporic Judean communities during Paul's time. These communities were in a precarious position. Due to their religious, ethnic, and national commitments they remained on the periphery of the broader civic and imperial communities in which they were embedded.[212] Despite the exemptions they had received from Julius Caesar and his heirs, their

207. Winter, *Divine Honours for the Caesars*, 110–12.

208. Winter, *Divine Honours for the Caesars*, 112.

209. Wright, *New Testament and the People of God*, 156.

210. Barclay, "Deviance and Apostasy," 119.

211. Barclay, "Deviance and Apostasy," 114–27.

212. See Kee, *Beginnings of Christianity*, 28; Barclay, "Diaspora Judaism," 48; Tellbe, *Paul Between Synagogue and State*, 35–63, 147–49.

monotheism was considered antipatriotic, antisocial, and antireligious, and their concomitant ban on images bordered on sedition when they refused to display images of the emperor.[213] Furthermore, the wealthier Judean communities were often seen as not contributing to the welfare of the city (the permission they received to send money to support the temple in Jerusalem only exacerbated this because that moved money out of the local community to support a foreign city), and their distance from local and imperial cults was seen as undermining the civic unity required to maintain the peace between the gods and the inhabitants of the empire.[214] The prevailing view was that anyone who jeopardized this unity put everyone at risk of suffering divine wrath in significant life-changing ways.

Therefore, in Greco-Roman culture and literature, we see Judeans treated with a mixture of disdain and suspicion as well as curiosity and attraction. During Paul's day, for example, we see Seneca complaining to Nero about the influence of Judaism within urban centers throughout the empire: "The customs of this accursed race have gained such influence that they are now received throughout the world. The vanquished have given laws to the victors."[215] Similarly, after Pompey brought several thousand Judean slaves back to Rome, Cicero characterizes them as a whole people "born to slavery."[216] The elite literature reflects the general Roman disdain for conquered people groups (as well as the suspicion that the Judeans were potentially more rebellious and exclusive than others), but it also notes significant popular levels of attraction to diasporic expressions of Second Temple Judaism.[217]

In order to not be targeted when distrust turned into outbursts of violence (to which some local magistrates were sympathetic or willing to turn a blind eye), the Judeans tried to both court favor from the authorities and

---

213. See Kahl, *Galatians Re-Imagined*, 211–16.

214. See Tellbe, *Paul Between Synagogue and State*, 39–41.

215. Quoted by Elliott in Horsley, *Christian Origins*, 177. I will return to the importance of the categories of victor/vanquished and law in Roman imperial ideology in volume 2. It should be noted that these attitudes persisted both among the common people and the Roman elite, despite the personal favor of the Caesars expressed especially by Augustus to Herod the Great and then by Claudius to Herod Antipas.

216. Horsley, *Christian Origins*, 177.

217. See Keresztes, *Imperial Rome and the Christians*, 24; Tellbe, *Paul Between Synagogue and State*, 59–63; Barclay, "Diaspora Judaism," 50–52, 56–58, 60–61; Wrede, *Paul*, 49.

keep a low profile.[218] Shortly before Paul's time, the Judeans had done this with some success at the imperial level. Julius Caesar afforded them the rights granted to a *collegium licitum*—permitting them to gather in a place for cultic and social functions, allowing them to provide for the burial of their dead, administer their own finances, elect officers with titles, and even permitting them privileges not granted to other *collegia*: the ability to meet weekly (instead of monthly), permission to gather an international temple tax, exemption from prayers to the emperor (praying, instead, for his welfare) and exemption from the military.[219] Augustus, who was a personal friend and patron of Herod the Great, then extended these benefits. He permitted Judeans at Rome to gather their grain share after the Sabbath, and he personally helped to fund the building of Herod's Temple in Jerusalem.[220]

However, after Augustus and the dissolution of Herod's kingdom in Judea, along with the increasing number of popular uprisings that were occurring in Judea, the situation of the Judeans began to worsen across the empire. Tiberius began to target them as an expanding oriental religion and expelled some Judeans from Rome in 19 CE.[221] Under Claudius, when major rioting broke out in Alexandria, resulting in the murder of many of the Judeans living there, as well as the theft or destruction of their property, Claudius intervened and blamed the Judeans for inciting the riot by seeking to gain civic citizenship (which would exempt them from certain taxes). He declared them "aliens and strangers" and "a general plague for the whole world."[222] As the Judeans became increasingly viewed as those who disturbed the civic order, Claudius first placed a ban on their meetings in Rome in 41 CE and then in 49 CE he expelled a number of Judean

---

218. See Hardin, *Galatians and the Imperial Cult*, 13, Jeffers, *Greco-Roman World*, 215.

219. See Meeks, *First Urban Christians*, 34–38; Horsley, *Christian Origins*, 183; Tellbe, *Paul Between Synagogue and State*, 42–49, 59; Dunn, *Beginning from Jerusalem*, 618–19; Sanders, *Paul: The Apostle's Life*, 62–65; Winter, *Divine Honours for the Caesars*, 105–6. This is not to say that all expressions of Second Temple Judaism were granted the status of a *religio licita*—as used to be a common assertion in New Testament scholarship (which also tended to see Second Temple Judaism as a more singular or monolithic thing).

220. Horsley, *Christian Origins*, 183; Dunn, *Beginning from Jerusalem*, 172–73.

221. Tellbe, *Paul Between Synagogue and State*, 151.

222. Horsley, *Christian Origins*, 184–86; the last quote is cited in Keresztes, *Imperial Rome and the Christians*, 25.

"troublemakers" from the city.[223] Under Nero, the Judeans may have regained some peace and influence, but their situation remained precarious.[224]

It is clear that maintaining friendly terms with those in power, and appearing as good citizens, was crucial to the safety and survival of the diasporic communities in Paul's day.[225] Therefore, it is neither surprising to see Judean synagogue officials in Rome who have been named after emperors or high-ranking imperial officials, nor is it surprising to see inscriptions, shields, wreaths, and pillars dedicated to civic or imperial rulers (and patrons) at various synagogues throughout the empire.[226] It was very important to Judean survival to appear as model citizens for popular and elite sentiments never totally abandoned the notion that they were seditious rebels who would never fully accept imperial law and order. Thus, Juvenal writes: "[The Judeans] look down on Roman law, preferring instead to learn / And honor and fear the [Judean] commandments."[227] As we shall see, this is a very serious charge.

This, then, relates back to the suggestion that "jealousy" was at the heart of Judean opposition to the work of the Pauline faction. A much stronger hypothesis is the suggestion that the early Jesus movement, of which the Pauline faction was a part, was jeopardizing the precarious safety of the diasporic Judean communities.[228] For a variety of reasons I will explore in detail later—the proclamation of a state-executed terrorist as the true Lord of all, the suggestion that the rulers of this present age are both evil and foolish, the desire to bring together parties from a multitude of vanquished cities and nations under a rule different than that of the empire, and so on—it was likely that the early Jesus movement as understood by the Pauline faction was either a seditious movement or was very easily mistaken for one by the authorities. Judean communities would have good reason to distrust any who came into their midst speaking about such things and

223. Horsley, *Christian Origins*, 186–87; also Tellbe, *Paul Between Synagogue and State*, 151, 154–56; Jewett, *Romans*, 59–60.

224. Horsley, *Christian Origins*, 191; Tellbe, *Paul Between Synagogue and State*, 151.

225. See Tellbe, *Between Synagogue and State*, 51–54; Pilgrim, *Uneasy Neighbors*, 22–24.

226. See Tellbe, *Between Synagogue and State*, 149–50; Pilgrim, *Uneasy Neighbors*, 22–24.

227. Juvenal, *Satires* 14.100–101.

228. See Fredriksen, *From Jesus to Christ*, 145–56; Horsley and Silberman, *Message and the Kingdom*, 120–21; Taubes, *Political Theology of Paul*, 17; Tellbe, *Paul Between Synagogue and State*, 66–67, 152; Munck, *Paul and the Salvation*, 218–319, 324.

trying to organize people anew, and would likely be very keen to distance themselves from any such obvious troublemakers.[229] No wonder, then, that Paul received the thirty-nine lashes on five separate occasions. He had to be clearly marked as not representative of the Judean communities lest the Roman authorities mistook him from a representative thereof and responded with devastating violence against other Judeans living in the diaspora.

Yet here is the catch: while the members of diasporic Judean gatherings would want to distance themselves from the early Jesus loyalists, lest the (either real or apparent) seditious nature of their beliefs and practices caused the Judeans to lose not only the privileges they had been granted but possibly also their property and their lives, the early Jesus loyalists would want to fall under the protective (albeit still precarious) umbrella of privileges offered to the diasporic Judean communities as this would allow them to continue to meet weekly and avoid participation in other civic and imperial cultic activities. Mikael Tellbe summarizes the two sides of this: "It must have been of the utmost importance for Jewish communities in the Diaspora to safeguard their continued social and legal status by avoiding activities that would unnecessarily draw Roman attention to them and identify them as troublemakers."[230] But, at the same time, "the early Christian movement could not develop an identity separate from the Jewish one without being reckoned as suspicious by the Romans."[231]

It is precisely this tension that gives rise to the conflict over circumcision between the Pauline faction and the so-called "Judaizers" in Galatia. Circumcision was appealing because it permitted the Jesus loyalists to remain within the safety net of diasporic Judaism. The letter to the Galatians is very clear that this is the reason why people are being circumcised there. In Gal 6:12, the Pauline faction writes that their opponents try to compel the Galatians to be circumcised so that they will not be persecuted for the cross of the Anointed. In other words, circumcision becomes the means of avoiding being labeled an illegal gathering and of avoiding the confrontation with neighbors, and civic authorities, that would result from this.[232]

229. See Sanders, *Paul: The Apostle's Life*, 194–95, 494–95.

230. Tellbe, *Paul Between Synagogue and State*, 63.

231. Tellbe, *Paul Between Synagogue and State*, 71; also 287. For others who make similar arguments see Munck, *Paul and the Salvation*, 318–19, 324; Hardin, *Galatians and the Imperial Cult*, 110; Dunn, *Beginning from Jerusalem*, 642, 647–48.

232. A point made by Winter, *Seek the Welfare of the City*, 124, 131–40; Winter, *Divine Honours to the Caesars*, 227, 241–43; Hardin, *Galatians and the Imperial Cult*, 12–13, 85–115, 142; Kahl, *Galatians Re-Imagined*, 211, 224–28; Theissen, *Fortress Introduction*,

What is remarkable and politically significant about this conflict, is that the Pauline faction zealously argues that "strategies to avoid persecution characterize those who are opponents of the gospel."[233] Instead of avoiding persecutions, Paul and his coworkers, here and elsewhere, urge Jesus loyalists not to flee from them but to welcome them joyfully![234]

Two points, then, bear repeating in light of this discussion: first, we can see how the persecutions—the punishments—that Paul received from Judean officials reflect his vulnerability to being punished in this way. This suggests that he and his coworkers (who could not prevent him from being punished in this way), possessed little or no status within those communities. Second, we also see that these punishments were most likely politically motivated and driven by a Judean concern to maintain both the safety and survival of their communities. The Judeans wanted to distance themselves from the early Jesus movement and, while some members of that movement wanted to shelter under the relatively safer umbrella of officially sanctioned forms of Second Temple Judaism, the Pauline faction seems to be eager to have the movement go in a more radical—and more dangerous—direction.

Persecutions Arising from Greco-Roman Civic and Imperial Authorities

Having examined the ways in which Judean officials punished Paul, it is worth looking in more detail at why the Greco-Roman civic and imperial authorities might be concerned by the spread of the Jesus movement. We have already noted how the diasporic Judean communities were granted the exceptional right to refrain from participating in local expressions of the imperial cult. This was granted despite the fact that, as we will see in volume 2, the imperial cult was absolutely fundamental to the structuring of public (political, social, economic, and religious) life within the cities visited by the Pauline faction. Therefore, any who chose to withdraw from the imperial cult, without being granted clear imperial permission to do so, would be seen as a black mark against the community at best, or, more probably, as immoral, impious traitors and rebels.[235] Yet, as our subsequent

62–63; Sanders, *Paul: The Apostle's Life*, 492–93.

233. Cousar, *Letters of Paul*, 16.

234. On the close connection between joy and suffering in Philippians, see Engberg-Pedersen, *Paul and the Stoics*, 96–114.

235. Price, *Rituals and Power*, 122–23; Tellbe, *Paul Between Synagogue and State*, 72;

discussion of the Pauline response to the imperial cult will make clear, Paul and the other members of the assemblies of Jesus loyalists did precisely this. They urged others to withdraw from participation in the imperial cult and, instead, offer their allegiance solely to Jesus the Anointed (and the God whom they refer to as the Father of Jesus). This would cause complications for the early Jesus loyalists and their participation in every area of life— from public festivals, to attending the baths, to possible memberships in trades-based *collegia*, to being unable to participate in certain sacrifices— their day-to-day lives would be markedly disrupted.[236] Furthermore, given the high population densities of these cities, and given the cramped urban living conditions, it would have been impossible to withdraw unobserved from the imperial cult.[237] Consequently, in situations where the early Jesus loyalists were sufficiently removed from diasporic Judaism in order to merit attention as a unique entity, they almost immediately encountered persecution from the local civic or provincial authorities.[238]

Regarding this point, two things should be emphasized given prior scholarly discussion. First, it should be emphasized that the small and local nature of the early authority-inspired persecutions of the Jesus loyalists does not negate the political nature of that persecution.[239] That this is not an empire-wide, state-sponsored persecution, does not mean that Paul and his coworkers were not facing very serious political charges within the cities when they were brought before the authorities. To suggest otherwise and argue that the absence of a sweeping state-sponsored persecution shows the early Jesus movement to be apolitical forgets both that the early Jesus movement was very far from being empire-wide (and meriting this kind of attention), and that wherever the Jesus movement did go in Paul's day, it tended to meet with political opposition and resistance from the rulers and the socioeconomic elite (and this predates Paul—Jesus, himself, was justly condemned according to the rule of law and executed as a terrorist by the elite in Judea). Secondly, it should also be emphasized that the social consequences of these persecutions—from loss of status to loss of connections

Sanders, *Paul: The Apostle's Life,* 194, 201–4.

236. See Schnabel, *Early Christian Mission,* 2:1371–72; Price, *Rituals and Power,* 220–21; Carter, *John and Empire,* 262; Hopkins, *World Full of Gods,* 78; Judge, "Did the Churches," 519; Judge, *Social Distinctives of the Christians,* 101–2.

237. See Howard-Brook and Gwyther, 100–01.

238. See Dunn, *Beginning from Jerusalem,* 673, 677–80, 692–703, 763–65, 774–77.

239. See Hopkins, *World Full of Gods,* 84, 92, 111; Remus, "Persecution," 431–52; Thielman, *Theology of the New Testament,* 438–42.

within one's community—does not negate their political nature.[240] In this context, there is no sustainable divide between "the social" and "the political"—they are very deeply intertwined.

What, then, is the political charge faced by Paul and the early assemblies of Jesus loyalists? Nothing less than treason (*maiestas*).[241] As Garnsey and Saller observe: "[u]nauthorized religious cults and organizations that could not be controlled or eradicated were simply not allowed to exist."[242] It was considered treasonous to break the united civic consensus needed to maintain peace with the gods, with the empire, and with one another. To do so, from the Roman perspective, was to betray the civic body and "infect" it with a foreign "poison" that had to be drawn out and neutralized.[243] It was illegal and treasonous to gather an assembly of people on a weekly basis, unless one had official permission to do so. It was illegal and treasonous to try and create an international network of communities between members of nations vanquished (and both segregated and re-assembled in new ways) by Rome. It was treasonous (and pure folly!) to proclaim a state-executed terrorist as the one Lord over all. Thus, as the Pauline faction says and as Acts reaffirms, charges of political sedition were constantly brought against Paul.

Here, we should note that the later Roman classification of the Jesus movement as a "superstition" (*superstitio*, being the term employed by both Tacitus and Suetonius) does not take away from its politically offensive status. As we shall see in our discussion of the ideo-theology of Rome, true religion was fundamental to the Roman vision of peace and victory. Piety, understood as faithfully following the law and respecting the gods, was crucial to the maintenance of law and order. Piety produced peace with the gods who, in turn, provided security and stability for the empire.[244] Any superstition, any false religion, jeopardized this security and was considered

---

240. Contra the likes of Judge, *Social Distinctives of the Christians*, 44–52; Malherbe, *Social Aspects of Early Christianity*, 21–22; Tenney, *New Testament Times*, 124–26, 292.

241. See Georgi, *Theocracy*, 103–4; Horsley and Silberman, *Message and the Kingdom*, 195; Horrell, "'Becoming Christian,'" 318–20; Deissmann, *Paul*, 251–52; Jeffers, *Greco-Roman World*, 109.

242. Garnsey and Saller, *Roman Empire*, 174. The Roman state, in other words, tolerated religious cults and organizations that were willing to work with the state or be controlled by the state or acknowledge the supremacy of the state—often by working imperial cultic figures and sacrifices into the worship of other local gods.

243. See Ando, *Imperial Ideology*, 393.

244. See Remus, "Persecution," 436–37.

a very real political threat.[245] Furthermore, the Caesars were prone to classify seditious political movements as ignorant superstitions in order to undermine the political threat that these movements could pose to their authority. Because the Caesars wanted to be *sui generis*, they could have no rivals. Thus, if rival political movements arose that recognized Lords who were seen as possessing equal or greater authority than Caesar, they were never recognized as such in imperial propaganda. Instead, they were mocked as superstitions—and crushed.[246]

This is why the Jesus movement is increasingly targeted by the Roman authorities as it gains momentum. Its small size provides the movement with some protection and the ability to at least survive early on.[247] But, even from the beginning, it does not escape unscathed. Thus, Jesus is executed and, according to John's Gospel, mockingly placarded as "the King of the Jews" when he is killed.[248] Not long after, the members of the Jesus movement in Antioch are labeled "Christians" (as per Acts 11:26) by civic authorities as they tried to make sense of the new movement of "Christ" loyalists that had appeared in their city.[249] The suffix of this word (*-ianoi* or *-ianus*) was not applied to followers of a god, but was used to classify people who were partisans of a specific political leader or military general.[250] Thus, from the beginning, the censors were wary of "Christianity." Consequently, as the movement spreads and gains popular support among the lower levels of society (those whom the elites always treat with suspicion), it became

245. See Tellbe, *Paul Between Synagogue and State*, 71.

246. Contemporary discourses around terrorism that refuse to understand how members of oppressed, colonized, impoverished, or dispossessed groups might be willing to act in certain ways mirrors this.

247. Garnsey and Saller, *Roman Empire*, 174.

248. Placarding Jesus as "King of the Jews" was a cynical and mocking act. It reminds the Judeans that any of their hopes for independence will meet a similar fate. A comparable act today would be to imagine a member of the American special forces holding a sign that said "Freedom Fighter" over the corpse of Osama bin Laden (and, indeed, in 2012 some American soldiers were discovered posing for pictures, in an equally cynical and mocking way, with the bodies of dead Afghani civilians who had been killed for sport).

249. See Judge, "Did the Churches," 515–16; Winter, "Roman Law and Society," 70–71.

250. See Judge, "Did the Churches," 515; Malina, "Social Levels, Morals and Daily Life," 269; Winter, "Roman Law and Society," 70–71, 82–98. Judge also suggests that this is why the early Jesus loyalists demonstrate some circumspection in their own deployment of this term ("Did the Churches," 517).

the ideal target for a person like Nero to blame for setting fire to Rome in 64 CE.[251] By this point, the imperial authorities at the highest levels demonstrate an increasing awareness of the movement and they continually conclude that the Jesus loyalists are disloyal, averse to human society, derelict in their duties towards their communities, commonly associated with disorder and crime, and enemies of the state.[252] Thus, over the course of Paul's life, the Jesus movement begins by facing political charges at the local level and goes on to face political charges within Rome itself, at the behest of the emperor.

This understanding of the political nature of Pauline suffering is strengthened when we look more closely at the persecutions mentioned in the non-contested letters. I have already mentioned the political nature of the conflict that arose in Galatia. I will now turn to the persecutions experienced by the Thessalonians and the Philippians. In Thessalonika, a provincial capital, the rulers of the city actively cultivated Roman favor and benefaction and sought to distance themselves from occasional uprisings that occurred elsewhere in the province of Macedonia. The city was deeply immersed in the ideology of Rome—publicly praising the Roman general Metellus as "Savior" for crushing an anti-Roman Macedonian revolt (i.e., for killing their compatriots!), minting coins praising Augustus and Antony as liberators of the city, minting other coins honoring the deified Julius, building statues of the divine Claudius, and establishing central temples to the imperial cult. All of this makes it clear that imperial benefaction was of the utmost importance for the Thessalonian elite.[253] In such a city,

251. Suetonius says that Nero uses the Christians as scapegoats (see Suetonius, *Twelve Caesars* 6.37, 69–140) and subsequent scholarship has followed this line but it is interesting to ask a few questions. Was Suetonius wrong and Nero right? Or did Nero have people infiltrate the Christian community at Rome and provoke them to set the fire (empires, after all, have always had their *agents provocateurs*, and have often found ways to twist seditious movements in order to have them meet imperial objectives)? Or if Suetonius was right, what was it about early Roman Christianity that made it susceptible to this charge? More recently, Brent D. Shaw has questioned if there was any widespread Neronian persecution of Christians after the fire in Rome (See "Myth of Neronian Persecution," 73–100). However, one need not posit such a cataclysmic persecution to still suspect that Paul was executed in Rome (as per 1 Clement) given that he may have, yet again, come to the attention of the local authority and, this time, not escaped with his life.

252. See Jeffers, *Greco-Roman World*, 319; Dunn, *Beginning from Jerusalem*, 60; Kahl, *Galatians Re-Imagined*, 297; Wengst, *Pax Romana*, 72–76; Keresztes, *Imperial Rome*, 69–73; Tellbe, *Paul Between Synagogue and State*, 63–77. Of course, this only continues into the second century CE (see Grant, *Early Christianity*, 2–3).

253. See Smith, "'Unmasking the Powers," 57; Tellbe, *Paul Between Synagogue and*

the sensitivities of the rulers would be very high in relation to anything that was or could be perceived of as anti-imperial or seditious. Therefore, the emergence of a community of Jesus loyalists separate from the Judean assemblies—a separation that the Pauline faction appears to encourage despite the danger—could have been viewed as a threat to the benefaction and status granted to the city.[254] Persecution seems inevitable and, indeed, in 1 Thessalonians, we see Paul writing a letter to assemblies defined by the experience of persecution, hostility, and suffering.[255] It is clear that membership in the Jesus movement resulted in strained relationships among families and coworkers, as well as producing economic isolation and experiences of violence. The movement seems to be understood as a political and religious threat to the city and the common good.[256]

The same holds true for the experiences of Jesus loyalists at Philippi. The Pauline faction writes to Philippi, emphasizing that Paul himself takes part in this process as a political prisoner writing to those who are experiencing a suffering similar to his own—i.e., a political persecution.[257] Yet here, when the stakes for Paul himself may be even higher than those he faced in Galatia or Thessalonika, we see the Pauline faction refusing to back down from conflict with the authorities. Instead, being united while persevering through suffering is emphasized.[258] As elsewhere, the problem in Philippi is that the Jesus loyalists could be (perceived of as) disloyal troublemakers, who would then risk becoming social and economic pariahs, and the targets of opposition, exploitation, or violence from their neighbors and the local magistrates.[259] Given that the Jesus loyalists were situated at or near the subsistence level, the smallest amount of persecution could have a ripple effect with potentially fatal consequences. Hence the ongoing appeal

---

State, 81–86, 118.

254. See Donfried, "Imperial Cults," 215–20; Meeks, *First Urban Christians*, 31; Tellbe, *Paul Between Synagogue and State*, 86–89, 109–10, 118–19, 121–22, 131–37; Theissen, *Fortress Introduction*, 59.

255. See Tellbe, *Paul Between Synagogue and State*, 94–96, 103–4.

256. See Carter, *Roman Empire and the New Testament*, 53–56.

257. See Oakes, *Rome in the Bible*, 126–41; Harink, *Paul Among the Postliberals*, 111–14.

258. See Carter, *Roman Empire and the New Testament*, 60–62; Oakes, *Philippians*, 77–89, 136; Tellbe, *Paul Between Synagogue and State*, 22–31.

259. See Oakes, "God's Sovereignty," 128–30; Tellbe, *Paul Between Synagogue and State*, 233–37. Hence the importance of unity for basic survival (see Oakes, *Philippians*, 99–102).

of the "Judaizers." As Tellbe writes: "'Christian-identity' [*sic*] means suffering in contrast to Jewish identity which in this context implies social safety and security . . . the most likely reason why the Judaizers' teaching appealed to the Philippians had to do with the achievement of social and political protections."[260] The "Judaizers," in other words, are simply those willing to make a strategic concession to legal systems for the sake of survival. The Pauline opposition to this route is remarkable. Paul and his coworkers respond by offering Paul as a model of suffering to be imitated, by arguing that God is sovereign even over Rome, and by claiming that those of lowly status now are actually also first-class citizens of heaven. When faced with political persecution, the Pauline faction does not compromise—they double-down in both Philippi and Thessalonika, as they did in Galatia.

Therefore, as with the persecutions Paul and others experienced from the hands of Judean officials, the persecutions they experienced from Greek and Roman civic officials reflects both the vulnerability and low status of the early Jesus loyalists as well as the political stakes involved. Paul and the early Jesus loyalists were forced to scramble to survive yet, even as they did so, they refused to give up their treasonous "superstition" about the Lordship of Jesus and how that reshaped the ways in which they shared life together.

Conclusion with a Self-Critical Postscript

This chapter began by looking at four issues related to Paul's personal life—his supposed citizenships, level of education, class-based sensitivities, and labor—and concluded that positing Paul as a person of high status and wealth is historically implausible and does not hold up in light of the evidence. The subsequent discussion of Pauline suffering verifies this. Although he was not among the very lowest members of society (like sex workers, slaves, and the starving rural poor), he was still a member of those considered both "lowly" and "poor."

We should also draw the same conclusion about the other members of the early assemblies of Jesus. Having examined the evidence offered by Theissen and the "new consensus" on socioeconomic matters, as well as the counter-evidence offered by Meggitt, and the models of Friesen, Oakes, and Longenecker, the most plausible conclusion to draw is that, while some variations of status and wealth were present in the early assemblies of Jesus

---

260. Tellbe, *Paul Between Synagogue and State*, 264.

loyalists, these are likely variations found between the poor, the very poor, and the utterly destitute. Again, a study of the sufferings ascribed to Paul and other members of the assemblies strengthens this conclusion. If one were to look for a contemporary analogy to this kind of diversity it would be found in an urban slum, not a suburban church.

I emphasize this because of the political implications that have been drawn from sociological studies of Paul and the assemblies associated with him. Generally (but not always), the higher the status ascribed to Paul and his peers, the more conservative their politics are said to be. Similarly, the lower the status ascribed to Paul and his peers, the more subversive or revolutionary their politics are said to be. This is based upon the idea that those who benefit from a certain system are not as likely to be critical of that system, whereas those who suffer under that system are more inclined to want to change it. Therefore, reflecting upon this, we can now see that those who wish to make any political statement based upon Paul and others having high status and wealth is undermined. In light of the evidence, it is historically implausible to assume that Paul and his peers were well situated in society and so this cannot be used as the basis of any sort of political argument related to Paul.

Having made that important point, I do want to exercise more caution than most do in terms of the conclusions I draw from this evidence. I am not convinced that those who suffer under a certain socioeconomic and political empire are *always* keen to subvert or change that empire. If anything, history teaches us that allegiances are always far more complicated. On the one hand, in order to sustain itself, all empires need to be backed by an ideology that causes people of all ranks to accept its divisions of labor, property, and power. Thus, a good many of those who are among the oppressed accept the broader ideology of the empire and seek to make do with what they can based upon the rules of the game. To use the words of Foucault, they become self-disciplining and internalize that which is required to keep them (and others) in check, thereby becoming subjected at the level of their subjectivities (i.e., as subjects).[261] Not all oppressed people are trying to create a new system or subvert the old one—and given the opportunity, many (but far from all) would choose to live the same way as any middle-class or wealthy person lives in our society.[262] Thus, while those

261. See Foucault, *Discipline and Punish*.

262. Sayak Valencia's fascinating study of the "endriago subjects" produced by "gore capitalism" is an excellent recent example of the sort of complications I have in mind here

like James C. Scott properly draw our attention to the plurality of ways in which those on the margins mock and subvert the values of those in the center, many of those on the margins are content to stop mocking and join the center if given the opportunity.[263] Therefore, while those on the margins are *more likely* to be subversive they are *not necessarily* that way, nor are they always deeply committed to that which is subversive.

On the other hand, a good many of those who have worked to overthrow corrupt systems came from the ranks of the elites (Moses came from the court of the pharaoh, Gandhi came from the elite schools of England, Kropotkin came from the intimate circles of the Tsar, and so on).[264] We cannot create a simplistic, one-to-one corollary between a level of socioeconomic status and a political position. Statistics and generalities help us in understanding things like probability and plausibility, but they do not provide us with certainty in relation to this-or-that specific case.

Therefore, this analysis of the socioeconomic status of Paul and the other members of the early assemblies of Jesus is somewhat limited in its value for our discussion of Pauline politics. It is valuable because it undercuts any who posit a conservative reading of Paul based upon an historically implausible socioeconomic reconstruction of Paul and his peers. However, it does not necessarily lead to the conclusion that Paul's politics were subversive or radical. While it certainly adds to the *plausibility* of this reading of Paul, a politically subversive understanding of Paul should not depend upon it.

In this regard, I want to pay attention to the criticisms raised by those who question the value of the social-scientific approach to Paulinism because it seems to be employed by people on all sides in order to support the already established political commitments of the interpreter. As David Horrell notes, "radical readings" of Paul are often presented as "an idealized reflection of contemporary commitments" and "'bourgeois' interpreters"

(see Valencia, *Gore Capitalism*). I am also reminded of a story Proust tells in *In Search of Lost Time*, when Marcel is talking with a lift-operator at a fancy resort and he (Marcel) is shocked that the lift-operator, who is very poor, does not want poverty to be eradicated because, as the lift-operator says, I want to have people to shit on when I'm rich (my paraphrase and, alas, I cannot find the passage now). Of course, the rich like to draw attention to stories like these because it makes them feel better about themselves. While they do express what some people think and feel, I have personally found a considerable percentage of people experiencing poverty and oppression think and feel differently.

263. See Scott, *Weapons of the Weak*.

264. And, in fact, it's worth noting that the purported subversiveness, or liberating potentiality, of all of those named here has been questioned.

are also working with "unacknowledged commitments which inevitably means that evidence is seen from a particular perspective."[265] Consequently, a lot of sociological exegesis is overly-determined by models and is too reductionistic.[266] Therefore, I do not want my own efforts to embody a lived commitment to people experiencing oppression today to cause me to draw firmer conclusions than are warranted by the evidence.

It is only with Pauline talk about suffering and persecution that we begin to move into a more explicitly political terrain that is specific, localized, and compelling. As we have seen, suffering, for Paul and other Jesus loyalists, was just as deeply a political issue as it was religious, social, and economic. Furthermore, this was suffering that was imposed by those with a high degree of status, wealth, and power—the authorities within local Judean assemblies, civic governors, military officers and, at the end of Paul's life, perhaps even the emperor. There is no doubt that local communities and authorities saw Paul and the assemblies of Jesus loyalists as a threat to their political well-being from the very beginning. The question we must then ask is whether this was an inaccurate perception or whether the persecutors of the assemblies actually did understand something about Paulinism that subsequent Christians have forgotten or denied. I will answer this question in subsequent volumes, but I must first turn to eschatological matters and their significance for our understanding of the politics of Paulinism.

265. Horrell, "Introduction—Social-Scientific Interpretation," 17–19; also 1–2, 21–24. Gerd Theissen is aware of the history of this (*Social Reality and the Early Christians*, 1–15, 20) but, despite that awareness, his own work does not entirely escape this line of criticism.

266. Horrell, "Introduction—Social-Scientific Interpretation," 10–12.

4

PAULINE APOCALYPTIC ESCHATOLOGY: TRADITIONAL THEMES

Introduction

BEFORE DIRECTLY EXAMINING WHAT I take to be Pauline apocalyptic eschatology, I think it is useful to spend some time framing that discussion and exploring how the terms "apocalyptic" and "eschatology" have been employed in prior debates. A great variety of competing, vague, or contradictory meanings have been put forward and so it is useful to explore those meanings, and the historical conditions that were related to their production, so that we can be clear about the way in which I employ this language.[1] First, I will explore these matters in relation to "eschatology" and, in the subsequent section, I will more fully develop the "apocalyptic" elements of this. I will then examine some of the traditional themes that have arisen in relation to Pauline eschatology—questions about its origins, about the possible "eschatological tension" found in Paulinism, about the role of the Spirit in Paul's life and writings, about the relationship that exists between

---

1. Aune notes how the word "eschatology" tends to operate as an "umbrella term" and so "its usefulness has become directly proportional to the extent to which it is carefully defined and qualified." Similarly, Collins notes that modern scholarship has made many judgments in relation to the word "apocalyptic," but then suggests that we forego judgment until we gain some clarity regarding what exactly we are talking about (see Aune, *Cultic Setting*, 1; Collins, *Apocalyptic Imagination*, 1–2).

Pauline eschatology and ethics, and about questions regarding judgment and the purported "imminence" of Jesus's return. I will pay special attention to the socio-political implications of traditional explorations of these matters. This will then pave the way for the next volume, wherein I will engage in a more detailed exploration of the apocalyptic nature of Pauline eschatology and how it, as a whole, confronts, conflicts, and overlaps with the imperial ideo-theology of Rome.

Eschatology

Eschatology's Loss and Recovery

With the rise of reason, science, and the modern period—let us imagine this to be a time spanning roughly from the beginning of the Enlightenment in eighteenth-century Europe up until the 1960s (leaving aside debates about whether or not "postmodernism" is truly *post*-modern or if it is, instead, better understood as *hyper*-modern)—traditional eschatological themes became increasingly marginalized in society, in Christian theology, and in biblical studies. The path to this marginalization had been paved by the Magisterial Protestant Reformers and the Roman Catholic neo-scholastics who deliberately relegated eschatological matters to the realm of doctrine. This was done in order to counteract more radical movements—like those inspired by Thomas Müntzer, the Franciscan Spirituals, or Joachim of Fiore—which claimed eschatology as the grounds for significant, disruptive action in the present.[2] In response to these movements, matters of eschatology were distanced from a person's lived existence and defined as *doctrines* which related to "The End" and what followed after—doctrines about such things as the return of Jesus, the resurrection of the dead, the final judgment of all humanity, the destruction of the earth and the start of new life in heaven (or in hell or purgatory). Then, with the rise of modern sensibilities, these doctrinal matters became increasingly embarrassing to Christians and were further marginalized as throw-away elements of a primitive pre-scientific mythology.[3] Thus, when eschatological issues

2. See Sauter, *What Dare We Hope?* 2–9; Taubes, *Occidental Eschatology*, 85–122. Taubes then demonstrates how the process of the individualization and de-historicization of eschatology is continued in the philosophies of Lessing, Kant, and Hegel (125–63) before Marx and Kierkegaard recover the more revolutionary root of the eschatological outlook (164–94).

3. Several authors note this embarrassment. See, for example, Hill, *In God's Time,*

are explored by modern theologians, they tend to be attached to the end of any given systematic theology, almost as an appendix, and carry little significance in relation to that which came before.[4] For many, eschatology *should be* surrendered because we now "know better" than the primitive Christians, and it *can be* surrendered because it makes no meaningful difference to daily life.

This discussion is further nuanced when the relationship between "eschatology" and "history" is explored. On the one hand, there are those who argue that eschatology is a problem because it requires us to flee from history and project our hopes into some possible (or imagined) spiritual future. Thus, Richard Horsley argues that "[the] eschatological is useful for those who want to avoid the historical" as it aids "a withdrawal from historical, political, and economic life into a purely religious realm."[5] This flight from the historical is then said to be rooted in the observation that the "early Christians" must have been deeply traumatized by the delay of the *parousia* and the failure of Jesus to return and fully implement the kingdom of God. Hence, Hans Joachim Schoeps argues that:

> the origins of all eschatological expectation are to be found in the disappointment of hopes focused on earthy history, i.e., the resigned recognition that any imminent realisation was impossible. Despair of earthly history caused what was impossible in the present either to be transferred to the future or to be projected into the sphere of the unearthly and supernatural.[6]

On the other hand, some scholars assert that the problem and embarrassment related to eschatology is not that it is ahistorical but that it is *too* historical. The issue, from this perspective, is that eschatology makes very specific historical claims—for example, that Jesus did, in fact, rise from the dead sometime around 33 CE and that the risen Jesus will return again at

---

7-9; Kee, *Renewal of Hope*, viii. The term "mythology" is employed here in a derogatory manner—implying that we know better—and not with the richness that the study of mythology has gained in more recent decades. See, for example, Ricoeur, *Symbolism of Evil*; Reynolds and Tracy, *Myth and Philosophy*.

4. Erikson's systematic theology is a good example of a work that follows this post-Enlightenment tradition (Erikson, *Christian Theology*). Of course, it should be noted that systematic theology is also a child of its age, as theologians began to attempt that which philosophers like Hegel or Kant were attempting to do—the creation of a clear, rational, and consistent system of studying and engaging the world.

5. Horsley, *Liberation of Christmas*, xiii, 2; see also 153.

6. Schoeps, *Paul*, 91.

some point in the future. From this perspective, abstracting eschatology from history based upon the content of the New Testament seems unwarranted. Consequently, according to those who hold this view, eschatology was marginalized in the modern period not because it was irrelevant but because it was *threatening* and posited an historical paradigm over against rationalism's disavowal of tradition, which led rationalism to ignore the past and "barely tolerate" the future.[7] Rationalism moves from the material domain of history into the mind of the individual who only knows what is experienced in the present.[8] So, is eschatology rooted in a flight from history or in history itself? We will explore that question in a moment, but for now we should ask another question: why does this matter?

It is helpful to see the 1960s as a break-through period when matters related to eschatology were resurrected. This occurred as one small part of the great questioning of modernity, rationalism, and scientific objectivity that began to break out *en masse* at that point of time. In part, this questioning arose because the devastation wrought by two consecutive World Wars helped to reveal some of the implicit assumptions, or blind-spots, of modern European thinking. It became apparent that European philosophy and politics were always already operating with a certain kind of eschatology. The grand narrative of Europe was pushing forward toward the end (*eschaton*) or goal (*telos*) of history. Eschatological claims were used as one component of an ideology self-avowedly oriented around the realization of enlightenment, liberty, equality, and fraternity—of peace and prosperity for all. The two World Wars made it clear that these goals had not been realized.[9] Thus, even among the most "enlightened" Europeans, eschatol-

---

7. Vos, *Pauline Eschatology*, vi.

8. This is Vos's line of criticism (*Pauline Eschatology*, vi–vii).

9. See Moltmann, *Coming of God*, 3–6. Of course, it almost (but not quite) goes without saying that, although European leaders employed the language of "liberté, égalité, et fraternité," they certainly weren't keen to see those things equally applied to the poor, those without property, the colonized, or other outsiders. For example, Susan Buck-Morss notes how both the French Revolution against the monarchy and the Haitian Revolution against France were inspired by the same ideals—only the French were happy to claim those things for themselves while simultaneously denying them to the Haitians (Buck-Morss, *Hegel, Haiti, and Universal History*). In this regard, one should also note that countries like Canada and the United States continue the colonization and abuse of the Haitian people, despite the rhetoric they employ about freedom, equality, and "universal human rights." See Hallward, *Damming the Flood*; Engler and Fenton, *Canada in Haiti*. That said, as atrocities committed by the Belgians in the Congo, or the French in Algeria, or the British in Zimbabwe, or the Dutch in Ghana, or the Portuguese in Angola, or the Spanish in Equatorial Guinea (to focus only the African continent)

ogy was never so much abandoned as reformulated into a more humanistic and less deistic mode of presentation. Hence, Jürgen Moltmann notes that "[t]he embarrassment and neglect related to Christ's *parousia* in modern theology has led to the proliferation of other fantasies."[10] Indeed, when understood in relation to the *telos* of history, eschatology seems inextricably linked to much broader questions about the search for meaning.[11] Ultimately, the issue might not be that of choosing or rejecting eschatology but of choosing which kind of eschatology one finds most compelling.[12] In this regard, it is worth exploring Moltmann's understanding of eschatology in more detail as he has done more than any other person to remap and restore this subject. Wolfhart Pannenberg has also been influential in this revitalization and his work will also be discussed.

The Eschatologies of Pannenberg and Moltmann

Both Moltmann and Pannenberg understand eschatology to be a *theology of history*. For Pannenberg this is an understanding of history centered upon the historical truth of the resurrection of Jesus, which proleptically

---

make very clear, the magnitude of the slaughter in the World Wars only really traumatized Europe because it took place in Europe and among Europeans.

10. Moltmann, *Way of Jesus Christ*, 313.

11. In this regard, I'm not convinced that even the most thoroughgoing postmodern nihilists (such as Jean Baudrillard) are able to completely escape this subject matter. Baudrillard adamantly rejects meaning, but I fail to see how this rejection is not itself making a particular claim about meaning. I do not intend to be disingenuous to claim that, for Baudrillard, the meaning of life is that there is no meaning. This becomes apparent when Baudrillard judges the death of meaning in ethical terms. He writes: "There is no more hope for meaning. And without a doubt this is *a good thing*" (emphasis added; *Simulacra and Simulation*, 164; see also 159–64).

12. Sauter, for example, challenges the understanding of eschatology as related to the telos of history, claiming that such a view collapses eschatology into a "teleology of history" and is bound by a progressive outlook, falsely believing things are gradually getting better as history advances and as human actions come to match what God desires (Sauter, *What Dare We Hope?* 9–18). Thus, he seeks to redefine eschatology as "*comprehensive theological argumentation*, whose task is to give an account of the 'hope that is in you'" (xi). It is giving an account of this "hope" that "rehabilitates the rather disdained doctrine of last things" and reconnects that doctrine to lived existence in new ways (209). I do not believe that Sauter's definition is the best, although eschatology and hope are deeply connected. Further, I neither think his criticisms are sustainable—the view he criticizes need not be progressivist in the sense he suggests—nor do I find anything worrisome about understanding eschatology as "teleology," so long as Pauline eschatological (or teleological) tension is maintained.

anticipates the eschaton.[13] In making this point, Pannenberg is counter-ing two different parties. On the one hand, he is arguing against Rudolph Bultmann who "demythologized" the historicity of the resurrection. On the other hand, he is arguing against Karl Barth who translated historical eschatology into more existential terms regarding the personal experience of the eternal within the realm of the temporal. Thus, while Barth and his followers emphasize that God's revelation is a pure and unmediated en-counter, Pannenberg argues that the revelation of God occurs indirectly, as a "reflex" of God's activity in history.[14] By focusing upon the revelation of God in the historical resurrection of Jesus, Pannenberg gives a new impetus and significance to the study of eschatology because resurrection is, itself, *the* eschatological event. Furthermore, Pannenberg's historical outlook also aids this renewed interest in eschatology because he believes that history is only completely comprehended at the end.[15] Thus, how one understands the end (the *telos*) transforms the way in which one understands the present.

Jürgen Moltmann's eschatological project has been much larger and more sustained than Pannenberg's.[16] In *Theology of Hope,* Moltmann begins his "systematic contributions to theology" by arguing that eschatology does not belong at the periphery of Christian thought and life; rather, it must be understood as the center and the foundation upon which everything else depends.[17] For Moltmann, eschatology names a *narrative-based historical and political orientation* that is grounded in the space created between the memory of God's past promises and the hope of God's in-breaking future. This is an historical orientation because, as with Pannenberg, faith in God is mediated by the experience of God in history.[18] It is also political, because

13. Sauter, *What Dare We Hope?* xii–xiii, 127–28.

14. Pannenberg, *Revelation as History,* 13–15; 125–31. In this regard, Pannenberg is closer to the "natural theology" opposed by Barth. In Pannenberg's view, revelation that is rooted in history is universal and open to any who have eyes to see it (135–39).

15. Pannenberg, *Revelation as History,* 131–35. In contradistinction to some kind of protology which gives meaning to history via an effort to get back to some kind of mythic, pristine, originary state.

16. A multitude of studies, summaries, and criticisms of Moltmann's eschatology exist. I have found the response of Richard Bauckham to be especially useful. See, for example, his identification of seven key elements in Moltmann's eschatology in "Escha-tology in *The Coming of God,*" in Bauckham, *God Will Be All in All,* 2–34.

17. Moltmann, *Theology of Hope.* Others have also tried to maintain this centrality of eschatology. See Hill, *In God's Time,* 9; Kee, *Renewal of Hope,* viii; Dawson, "Christian View of History," 30; Taubes, *Occidental Eschatology,* 3–4.

18. Moltmann, *Experiences in Theology,* 38–39. In this regard, Moltmann can refer

"remembrance of God's liberating act, hope for God's guidance into the future, the keeping of his commandments, and love of his presence" leads Jesus loyalists into the domain of struggle.[19]

By understanding eschatology in this way, Moltmann is also countering two previous perspectives. On the one hand, his historical and political understanding of eschatology leads him to reject the more personal or individualistic existential perspectives popularized by Barth and Bultmann. On the other hand, Barth and Bultmann were themselves responding to the influential "consistent" eschatology of Albert Schweitzer. Schweitzer argued that "the term eschatology ought *only* to be applied when reference is made to the end of the world as expected in the immediate future, and the events, hopes, and fears connected therewith."[20] The problem Barth and Bultmann have with Schweitzer is that his consistent eschatology leads to the conclusion that Jesus and Paul were mistaken about a good many important things and so they become problematical as figures for contemporary ethics. Hence, both Barth and Bultmann, in different ways, look to recover the significance of Jesus and Paul in more existential categories. Moltmann rejects this tactic. However, by making eschatology the foundation of Christian theology, he also rejects the view proposed by Schweitzer who, in Moltmann's opinion, robbed eschatology of its ongoing significance for daily life by orienting it so heavily around "the End."[21]

In his rejection of Schweitzer, Moltmann is not disregarding the significance of the future for eschatology. He speaks of "God's future" as "*adventus*"—a future that breaks into the present as a *novum*—rather than as "*futurum*," which is simply the development of that which already is.[22] In this way, Moltmann rejects the "false eschatology" of modernity's historical

---

to eschatology as "the doctrine and wisdom of hope" or as the "intellectus spei" in a way similar to Sauter, but without abandoning the historical element (*What Dare We Hope?* 51, 53).

19. Moltmann, *Experiences in Theology*, 39.

20. Schweitzer, *Paul and His Interpreters*, 11; emphasis added.

21. See Moltmann, *Theology of Hope*, 15; also Sugai, "Paul's Eschatology," 1. In many ways, Moltmann is recovering the socio-political significance granted to eschatology by the Radical Reformers and by Joachim of Fiore, who is often mentioned in Moltmann's writings.

22. This point is crucial to Moltmann and is repeated many times. See *Coming of God*, 25–29; "Liberation of the Future," 265; *God in Creation*, 132–35; also Bauckham, "Time and Eternity," in *God Will be All in All*, 163–64.

progressivism, and asserts the transcendence of God's eschatological or messianic time over the *futurum* of history.[23] This, then, brings a "kairological" understanding to time, wherein "time is determined by happening, not happening by time."[24]

This, in turn, leads Moltmann to reject the common linear conception of history as a single line moving from the past to the present to the future. Instead, Moltmann affirms an ontological view of time defined by different modalities: the past is the domain of the real, the future that of the possible, and the present is the moment where the real and the possible come into contact, and where the possible is or is not realized.[25] Within this understanding, there is a qualitative difference between the past and the future—the future receives an "ontological priority" and is the source of time.[26] Consequently, people are liberated from the past, opened to the future, and history itself is "de-fatalized" because it is the in-breaking advent of God that truly defines who people are, more so than anything people have been or done (or had done to them) in the past.[27]

Moltmann provides us with a truly fascinating and liberating theological understanding of eschatology and its relevance. However, he writes as a theologian and Richard Bauckham, a biblical scholar who has been profoundly influenced by Moltmann, argues that Moltmann's engagement with New Testament texts is "remarkably ignorant and incompetent."[28] Therefore, we will now turn to some key understandings of eschatology within New Testament scholarship, in order to see if a comparably relevant

---

23. Moltmann, *Experiences in Theology*, 44; Moltmann, *God in Creation*, 126; also Bauckham, "Time and Eternity," in *God Will be All in All*, 155–57.

24. Moltmann, *God in Creation*, 118.

25. Moltmann, "Bible, the Exegete and the Theologian," 227–28; Moltmann, *God in Creation*, 128–29; also Bauckham, "Time and Eternity," in *God Will be All in All*, 161–62. Khiok-Khng Yeo follows Moltmann closely in this regard when he asserts that biblical eschatology does not see the past, present, and future as tenses but as "modes of existence and aspects of action . . . *Present* describes our spontaneous and continuous experience of the holy despite our current historical ambiguity and despair. *Past* refers to the realized acts of God in history. *Future* is the coming (advent or *parousia*) of God's radically new creation, which is assured by the past and realized in the present" (*Chairman Mao*, 21).

26. Moltmann, *Coming of God*, 138–40; Moltmann, *God in Creation*, 129–30; Moltmann, *Experiences in Theology*, 31; also Bauckham, "Time and Eternity," in *God Will be All in All*, 163.

27. See Moltmann, *Coming of God*, 134; also Bauckham, "Time and Eternity," in *God Will be All in All*, 164; Sauter, *What Dare We Hope?* 117.

28. Bauckham, "Time and Eternity," in *God Will be All in All*, 179.

or liberating understanding of eschatology pertains to the Pauline letters. As we engage with biblical scholars, it is worth remembering the various perspectives about eschatology that have been mentioned—the eschatology that arose out of the Reformation focused upon the doctrines related to "the End," the "consistent" eschatology of Schweitzer, the existential eschatologies of Barth and Bultmann, Pannenberg's eschatology as a "doctrine of history" grounded in the event of Jesus's resurrection, and Moltmann's eschatology as a narrative-based historical and political orientation—because these perspectives have also deeply influenced biblical scholarship (indeed, Schweitzer and Bultmann were biblical scholars more than they were theologians).[29]

Eschatology within New Testament Scholarship

We can identity three closely related clusters of thought regarding eschatology in New Testament scholarship. First, the view of eschatology as that which is focused on the *telos* of history finds quite a bit of resonance here. Second, slightly shifting the emphasis, some argue that eschatology has to do with the *process* of history just as much as it has to do with history's ultimate purpose. Finally, there are scholars who take this second view and explore it in more detail under the notion of *Heilsgeschichte*—Salvation History. Obviously, there is considerable overlap among those who hold to these views, but it is worth taking some time to highlight each emphasis.

Eschatology defined as that which is concerned with the end and goal of history has already been explored in our survey of Pannenberg and Moltmann. Several biblical scholars also hold to this view. For example, Geerhardus Vos argues that eschatology relies upon the notion that history "tends towards a goal," Craig C. Hill defines eschatology as being concerned with the fulfillment of God's plan for human history, Lucien Cerfaux sees eschatology as "a divine intervention in time, which is definitive, and rounds off the history of the world," and Howard Clark Kee defines eschatology as "the way the group understood and affirmed its ultimate destiny."[30] Similarly, Paul Merkley argues that biblical eschatology is best understood

29. Although, as is often the case, the lines between "biblical studies" and "theology," as well as those between "theology" and "history" tend to blur and fluctuate depending on which ideologies are most dominant in popular culture and the academy.

30. Vos, *Pauline Eschatology*, 1; Hill, *In God's Time*, 3–4; Cerfaux, *Church in the Theology*, 47n92; Kee, *Beginnings of Christianity*, 1.

as history oriented towards a meaningful future and he distinguishes this from teleology because it places God at the center of the drive of history.[31] Hans Joachim Schoeps goes so far as to conclude that "[a]ll Jewish eschatology was and is exclusively concerned with the future."[32]

However, a good many biblical scholars disagree with Schoeps and argue that the eschatologies arising out of Second Temple Judaism(s) were not only concerned with the future—they were also concerned with the past and present.[33] A considerable amount of eschatology is not only about the *telos* of history, but it is about history itself. Thus, William J. Dumbrell argues that eschatology should be defined as both the goal of history *and* the "biblical factors and events bearing on that goal."[34] Indeed, it is argued that this is why the whole notion of history itself plays such a prominent role within Judaism. Over against more cyclical conceptions of time that dominated the ancient Near East, the Judeans developed a more linear conception of time based upon their eschatological perspective that God was guiding the course of history towards a certain goal.[35] In particular, the Judean view of history was especially focused upon God's various covenants—with Noah, with Abraham, with Israel, and with David—and it looks to the eschatological outworkings of these covenants.[36] Others, outside of the purview of these covenants, are brought into the overarching eschatological framework to the extent that they overlap or engage with

31. Merkley, *Greek and Hebrew Origins*, 249–52.

32. Schoeps, *Paul*, 97.

33. Aune goes so far in the opposite direction as to state that Jewish eschatology is so focused upon a perfect primal past that it might better be referred to as "protology" (*Cultic Setting*, 7). However, as with Schoeps, it is best to view this as an overstatement.

34. Dumbrell, *Search for Order*, 9. For similar statements, see Witherington, *Jesus, Paul and the End*, 9; Wright, *New Testament*, 81–120; Kee, *Renewal of Hope*, viii; Dawson, "Christian View of History," 31.

35. See Kee, *Christian Origins in Sociological Perspective*, 38; Meeks, *Moral World*, 91; Merkley, *Greek and Hebrew Origins*, 74–75, 117, 145; Taubes, *Occidental Eschatology*, 11–12; Vos, *Pauline Eschatology*, 61; also Moltmann, *Experiences in Theology*, 28–29. It should be noted that this distinction between "cyclical" and "linear" conceptions of time is often overplayed in biblical scholarship. It is more accurate to state that most cultures utilize both cyclical and linear conceptions of time simultaneously. Thus, for example, while the Judean people held to an eschatological perspective regarding God's goal for history they also celebrated cyclical festivals. I will explore this point in more detail in volume 2.

36. Merkley, *Greek and Hebrew Origins*, 132; Schweitzer, *Mysticism of Paul the Apostle*, 76–79.

Israel. Within this perspective people are active, history-making agents, not simply beings dominated and controlled by fate or other Powers.[37]

This then overlaps with our third cluster of thought and those who spoke of biblical eschatology as the narration of Salvation History. Those who hold to this view seek to identify decisive moments in history—particularly revealed in the interaction of God with the world, and of the world with God—in a trajectory spanning from creation to new creation. This view was largely popularized by Oscar Cullmann in the 1960s. Cullmann employs the term *Heilsgeschichte* as a way of referring to the New Testament word *oikonomia*, which refers to "the thought of a plan, of an administration, of a 'household', sometimes in the passive sense and sometimes in the active sense of 'keeping house'."[38] By defining eschatology as Salvation History, Cullmann believed that he was being faithful to the New Testament authors and their understanding of eschatology. The core of the New Testament, according to Cullmann, is "interpreted events."[39] Thus, Cullmann is clear that "Salvation History" is not history understood in the general sense (i.e., as an "objective" record of times, places, peoples, and events); rather, Salvation History focuses upon recognizing or establishing connections between a few specific events that are continually interpreted and reinterpreted based upon each subsequent event or revelation.[40] Consequently, he argues that this eschatological outlook is one that unites history and myth by viewing history from the viewpoint of prophecy.[41] As a result of this, Cullmann distinguishes the "early Christian" view of time and history from the view of the Greeks—the "early Christians" did not sharply distinguish time and eternity, nor were they dealing with strictly conceptual notions

37. See Merkley, *Greek and Hebrew Origins*, 102–3, 138–42.

38. Cullmann, *Salvation in History*, 75–76.

39. Cullmann, *Salvation in History*, 87. As an example of the practice of this, Cullmann references 1 Cor 15, which he believes to be the earliest known creed of "the church." Here, Cullmann stresses the usage of the term *Kairos* in the New Testament (which he defines a specific moment in time that is especially favorable for a specific undertaking). When the *kairoi* of history are joined together, the redemptive line appears (Cullmann, *Christ and Time*, 39, 43).

40. Cullmann, *Salvation in History*, 77, 91.

41. Cullmann, *Christ and Time*, 94, 97. Or, as he later writes, "Salvation history is not concerned with a philosophy of history, but a prophecy of history" (*Salvation in History*, 98).

of time or history; instead they were always addressing "filled" time and "purposeful" history.[42]

Although some have taken issue with Cullmann, his proposal has largely been accepted within New Testament studies, albeit with the addition of various nuances or emphases.[43] Thus, despite their differences, C. H. Dodd agrees that Christianity is rooted in events not ideas and, despite what he takes to be its transcendental significance, he does not deny its historical element.[44] Similarly, Ernst Käsemann asserts that nobody can "seriously dispute that "salvation history forms the horizon of Pauline theology."[45] Thus, Käsemann argues that Paul divides world history into various ages (*aiones*) from the age of Adam, to those of Abraham, Moses, and the Anointed.[46] However, Käsemann also emphasizes the element of struggle found within Salvation History, calling it "the battlefield between the *civitas dei* and the *civitas terrena*."[47] Here, Käsemann finds some resonance with Moltmann, and this is furthered by his emphasis that eschatology does not arise out of history but is defined by that which breaks into history.[48]

However, the dissenting voice of the Jewish scholar, Jacob Neusner, should also be noted. Neusner argues that history had nothing to do with the formation of Christianity—"The New Testament contains no history-writing"—and the same applies to the Jewish Scriptures.[49] History, he ar-

---

42. Cullmann, *Christ and Time*, 62, 67–68; *Salvation in History*, 15.

43. For some who both anticipate and follow Cullmann quite closely, see Kee, *Renewal of Hope*, 154; Brunner, *Eternal Hope*, 31–41; Daniélou, *Lord of History*, 1–5; Schoeps, *Paul*, 88–96; Merkley, *Greek and Hebrew Origins*, 12, 235–36; and Sauter, *What Dare We Hope?* 125–26. Moltmann, on the other hand, strongly objects to Cullmann's notion of Salvation History because he thinks it is overly modern and errs on the side of historical progressivism ("historical Deism") thereby trapping us within the limits of the future of the past (*futurum*) rather than allowing us to be liberated by the *novum* of God's advent (not to mention the further observation it takes no account of the prolonged delay of Jesus's return, a point which we will return to at the end of this chapter; see Moltmann, *Coming of God*, 10–13).

44. Dodd, *History and the Gospel*, 9–15. Dodd's alternate proposal will be explored in more detail below.

45. Käsemann, *Perspectives on Paul*, 66.

46. Käsemann, *Perspectives on Paul*, 65.

47. Käsemann, *Perspectives on Paul*, 67.

48. Käsemann, *Perspectives on Paul*, 68. Or, as Hans Urs von Balthasar phrases it, "Grace brings forth history" (*Theology of History*, 70).

49. Neusner, *Christian and Judaic Invention*, 3–4, 14. Although Neusner does note

gues, was invented much later, in the fourth century CE and it was invented to serve certain (imperial, Constantinian) political purposes.[50] To make this argument, Neusner is operating with a very specific definition of history. He takes "history" to refer to "the representation of intelligible sequences of purposeful events presented as narrative."[51] Thus:

> Prior to the fourth century, Christian writiers [sic] referred to past events, but they did not produce linear, harmonious, pointed historical narratives, formed around the theological teleology that later historians would frame. The New Testament tells stories and provides biography, *but it does not organize in a sustained historical narrative the history of its time or prior ages.*[52]

Neusner explicitly employs this definition of history against the "typological" (or eschatological) understanding of history he finds within Judaism and early Christianity.[53] However, at this point it is important to recognize the language-game that he is playing. By narrowing his definition of history in order to exclude blatantly eschatological elements, while simultaneously broadening his definition so that history must include a more comprehensive account of any given time (or of all times), Neusner is able to label biblical Judaism and Christianity as ahistorical. Essentially, Neusner is imposing a more recognizably modern definition of history onto texts that do not easily fit into a modern paradigm.

This is disappointing because Neusner's sensitivity to the political elements contained in the writings of (post-Constantinian) histories should help him to see that typology, of some sort, is always looming over our endeavors in this regard.[54] Yes, the New Testament writers read history eschatologically and from the perspective of the coming of God, but this does not mean that they have abandoned history altogether. Far from it. It

---

that some minority Jewish positions did start writing history earlier, he argues that they had no significant impact upon Judaism more broadly or upon Christianity.

50. Neusner, *Christian and Judaic Invention*, 3, 14–15.

51. Neusner, *Christian and Judaic Invention*, 3.

52. Neusner, *Christian and Judaic Invention*, 5–6. Emphasis added.

53. Neusner, *Christian and Judaic Invention*, 9.

54. After all, as post-colonial studies have reminded us, all histories are written arbitrarily—the historian chooses what to speak about, what to ignore, who to highlight, what connections to bring forward, and so on. A great example of this kind of analysis as it pertains to Haiti is provided by Michel-Rolph Trouillot in *Silencing the Past: Power and the Production of History*. As he reminds us, "historical production is itself historical" (*Silencing the Past*, 145).

means that they are contesting history, its meaning, and the sort of historical actions that are required in the present moment. Further, as we will see, this contestation of history arises in relation to other histories (like Virgil's *Aeneid*) which posit a different meaning to history resulting in different historical action(s) or ethics.[55] Therefore, while Neusner can help us to realize the political element of all histories, his assertions about Second Temple Judaism(s) and the early Jesus movement are not particularly helpful.

Summary

In this section, we have rapidly mapped out some of the dominant ways in which eschatology has been defined and how its importance has been understood. However, the reader will likely have noted that I have not yet provided a solid definition of how this term will be employed in what follows. In part, I have avoided doing so because I think that "eschatology" is simply a shorthand way of referring to a complex cluster of beliefs, orientations, and actions and a description of those things sometimes serves a better purpose than a definition. However, to be transparent, my own understanding of eschatology falls between Moltmann and Cullmann. I think Cullmann mostly captures the understanding of eschatology contained in the Pauline texts. However, I think Moltmann provides an important corrective to Cullmann by emphasizing the subjective element of eschatology as a narrative-based historical and political *orientation* that leads to certain ways of *acting* in the world. I am not too concerned by the discrepancies that exist between the two (Cullmann's focus upon past, present, and future as tenses, and Moltmann's focus upon those things as modalities of being, for example). To put things slightly differently, I think Cullmann helps us to understand the story that inspired the Pauline faction, while Moltmann helps us to understand how the Pauline faction sought to live within it. I think both of these elements—the story and its embodiment—are strongly present in Paulinism and so this discussion should be helpful when we turn to the cluster of thoughts found in Pauline eschatology. However, I think that Pauline eschatology is of the apocalyptic variety and so, before we go into more detail about specific eschatological themes and their relation to Pauline praxis, it is necessary to describe what I mean by the terms apocalyptic or apocalypticism.

55. Virgil's *Aeneid* is, in many ways, the narration of history that undergirds Roman Imperial ideology. I will explore this more in volume 2.

Apocalyptic

A Similar Trajectory: Losing and Recovering Apocalypticism

Just as with the discussion of matters related to eschatology, matters related to apocalypticism were treated with embarrassment and marginalized within much of modern scholarship. Apocalypticism, from the dominant modern perspective, is that which is caught up in cataclysmic and imminent end-times scenarios. The basic motifs within this understanding are the destruction of the earth, the coming of horrendous beasts, along with pestilence, war, famine, death, and the anti-Christ. Consequently, apart from the populist appeal that this view holds for some (who incline to anti-modernism), most in the mainstream have attempted to distance themselves from apocalypticism.[56] Thus, as Klaus Koch notes, modern European New Testament scholars attempted to save Jesus from the apocalyptic perspective while modern systematic theologians simultaneously tried to develop a non-apocalyptic eschatology focused on the categories of time and eternity instead of engaging in speculation about various ages.[57] Thus, "legitimate" and rational Christian scholarship attempted to distance itself from "mad" and irrational speculation.[58]

However, the work of Albert Schweitzer at the turn of the twentieth century seriously disrupted these bourgeois scholarly efforts. Schweitzer argued that Jesus and his message (along with Paul, although in a slightly altered fashion) were thoroughly, inescapably, and cataclysmically apocalyptic.[59] This, then, provoked the existential turn already mentioned in

56. The ongoing appeal of this sort of "apocalyptic" outlook is evident in the success of books like Hal Lindsey's *The Late Great Planet Earth* and the *Left Behind* series by Tim LaHaye and Jerry Jenkins. Of course, the ways in which most mainstream Christians respond to things like the *Left Behind* series demonstrates that a certain sense of embarrassment in relation to this understanding of the apocalyptic is also still alive and well today.

57. Koch, *Rediscovery of Apocalyptic*, 57–101.

58. Koch, *Rediscovery of Apocalyptic*, 18. It is also worth noting, as Koch does, that the European Christian rejection of apocalyptic literature may have been, at least in part, inspired by the church's rejection of Judaism as the early church began to embrace more Hellenistic ways of viewing the world (20).

59. See Schweitzer, *Quest for the Historical Jesus*; Schweitzer, *Mysticism of Paul the Apostle*. Other scholars, including E. P. Sanders, P. M. Casey, and Bart Ehrman, have continued to reassert or reinvigorate Schweitzer's thesis in more recent decades (see Sanders, *Jesus and Judaism*; Sanders, *Historical Figure of Jesus*; Casey, *From Jewish Prophet*; Ehrman, *Jesus*).

Barth, Bultmann, and early twentieth century Christian scholarship, which tried to find a new way of escaping apocalyptic thinking without abandoning the relevance of the New Testament texts for contemporary life.

However, as with matters related to eschatology and for comparable reasons, a renewed interest in apocalyptic material was sparked in the middle of the twentieth century. Again, both Wolfhart Pannenberg and Jürgen Moltmann played important parts in reviving this interest. On the one hand, Pannenberg explicitly endorsed a connection between the apocalypse (or revelation) of God in history and his eschatological outlook.[60] On the other hand, Moltmann wished to distance his eschatological theology from what he understands to be an apocalyptic focus on "last things" or (more polemically) "final solutions."[61] Be that as it may, by recovering eschatology, both Pannenberg and Moltmann contribute greatly to the revival of apocalypticism.

However, Ernst Käsemann is probably the most influential person involved in this resurgence, especially as it relates to Paulinism. In 1960, he (in)famously asserted (over against existential interpretations) that early "Jewish-Christian apocalyptic" was "the mother of all Christian theology."[62] Käsemann argued that Pauline reflections upon the righteous justice of God (*dikiosyne theou*) was rooted in the belief that "God's sovereignty over the world [was] revealing itself eschatologically in Jesus."[63] In this way, Käsemann provoked a debate and a trajectory in scholarship that has continued until now.[64] One of the important points that has emerged from this is the understanding of apocalypticism's close relationship to eschatology. Rather than positing a gap between the two, a more nuanced understanding of what apocalypticism was at the time of Jesus and Paul has

---

60. See Moltmann, *Revelation as History*.

61. See Moltmann, *Coming of God*, xi. Moltmann, it should be remembered, had been conscripted into the German army when he was young (at the close of World War II) and only had his vision of "the crucified God" after visiting Auschwitz upon his return to Germany (from a POW camp in the UK) when he was asking himself questions about the possibility of continuing to be a German Christian after the events of the war.

62. See Käsemann, *New Testament Questions of Today*, 102.

63. Käsemann, *New Testament Questions of Today*, 180.

64. Käsemann draws strong reactions from many others—from Bultmann to Sanders, Conzelmann to Malherbe, and many more—but he has also drawn an increasing number of scholars into his orbit over the years. Summaries of Käsemann's influence exist in many New Testament introductions and other studies of Paul (see, for example, Ladd, "Place of Apocalyptic," 25–85; Campbell, *Paul and the Creation*, 23–26; Way, *Lordship of Christ*).

led the majority of contemporary scholars to understand it as *a specific kind of eschatology which understands history in a particular way*.[65] Thus, Maurice Goguel explains: "Toute apocalyptique implique une eschatologie mais toute eschatologie n'est pas nécessarement apocalyptique [All apocalyptic implies eschatology, but all eschatology is not necessarily apocalyptic]."[66]

Furthermore, the key features of this apocalyptic form of eschatology have also become increasingly clear. Of primary importance is the understanding of history—in all its religious, political, ethical, social, economic, and ultimately cosmic expressions—as the domain of conflict and war between God and the forces of good and the united Powers of evil.[67] The centrality of this conflict then leads to what is generally a dualistic perspective: history is divided into two primary ages—the present age, dominated by the chaotic and death-dealing Powers, and the coming age of God's justly ordered and life-giving reign.[68] Consequently, this dualism frequently leads to a marked historical pessimism given, once again, the dominance of evil Powers, despite one's longing for the restoration of a supposedly perfect primordial state.[69] However, the reason for the rise of a particular apocalyptic outlook tends to be the belief that God has done something, or is about to do something, that breaks into the present age, signaling its end and the demise of the powers that rule it (this tends to be expressed in symbolic language that more superficial readings can take as references to an imminent "end of the world").[70] Pessimism in relation to the current

65. See Käsemann, *New Testament Questions of Today*, 109n1; Kümmel, *Introduction to the New Testament*, 453; Schoeps, *Paul*, 41; also Dawson, "Christian View of History," 32; and Taubes, *Occidental Eschatology*, 5.

66. Goguel, "Le Caractere," 322. Translation mine.

67. See Gorman, *Apostle of the Crucified Lord*, 22; Kee, *Beginnings of Christianity*, 41–42; Aune, *Apocalypticism, Prophecy, and Magic*, 107–14; Pate, *End of the Age*, 45.

68. See Koester, *Introduction to the New Testament*, 221–22; Beker, *Paul the Apostle*, xv, 136; Wright also points out how this historical dualism is combined with a theological and ontological dualism (between supernatural beings and earthly beings) and a moral dualism (between good and evil) (*New Testament and the People of God*, 297–99). However, while this is a helpful model, it should be noted that an over-emphasis upon these dualities can end up missing: (a) more complex understandings of history; (b) more complex ontologies (that sometimes incorporate semi-divine and semi-demonic characters—Messiahs, anti-Messiahs, and beastly people); and (c) more complex moral constructs of, for example, people who are evil who end up being used by God for good.

69. See Koester, *Introduction to the New Testament*, 221–22; Aune, *Apocalypticism, Prophecy, and Magic*, 13, 37.

70. See Koester, *Introduction to the New Testament*, 221–22; Beker, *Paul the Apostle*, xv, 136, 149; Taubes, *Occidental Eschatology*, 32. Jacob Taubes expresses this in a

order of things is supplemented by hope that change is taking place, and this inspires revolutionary action.

There are also several other more specific features common to the Judean apocalypticism of Paul's day, and listing these will provide us with some helpful points of reference.[71] In addition to the characteristics described above, Second-Temple Judaism(s)'s apocalypticism also tended to exhibit some combination of these features:

- the expectation of the restoration of the land;

- the expectation of a restoration of the Davidic kingship;

- the expectation of the regathering of Israel and the return of the people from exile;

- a focus upon Jerusalem and the temple;

- the expectation that YHWH would return to Zion to reign as King, to defeat the pagan idols and their devotees, and engage in the judgment of the nations and the vindication of Israel;

- the occurrence of the resurrection of the dead (perhaps only the faithful, perhaps all people);

- the expectation that the lost primordial paradise would be regained;

- the expectation of the restoration of the cosmos;

- the expectation that these things were already beginning to happen, or would begin soon.

Understood in this way, Second-Temple Jewish apocalypticism is very much defined by a focus upon the climax of Israel's covenant taking place *within space-time history* and not outside of it.[72]

---

particularly poetic manner when he asserts that apocalypticism speaks of the triumph of eternity in an End that brings an end to time, which is the Prince of Death, just as eternity is the Prince of Life (Taubes, *Occidental Eschatology*, 4). This, it should be emphasized, is more about the *transformation* of the cosmos than it is about the annihilation of the cosmos, a point also made repeatedly by N. T. Wright in *Surprised by Hope*.

71. The list that follows is drawn from Aune, *Apocalypticism, Prophecy, and Magic*, 16–38; Wright, *Paul*, 131–35; Wright, *Jesus and the Victory of God*, 202–4, 208; Schoeps, *Paul*, 104; Wilkens, "Understanding of Revelation," 65.

72. See Wright, *Jesus and the Victory of God*, 208; contra Collins, *Apocalyptic Imagination*, 12.

Apocalyptic Literature

Apocalypticism was expressed in two primary and interrelated ways—specifically, literature and movements. We will begin by looking at apocalyptic literature, before turning to apocalyptic movements. Given the complex issues related to defining and describing what exactly can be called "apocalyptic," a good many scholars have found comfort in focusing upon it as a certain genre of literature.[73] This apocalyptic genre of literature tends to be (roughly) defined by a combination of distinctive literary features, by being written for a particular purpose, and by its origins in a particular context. Thus, according to John J. Collins, apocalyptic literature is:

> a genre of revelatory literature, with a narrative framework, in which a revelation is mediated by an otherworldly being to a human recipient, disclosing a transcendent reality which is both temporal, insofar as it envisages eschatological salvation, and spatial insofar as it involves another, supernatural world.[74]

This description aligns closely with that of another noted expert, David Aune, who understands apocalyptic literature to be a type of supernatural, visionary, catastrophic, and pseudonymous literature, taking the form of a first-person recital of revelatory dreams, visions, or communications from heavenly beings.[75] This genre then tends to break down into two main types: historical apocalypses (which focus upon explaining things like the rise and fall of empires) and otherworldly journeys (which see the author lifted out of the earthly realm into another sphere, in order to gain a new perspective on the earthly).[76] Thus, the apocalyptic genre is a literary type

---

73. N. T. Wright is a good example of this. In his earlier writing, he holds back from offering a "definition" of apocalyptic and instead offers a "description" of a particular form of literature (*New Testament and the People of God*, 281). Later, he argues that the language of apocalyptic is so "slippery" that he is tempted to "declare a moratorium on it altogether" (*Paul: In Fresh Perspective*, 50). Of course, it almost goes without saying that the idea of a single scholar having the ability to declare this kind of moratorium is decidedly odd.

74. Collins, *Apocalyptic Imagination*, 5; emphasis removed.

75. See Aune, *Apocalypticism, Prophecy, and Magic*, 1–6; Aune, *Prophecy in Early Christianity*, 107–14. I take Collins and Aune to be two of the most recognized experts in this field. For other, mostly parallel, descriptions of the generic features of apocalyptic literature see Hill, *In God's Time*, 59–93; Koch, *Rediscovery of Apocalyptic*, 23–28; Lohse, *New Testament Environment*, 65–66; Ladd, *Presence of the Future*, 79–99.

76. Collins, *Apocalyptic Imagination*, 6–7.

that lays claim to a particular means of knowledge—revelation.[77] This revelation tends to be relayed pseudonymously and a great deal of symbolism, images, code words, and numerology are employed.

The purpose of this literature is to address some sort of problem, in order to exhort, console, and reshape the listener's imagination thereby providing the basis for a new course of action.[78] It is commissive literature: "it commits [the listener] to a view of the world for the sake of the actions and attitudes that are entailed."[79] Thus, it employs the voices of authoritative heavenly beings in order to legitimate its message and encourage modifications in behavior that often end up challenging or subverting whatever ways of being in the world were dominant.[80]

The subversive nature of apocalyptic literature is closely linked to the context in which it arose. As has been widely noted, this type of literature bloomed within Palestine from approximately 200 BCE until 135 CE. At this time, the Judeans, apart from a few brief moments, lived continually under the control of oppressive, international regimes. Suffering, struggle, exile, alienation, and ongoing revolt marked the Palestinian Judean experience at this time, and it was these dynamics which brought about the rise of Judean apocalypticism.[81] For, as Paula Fredriksen notes, apocalyptic literature expresses "a memory and a hope of liberation that no astute ruling foreign power could fail to perceive as threatening."[82] This, then, explains some of the more mystifying features of the literature. By laying claim to heavenly voices, apocalyptic writers were able to claim allegiance to a power

77. See Cullmann, *Salvation in History*, 80–81. "Revelation," of course, is the meaning of the word "apocalypse."

78. See Collins, *Apocalyptic Imagination*, 41–42.

79. Collins, *Apocalyptic Imagination*, 283.

80. See Aune, *Apocalypticism, Prophecy, and Magic*, 1–6; Aune, *Prophecy in Early Christianity*, 107–14.

81. See Fredriksen, *From Jesus to Christ*, 82–83; Taubes, *Occidental Eschatology*, 15, 24–29, 43–47; Wright, *New Testament*, 287; Lohse, *New Testament Environment*, 55–56; Cousar, *Letters of Paul*, 96. Collins and Aune both note that this type of resistance literature was not unique to Judaism but tended to bloom among oppressed and powerless people who suffered under Greece and Rome in the ancient Near East (Collins, *Apocalyptic Imagination*, 23–37; Aune, *Prophecy in Early Christianity*, 110).

82. Fredriksen, *From Jesus to Christ*, 86. For example, the Sibylline Oracles are marked by an anti-Roman polemic, and a particularly animosity towards Nero (see Collins, *Apocalyptic Imagination*, 234–41). The apocalypse of John has also received a great deal of attention for its anti-Rome, anti-imperial perspective (see, for example, Howard-Brook and Gwyther, *Unveiling Empire*).

greater than (for example) Athens, Antioch, Rome, and even the Jerusalem temple authorities. By writing pseudonymously, and by employing heavily symbolic and coded language, these authors were able to write subversive literature in a way that did not obviously jeopardize their lives and in a way that might be able to get past imperial censors.[83]

Apocalyptic Movements

Within this context, the close relationship between the production of this literature and the birth or development of apocalyptic (socio-political) movements becomes more apparent. Here, however, disagreements must be noted. On the one hand, scholars such as Aune, Calvin Roetzel, and Jacob Taubes argue that apocalyptic literature, based on the characteristics described above, gives rise to movements committed to radical change, liberation, and revolution.[84] On the other hand, scholars such as G. E. Ladd and Klaus Koch argue that the apocalyptic paradigm leads to ethical passivity because it is only God who is capable of transforming history and overthrowing the death-dealing Powers. [85] Thus, a reshaped imagination does not produce any new (personal or collective) action and so apocalypses remain descriptive and theoretical, rather than concretely prescriptive. Collins, aware of both of these poles, argues that apocalyptic literature does not lead definitely to either one of these alternatives. Rather, it holds the potential to give rise to either and its ability to do one or the other varies from apocalypse to apocalypse.[86]

With Collins's proviso in mind, we should note that apocalyptic revolutionary movements flourished within many forms of Judaism that

---

83. See Wright, *New Testament*, 288.

84. See Aune, *Apocalypticism, Prophecy, and Magic*, 1–6; Aune, *Prophecy in Early Christianity*, 107–14; Roetzel, *Paul*, 36; Taubes, *Occidental Eschatology*, 9–10.

85. See Ladd, *Presence of the Future*, 99–101; Koch, *Rediscovery of Apocalyptic*, 131. Collins, however, does note that "the revolutionary potential of such imagination should not be underestimated" (*Apocalyptic Imagination*, 283).

86. Collins, *Apocalyptic Imagination*, 9–13; 280–83. Rather than relating apocalypticism to radical action or ethical passivity, Collins argues that it is more universally defined by its goal of putting a certain problem into a perspective shaped by revelation and the nature of one's response will be determined by the nature of the problem under discussion (this varies, as he notes, from addressing the inevitability of death to addressing the experiences of persecution, culture shock, and social powerlessness).

existed at the time when apocalyptic literature arose.[87] These were movements that incorporated the apocalyptic perspective into their daily lives and, significantly, believed that their actions played an important role in bringing about the imminent coming of God or the change that God was creating. Thus, while Collins exercises a useful caution when approaching each individual apocalypse, it seems safe to say that, on the whole, Palestinian Judean apocalypticism tended to express itself in closely related literature and movements. Thus, Helmut Koester strikes me as essentially correct when he argues that the "apocalyptic movement became the single most important factor in the religious development of Israel in the Hellenistic period" and that "apocalypticism remained an essential factor in movements of protest, renewal, and liberation" from the Maccabees down to early Christianity.[88] That scholars like Ladd and Koch see apocalypticism as resulting in passivity suggests, then, that they are importing modern notions of apocalypticism back into the intertestamental and New Testament periods.

Summary

Within this subsection, I have provided an understanding of apocalypticism as a particular form of eschatology especially prominent immediately before and during Second Temple Judaism. It was shaped, most notably, by the experience of suffering, oppression, and colonization, which contributed to an understanding of history and the cosmos as a domain of conflict between heavenly good and monstrous evil. Moments of revelation provide people with the means of understanding this conflict, as well as providing insight into the stage of conflict in which they (personally and corporately) existed, and the actions they were called to at that stage (if any).

At this point, we have now prepared the way for looking at Pauline eschatology. Is it an apocalyptic eschatology? What are the dominant themes within Pauline eschatology? If this is an apocalyptic eschatology, is it one that calls for the creation of an apocalyptic movement in order to engage in certain subversive actions, or is it an apocalyptic eschatology that leads to passivity as one waits for God to act? We will explore the first two questions

87. See Koch, *Rediscovery of Apocalyptic*, 21–22; Collins, *Apocalyptic Imagination*, 9, 39; Merkley, *Greek and Hebrew Origins*, 160; Aune, *Apocalypticism, Prophecy, and Magic*, 110.

88. Koester, *Introduction to the New Testament*, 219–20.

here, and will look at the third question in more detail in the next volume of this series.

Pauline Apocalyptic Eschatology

I will argue that Pauline eschatology arises predominantly out of a variation of apocalyptic Judaism, which is understood anew after revelatory encounters with Jesus as the risen Anointed and Lord. In this way, I hope to demonstrate that a particular form of apocalyptic eschatology is the ideological framework of the Pauline faction's commission to live and work as God's ambassadors to the nations.

Arising Out of Jewish Apocalypticism
and Central to the Pauline Faction

Given some of the prominent features of Judean apocalyptic literature, it may initially strike the reader as odd or false to claim that the Pauline faction espouses an apocalyptic way of thinking and acting. Their letters do not read in the same way as the *Book of Daniel*, the *Apocalypse of John* or other representative apocalyptic texts from the Second Temple period. For this reason, E. P. Sanders argues that the general absence of apocalyptic methods, symbols, and visions in Pauline letters leads to the conclusion that the conventions of apocalypticism had little influence upon Paul.[89]

However, matters related to the apocalyptic are broader than basic representative literary features. Further, it is important to remember that apocalyptic eschatology could be found within all the diverse streams of Second Temple Judaism. Thus, that Paul is described as a "Pharisee" in Phil 3:5, does not, a priori, exclude him from the apocalyptic outlook.[90]

---

89. Sanders, *Paul and Palestinian Judaism*, 543. Sanders does grant a general, but not detailed, correspondence between Paul and Jewish apocalypticism, but prefers to see Paul as operating within more Hellenistic categories (*Paul and Palestinian Judaism*, 423–24, 553–54). Ben Witherington engages in a similar move when he argues for a sharper bifurcation of eschatology and apocalypticism—with Paul rooted in the former, but not in the latter (Witherington, *Jesus, Paul and the End*, 19).

90. As W. D. Davies emphasizes: "That Paul was a Pharisee did not exclude him from an extraordinarily rich apocalyptic tradition . . . To understand Paul's Pharisaism is not to exclude him from a context of Apocalyptic" (*Paul and Rabbinic Judaism*, xxvi). For others who make this point more broadly and ground Paul in Jewish apocalypticism, see Schoeps, *Paul*, 43; Elliott, *Arrogance of Nations*, 143; Gorman, *Apostle of the Crucified*

We can briefly identify five features that the Pauline Epistles share with apocalypticism. First, and most obviously, is the Pauline faction's understanding of history as being divided into two ages—the first marked by evil powers and the second defined by the presence of divine justice.[91] Although they nuance this view in some creative ways in light of the resurrection of Jesus and the uprising of the Spirit of Life within their assemblies, we should note their emphasis upon "this age" (Rom 12:2; 1 Cor 1:20; 2:6, 8; 3.14; 2 Cor 4:4), "this world" (1 Cor 3:18–19) and "the present time" (Rom 3:26; 8.18; 11:5; 2 Cor 8:14) which is ruled by death-dealing, anti-God Powers, and which will give way to the new age, the transformed world, and the coming time of God's justice and Jesus's rule (cf. 1 Cor 15:20–27, 51–57; 1 Thess 4:13–18).

Second, the language of "mystery" that Paul and his coworkers employ (particularly in relation to the outworking of God's plan in history) is a key apocalyptic marker.[92] Thus, in Rom 16:25, in thoroughly apocalyptic language, they speak of the gospel as "the revelation [i.e., apocalypse] of a mystery hidden for long ages." Similarly, when mapping out God's plan in relation to both Israel and other nations in Rom 11:25, they employ the language of the revelation of a mystery. Finally, in 1 Cor 15:51, they also use the language of mystery to speak of the revelation of the resurrection of the dead and the triumph of Jesus over death.

Lord, 21–23; Kümmel, *Introduction to the New Testament*, 454–55; Horrell, *Introduction*, 69; Marshall, *Concise New Testament Theology*, 163; Martyn, *Theological Issues*, 87; Wilkens, "Understanding of Revelation," 82–83; Lohse, *New Testament Environment*, 64–65. Consequently, Aune notes that it is now clear that Paul was "an apocalypticist" so the debate is really about to what degree Paul is rooted here (*Apocalypticism, Prophecy and Magic*, 8). Although this is the consensus, divergent perspectives should be noted. Sanders's preference for rooting Paul in Hellenistic ways of thinking has already been mentioned. Daniel Boyarin also roots Paul's thinking—and specifically his dualisms—in Greek Pythagorean thought and the Hellenistic drive for universalism (*Radical Jew*, 30–31, 57–59). However, as with those who belong to the consensus view, I find these perspectives to be unconvincing. While finding parallels of this sort is an interesting and sometimes enlightening exercise, given Paul's upbringing within Judaism (a point Paul emphasizes in Gal 1:13–14 and Phil 3:3–6) it seems much more historically plausible to understand Paul's foundation to be there.

91. Furnish, *Theology and Ethics in Paul*, 115.

92. See Cerfaux, *Church in the Theology*, 312–16. This emphasis upon mystery comes through even more strongly in the contested epistles, which suggest that the authors of these letters are following through on apocalyptic emphases that were found, originally, in Paul himself (see Eph 1:9; 3:3–9; 5:32; 6:19; Col 1:26–27; 2:2; 4:3).

This leads to the third apocalyptic feature in Paulinism—a focus upon resurrection itself. Judean belief in the bodily resurrection of the dead, arose within apocalypticism in the intertestamental period (in part, as a response to persecutions and martyrdoms experienced during the Maccabean revolt). The legal but unjust, politically sanctioned executions of the just, led to an increasing emphasis upon the belief that God would vindicate the witnesses (martyrs) by raising them to new life in the coming kingdom of God (and also gave birth to the much less emphasized view that God might also raise the wicked, not least the unjust judges, in order to judge them according to the standards of divine justice). Paul and his coworkers affirm this emphasis. Indeed, the resurrection of Jesus from the dead (which reveals God's vindication of Jesus despite the judgment pronounced by the religious and political Laws and leaders of the world) is absolutely central for them. As they write in 1 Cor 15:16–19: "if the dead are not raised, then [the Anointed] has not be raised either. And if [the Anointed] has not been raised, your [loyalty] is futile. . . . If only in this life we have hope in [the Anointed], we are to be pitied more than all people."

By emphasizing resurrection, the Pauline faction is not just engaging in a form of theoretical apocalyptic consistency. They are not merely staying true to a foundation in Judean apocalyptic eschatology. Rather, Paul and his coworkers emphasize the resurrection of Jesus because they (especially Paul himself, but no less the others as well) believe they have been encountered by the resurrected Jesus. This, then, points to the fourth marker of apocalypticism we see in Paulinism—the relation of dramatic, supernatural experiences that give a certain authority to the one who is shaped by those experiences. Here, of course, one thinks of the dramatic revelation (apocalypse) of Jesus to Paul, mentioned in Gal 1:11–16, 1 Cor 9:1, and 1 Cor 15:8.[93] Notably, it is this experience, the personal revelation of the risen Jesus to Paul, that transforms him into God's ambassador to the nations (see Rom 1:1–5). Further, as 2 Cor 12:1–6 and 1 Cor 12–14 suggest, this was not the only dramatic spiritual experience had by Paul. Thus, it seems clear that Paul had apocalyptic experiences.

Finally, the fifth apocalyptic marker in Paulinism is the eager longing for the imminent return of Jesus to judge the nations, vindicate those loyal to him, and transform creation into the just and beautiful realm of God's reign. As Calvin Roetzel argues:

93. The accounts of this event that are related in Acts—9:3–19, 22:6–21, and 26:12–18—are probably a fairly reliable fuller account of that occurrence.

> Both [Judean apocalypticism and Paulinism] are dominated by an eager longing for or an earnest expectation of the messianic kingdom. In both burns the intensity that comes from living on the boundary between the worlds. Both share a link with Israel's past, and both hope for the imminent fruition of God's promises.[94]

There has been much debate as to whether or not the Pauline faction actually expected the return of Jesus to take place within their lifetimes, and what the implications of that expectation might be for Pauline ethics. We will explore that discussion momentarily. For now, however, I am simply emphasizing that, at the very least, they seem to be *longing* for the imminent return of Jesus and the cataclysmic rebirth of God's good creation, and this is in keeping with Judean apocalyptic thought. Furthermore, as with several other Judean apocalypses, this longing or expectation led Paul and his coworkers to invest their actions with eschatological significance. In particular, it is likely that they understood their mission to the nations as an action that prepared the way for the coming of God.[95] Hence, in Rom 9–11, the Pauline faction speaks of participating in the ingathering of foreign nationals so that God's eschatological salvation may come to all of Israel and, ultimately, to all the people of the earth.

Thus we see five prominent apocalyptic markers found in Paulinism: (1) a dual account of history, marked by a battle between the God of Life and all the powers operating in the service of Death; (2) talk of the revelation (i.e., apocalypse) of matters that were previously understood as mysteries; (3) a focus upon resurrection; (4) the narration of supernatural occurrences; and (5) the longing for the imminent consummation of the new age coupled with personal participation in the events that would lead to that consummation. In light of these things, I think that it is safe to say that Jewish apocalyptic eschatology is, in the words of Gordon Fee, "the essential framework" of Paulinism.[96]

---

94. Roetzel, *Letters of Paul*, 44.

95. Beker, *Paul the Apostle*, 160; Fitzpatrick, *Paul*, 80; Fredriksen, *From Jesus to Christ*, 135, 165; Roetzel, *Letters of Paul*, 44; Horsley and Silberman, *Message and the Kingdom*, 131.

96. See Fee, *God's Empowering Presence*, 13. Fee makes this statement in relation to "eschatology" more generally. I have added the further terms "Jewish apocalyptic" in order to sharpen the point being made. For others who also make this point, see Cullmann, *Salvation in History*, 255; Kümmel, *Theology of the New Testament*, 142–46; Ridderbos, *Paul*, 44; Schoeps, *Paul*, 88; Vos, *Pauline Eschatology*, vi, 11; Schweitzer, *Paul and His Interpreters*, 243; Daniélou, *Lord of History*, 6–9; Schnackenburg, *Moral Teaching*, 278, 282.

Of course, given the pivotal role of Jesus, the Pauline faction does not simply adopt prior or contemporary models of Judean apocalypticism—they also modify that framework in some central ways. These modifications occur because their way of thinking and living is: (1) reshaped around the revelation of Jesus as the Anointed Lord over the nations; and (2) reshaped by the outpouring of the eschatological Spirit of Life into transnational assemblies composed of all of those whom Rome and her allies defeated, dispossessed, colonized, enslaved, and left for dead. These distinctive modifications will now be explored in more detail.

Features of Pauline Messianic and Pneumatological Apocalyptic Eschatology

Here, I will explore five central features of Pauline apocalyptic eschatology. I will first explore its so-called "eschatological tension" or "overlap" and the implications that prior understandings of this have for political understandings of Paulinism. I will relate this theme to discussions that have occurred regarding the role of the indicative and the imperative in Pauline ethics. Second, I will explore the role of the Spirit—a distinctively eschatological feature in Judean thought—in relation to Pauline eschatology. Third, this will provide us with the foundation for looking at the relation of Pauline eschatology to Pauline ethics more generally. Fourth, I will briefly highlight the theme of judgment and, fifth, I will explore the discussion of the *parousia* of Jesus and its possible immanence or delay. This will require us to look at the possibility that the Pauline faction is formulating of an "interim" ethics and what implications that might have.

Eschatological Tension and the Overlap of the Ages

Perhaps the most obvious way in which Paul and his coworkers modify the apocalyptic eschatology of Second Temple Judaism is the way in which they reorient its historical dualism (which posited a past and current age, defined by the dominance of death-dealing Powers, and a future and coming age, defined by the life-giving and properly-ordered reign of God). This conception of history was re-interpreted in light of the (ongoing) Jesus-event. Jesus, as has been frequently observed, did not align with popular conceptions of what Israel's eschatological Anointed would be or do. Jesus did not militarily overthrow the kingdoms of the world and he did not drive the Romans out of Israel. Instead, Jesus suffered, was crucified, and died. By all standard accounts, Jesus should have simply been understood as another failed revolutionary or messianic pretender and, in fact, this is likely what Paul believed prior to (what he takes to be) his encounter with the risen Jesus. After encountering Jesus, Paul's understanding of the person of Jesus and of God's eschatological timetable are radically altered. The resurrection of Jesus from the dead, demonstrated to Paul that God had, despite standard and reasonable expectations, vindicated Jesus as the Anointed.[97] Yet the coming of the Anointed and the resurrection of the dead are both eschatological events (as is the outpouring of the Spirit). Therefore, in light of his encounter with Jesus (and the Spirit), Paul was bound to conclude that God's new age had now burst into history. However, as with Jesus, this new age had not come in the way in which it was expected. A total rupture with the old age had been expected but this had not happened. The Romans still ruled over Israel, death-dealing Powers were still abundant, and the just continued to suffer and die. Thus, the Pauline apocalyptic eschatological dualism, and its entire view of history, had to take into account these unexpected developments. In order to do this, the Pauline faction posits an overlap between the ages, a time of eschatological tension wherein the new has come and will continue to come, and where the old exists but is passing away.[98] To employ Cullmann's famous World War II analogy, it is as though the life, death, and resurrection of Jesus were Victory over Europe day in God's war against death, but Victory over Japan day still remains in the future—the war is essentially won, but it has not finished.[99] Or, to use J. Paul Sampley's language, in Jesus, "God's redemptive purposes gained a

---

97. No wonder, then, that Paul stands in absolute awe of the revelation—an awe that one can see clearly in the hymn that Paul writes (or quotes) in Phil 2:5–11.

98 A good many have observed this tension or overlap in Paul. Oscar Cullmann has been particularly influential here and played a key role in establishing this view as a dominant position in New Testament studies (see Cullmann, *Salvation in History*, 79, 173). See also Dunn, *Theology of Paul the Apostle*, 462–72; Gorman, *Apostle of the Crucified Lord*, 137–38; Hill, *In God's Time*, 182–94; Ladd, *Presence of the Future*, 23–42; Ladd, *Theology of the New Testament*, 407–13; Ridderbos, *Paul*, 53; Schoeps, *Paul*, 99; Pate, *End of the Age*; Strom, *Reframing Paul*, 87–91.

99. Cullmann, *Christ and Time*, 84. Of course, this analogy is more than a little flawed given how it fails to take into account the many atrocities and war crimes committed by the Allies. To pick just a few: the fire-bombings of Hamburg, Dresden, and Tokyo, and the use of atomic bombs at Hiroshima and Nagasaki.

beachhead . . . But neither the end of sin nor the fullness of the new age is completely present."[100]

In this way, reshaped around Jesus, the age of God's reign receives a newly demarcated moment of inauguration and another, separate, moment of consummation. The new age begins with the Jesus-event more generally, and the resurrection of Jesus in particular, which anticipates the general resurrection of the dead.[101] However, this age will not be consummated until the *parousia* of Jesus, when he returns to judge the world and establish the justice of God.[102] Thus, Paul and others loyal to Jesus now live within the now and not-yet of God's eschatological age, apocalypsed in Jesus and the coming of the Spirit.

This impacts the Pauline faction's understanding of the whole course of history. They now understand the Jesus-event as the climactic turning point of all history, and all other moments of history, both before and after, derive their significance from their relation to this event.[103] In this way, the Jesus-event becomes "the fullness of time" (Gal 4:4).

It is important to note that this focus upon history, and the historical apocalypse of the Jesus-event, counters anti-historical attitudes that can

100. Sampley, *Walking Between the Times*, 10; see also, 7–17). Here, Sampley is likely relying on Beker's prior use of this term in his apocalyptic reading of Paul.

101. See, for example, Beker, *Paul the Apostle*, 153; Bornkamm, *Paul*, 196–200; Kümmel, *Theology of the New Testament*, 150; Sampley, *Walking Between the Times*, v, 7; Vos, *Pauline Eschatology*, 36; Cadoux, *Early Church and the World*, 74; Cullmann, *Salvation in History*, 169–71. Here some scholars focus upon the Jesus-event as a whole as the moment of inauguration while others focus more exclusively upon the resurrection of Jesus as the moment of inauguration. I am inclined to agree with the former. Of course, the eschatological significance of Jesus's whole life can only be understood from a post-resurrection perspective but, given that perspective, it does gain that eschatological significance.

102. On the *parousia* as Paul's new eschatological "end-point" see, for example, Bornkamm, *Paul*, 196–200; Ladd, *Blessed Hope*, 6, 11; Ridderbos, *Paul*, 90; Cullmann, *Salvation in History*, 169–71; Sampley, *Walking Between the Times*, v.

103. On this point, see, Cullmann, *Christ and Time*, 17–21, 32–33, 71–72, 81–84, 107; Cullmann, *Salvation in History*, 166, 169, 171, 255; Sugai, "Paul's Eschatology," 75–108; von Balthasar, *Theology of History*, 61–64. Moltmann, as we have already seen, challenges this view and, in this regard, argues that history is not centered at any one point but is grounded ex-centrically in God's future (*Experiences in Theology*, 127). Here, Moltmann is likely (admirably) motivated by his desire to build bridges with (among other things) contemporary expressions of Judaism, but I do not think his perspective on this issue is the same as Paul's.

be prominent in various religions.[104] Gerd Theissen captures the historical significance of this when he writes that:

> according to the conviction of primitive Christianity, something as decisive happened in the midst of history as had happened in primal times and would happen in the end-time . . . The history of Jesus was transformed into mythical statements; mythical expectations were transformed into history.[105]

Cullmann, then, summarizes a common way of understanding the Pauline view of history reinterpreted in light of Jesus: in a process of fall and redemption, history begins broadly with humanity, it then begins to focus more narrowly upon humanity's representation in Israel, and that representation is narrowed even further from a focus upon a remnant to an exclusive focus upon the person of Jesus, and then after Jesus, this explodes back out again into the assembled membership of the body of the Anointed, working its way out to all of creation.[106]

Having outlined this presentation of an eschatological tension or overlap Paulinism, it is necessary to engage those who challenge this view and who offer different perspectives. I will outline some of those challenges, and their implications, before turning to the subject of the use of the indicative and imperative in the Pauline letters.

A Realized Eschatology?

C. H. Dodd (in)famously argued that Paul's letters exhibit a "realized" eschatology. By this he means that Paul's focus is entirely upon the experience of liberation and life within the *now present* kingdom of God. History has reached its conclusion in the Jesus-event, and so a focus upon the future—apart from looking forward to the enjoyment of immortality in the company of God, which occurs after death—is unimportant.[107] Granted, there

---

104. This point is made in Aune, *Cultic Setting*, 7. Thus, Cullmann also writes that "all Christian theology in its innermost essence is Biblical history" (*Christ and Time*, 23; emphasis removed).

105. Theissen, *Religion of the Earliest Churches*, 286. As we will see in volume 2, this is not unprecedented—the same thing is said to take place with the coming of the Caesars.

106. See Cullmann, *Christ and Time*, 115–17. The troubling anthropocentrism here should be noted although I lack the space to question that in detail (but it certainly should be questioned).

107. See Dodd, *History and the Gospel*, 38, 42; Dodd, *Apostolic Teaching*, 79–85.

is still a "residue" of a "futurist" eschatology in Pauline theology—notably, talk about Jesus's *parousia*—but this is largely insignificant and Jesus's second coming can be best understood as Jesus coming for believers after they die.[108] Thus, Dodd writes that any supposed end to history is "no more than a fiction designed to express the reality of theology within history."[109]

In this way, Dodd shifts the future of eschatological possibility from the realm of the historical to the realm of the mystical or spiritual—something that he believes Paul already does, for example, in his "suprahistorical" understanding of the Eucharist.[110] However, Dodd engages in this shift in order to try and make "the Gospel" relevant to his present moment and the ethical decisions faced by his contemporaries.[111] Instead of relying upon seemingly "primitive" beliefs regarding miracles, the "end of the world," or the traditional post-Reformation content of the doctrine of last things, Dodd focuses upon the way in which the eternal constantly enters into, and disrupts, the historical and so a "vertical" movement (from the divine to the material) replaces a "horizontal" movement (of historical ages).[112] Thus, he writes:

> Whenever the Gospel is proclaimed, it brings about a crisis . . . Out of that crisis comes a new creation, by the power of God. Every such occasion is the "fullness of time" in which the Kingdom of God comes . . . Every situation is capable of being lifted into the order of "sacred history.[113]

Given this realized eschatology, Dodd argues that Paulinism exhibits an "ethics of crisis" wherein each moment is confronted by the challenge of "the Gospel" and one must constantly, and strenuously, confront the choice between new creation (now) or destruction (now).[114]

Goguel agrees with Dodd here (see "Le Caractere," 432).

108. See Dodd, *History and the Gospel*, 43–44; *Apostolic Preaching*, 62–63, 93; Dodd, *Coming of Christ*, 24.

109. Dodd, *Apostolic Preaching*, 201.

110. See Dodd, *History and the Gospel*, 42; Dodd, *Apostolic Preaching*, 93–94. As Goguel asserts, finding this realized eschatology in Paul means that Paul has "emptied" eschatology of its historical content (Goguel, *Primitive Church*, 448).

111. See Sugai, "Paul's Eschatology," 52; Dodd, *Apostolic Preaching*, 64.

112. See Dodd, *History and the Gospel*, 124; Sugai, "Paul's Eschatology," 50–51.

113. Dodd, *History and the Gospel*, 125.

114. Dodd, "Ethics of the Pauline Epistles," 304.

By arguing in this way, Dodd is responding to the challenge posed by Schweitzer and following the trajectory represented by Johannes Weiss. As has already been noted, Schweitzer argued that both Jesus and Paul adhered to a form of "consistent" eschatology that proclaimed the imminent and cataclysmic end of the world. However, Schweitzer argued (and, from his perspective, history proved) that both Jesus and Paul were wrong about this. Thus, a crisis is created related to the relevance of Jesus and Paul for the present time and it is this crisis that Dodd seeks to overcome by returning to Weiss, Schweitzer's precursor.

Weiss had argued that Paul proclaimed a "new *Religion of the Present*" which was expressed in a form of "Christian mysticism."[115] For Weiss, Paul understood Jesus as the present Lord, and living "in Christ" in the present becomes the focal point of Paulinism.[116] Here, Weiss posits a break between Jesus and Paul: Jesus's eschatology was basically future-oriented, but Paul's focus is upon the past (especially the past events of Jesus's life, death, and resurrection) and the present (of Jesus's rule).[117] Thus, by returning to and further developing the thought of Weiss, Dodd hopes to overcome the crisis of relevance popularized by Schweitzer.

Two other prominent scholars contemporary to Dodd, Bultmann and Barth, also follow this trajectory of thought, albeit in different ways. Bultmann posits a realized eschatology in Paul, but he translates this eschatology into the domain of a realized, and spiritualized, anthropology. Thus, Jesus is understood as the eschatological act of God, providing people with a new model of what it means to be human—he is the transfer point from an old to a new self-understanding.[118] From this perspective, the "salvation-occurrence" (i.e., Jesus's death and resurrection) puts an end to the old age, and gives birth to "the church" as the "eschatological

---

115. See Weiss, *Earliest Christianity*, 1:1976–77.

116. See Weiss, *Earliest Christianity*, 2:425, 446. Dodd also follows Weiss in recognizing that elements related to the future are still present in Paul but their significance is minimized (see Weiss, *Earliest Christianity*, 2:447).

117. See Weiss, *Paul and Jesus*, 104–7. In this discussion Weiss actually anticipates a "now and not-yet" eschatology in Paul, but he does not follow through on this.

118. See Bultmann, *Theology of the New Testament*, 1:294, 301–2. Of course, this is a part of Bultmann's larger task of "demythologizing" the New Testament but, it should be noted, it is a project of demythologization that he argues is present in Paul himself and thus not simply a "modern" scholarly project. (This is something conservative readers of Bultmann should keep in mind. Their a priori rejection of Bultmann as some sort of liberal boogey-man causes them to miss a good deal of the positive challenges and contributions found in his writings.)

congregation" of God's new humanity, regardless of what is taking place in society or in the world at large.[119] Thus, Bultmann's realized eschatology is not about the transformation of the world—or about lived resistance to unjust socioeconomic or political structures—but is focused upon the transformation of the individual within the church. Therefore, although the "aeon of sin" continues in the present, the freedom initiated by Jesus is understood as an existential "freedom from sin" and freedom from one's past as a sinner.[120] Bultmann's existential approach is summarized in the statement: "Freedom from the past, openness to the future."[121] In this way, "eschatology has wholly lost its sense as goal of history and is in fact understood as the goal of the individual human being."[122] Further, Bultmann argues that this shift from eschatology to anthropology occurs in Pauline thinking due to the delay of the *parousia*.[123] Thus, like Dodd, Bultmann argues that the present moment of the believer is constantly a moment of decision—the person of faith must continually choose to embody the realization of his or her new human existence within the conditions of the old age.[124] In this way the eschatological gives way to the anthropological, the historical to the spiritual, and the political to the existential.

Similarly, Barth also shifts the focus from an historical understanding of eschatology into the existential category of one's present encounter with the eternal within the realm of the temporal.[125] Again, this creates a crisis for people here and now.[126] However, Barth's approach to history is, perhaps, more complicated than the positions taken by Dodd, Weiss, or Bultmann. On the one hand, Barth appears to completely denigrate history

---

119. See Bultmann, *Theology of the New Testament*, 1:208–9, 306–9.

120. See Bultmann, *Existence and Faith*, 301.

121. Bultmann, *Primitive Christianity*, 189. Here freedom is understood in a very highly individualized manner, paired with a very highly spiritualized understanding of sin.

122. Bultmann, "History and Eschatology," 13.

123. See Bultmann, *History and Eschatology*, 41. As with Dodd and Weiss, Bultmann does not completely negate talk of the future coming of Jesus or "the end of the world" in Paulinism (see Bultmann, *Theology of the New Testament*, 1:306), but he does negate its significance for the present experience of the person of faith.

124. See Bultmann, *History and Eschatology*, 141. Also, commenting on Bultmann's point here, see Sauter, *What Dare We Hope?* 81–83; Moltmann, *Coming of God*, 19–22; Conzelmann, *Outline of the Theology*, 185n2.

125. See Moltmann, *Coming of God*, 13–16.

126. See Sauter, *What Dare We Hope?*, 71–76.

in light of the present experience of the apocalypse of eternity. Thus, in his famous commentary on Romans, he writes:

> History is the display of the supposed advantages of power and intelligence which some men [sic] possess over others, of the struggle for existence hypocritically described by ideologists as a struggle for justice and freedom, of the ebb and flow of old and new forms of human righteousness, each vying with the rest in solemnity and triviality. Yet one drop of eternity is of greater weight than a vast ocean of finite things . . .
>
> The judgement of God is the end of history, not the beginning of a new, a second epoch. By it, history is not prolonged, but done away with.[127]

Therefore, Barth also seems to hold little regard for historical-critical readings of the New Testament. Again, in a preface to the first edition of his Romans commentary, he writes:

> Paul, as a child of his age, addressed his contemporaries. It is, however, far more important that, as Prophet and Apostle of the Kingdom of God, he veritably speaks to all [people] of every age. The differences between then and now, there and here, no doubt require careful investigation and consideration. But the purpose of such investigation can only be to demonstrate that these differences are, in fact, purely trivial.[128]

These quotations may lead the reader to conclude that Barth has wholly abandoned history in favor of a focus upon the present moment of crisis and decision as one encounters the eternal within the temporal, but this conclusion may be overly hasty. In his *Church Dogmatics*, Barth engages in a more nuanced description of the role history plays in his understanding of faith.[129] Here, Barth comes very close to describing a salvation-historical approach akin to Cullmann's. He writes that the "aim of creation is history" but this is not "pure" history; rather, it is "the history of the covenant of grace instituted by God between himself [sic] and [humanity] . . . This history is from the theological standpoint *the* history."[130] In this way, Barth

---

127. Quoted in Harink, "Time and Politics in Four Commentaries on Romans," in *Paul, Philosophy, and the Theopolitical Vision*, 297.

128. Also quoted by Harink in "Time and Politics in Four Commentaries on Romans," in *Paul, Philosophy, and the Theopolitical Vision*, 299.

129. Barth, *Church Dogmatics* 3.1, 42–94.

130. Barth, *Church Dogmatics* 3.1, 59; 78–81.

emphasizes that this "history of salvation" is not simply "one history or element among others"; rather, it is the "true history which encloses all other history."[131] This is a perspective that challenges modern secularized approaches to time. For Barth, this is time with a beginning, an end, and a foundation in eternity—time with what Barth refers to as a "genuine temporal past and future . . . it is fulfilled time."[132]

Therefore, like Dodd but in contradistinction to Bultmann, Barth argues that the actual occurrence of the events described in the Gospels are crucial for faith.[133] Barth, then, is focused upon the present encounter with the eternal, but this does not lead him to abandon history completely; instead, it leads him to read history exclusively through the lens of the "faith" which is inspired by that encounter. Not surprisingly, then, Barth ends up being more actively involved in the historical events that occurred in his lifetime and was, for example, an ongoing and vocal opponent to the death-dealing Powers of his day.

However, historically, Barth is something of an exception here. The focus upon a realized eschatology that we find in Weiss, Dodd, Bultmann and others, tends to actually result in a form of conservative bourgeois moralism.[134] Joseph Ratzinger is a prime example of this.[135] Reacting to those who believe that Pauline apocalyptic eschatology carries subversive and even rebellious implications for contemporary engagement in society, Ratzinger argues that the task of eschatology is simply to pastorally strengthen faith and should not be confused with any sort of activism.[136] As

131. Barth, *Church Dogmatics* 3.1, 59–60.

132. Barth, *Church Dogmatics* 3.1, 72–75.

133. Barth, *Church Dogmatics* 3.1, 66.

134. I also fear that contemporary Barthian readers of Paul, who are now rereading Paul in conjunction with the philosophical project of Giorgio Agamben (whose reading of Paul strikes me as the most conservative of the post-Marxist scholars—even though it may be granted that his reading bears "radical" implications for those grounded in a Marxist form of materialism) risk losing the nuance we find in Barth in this regard (thus, for example, Ryan Hanssen tentatively suggests that we may need to abandon our talk of a "now and not-yet" eschatology in relation to Paul [see "Messianic or Apocalyptic," 198–223]).

135. Ratzinger's reading was undoubtedly influenced by his position as Grand Inquisitor (i.e., "God's Rottweiler") for the Roman Catholic Church at that time.

136. Ratzinger, *Eschatology, Death, and Eternal Life*. This point is highlighted in Sauter, *What Dare We Hope?* 165. Thus, Ratzinger has been instrumental in crushing many of the movements of Life that have arisen in the Roman Catholic Church over the last fifty years.

a result, traditional biblical scholars who adopt this point of view tend to provide an eschatological foundation for the conservative reading of Paul described previously.

That said, it should be noted that more recent biblical scholars who are engaged with philosophical readings of Paul—notably the readings arising from post-Marxist Continental philosophy—have begun to adopt this reading with different nuances. Giorgio Agamben's commentary on the letter to the Romans is the central text here.[137] Agamben sounds very much like Dodd when he writes that "[f]or Paul, the contraction of time, the "remaining" time . . . represents the messianic situation par excellence, the only real time."[138] This is not "the end of time, but *the time of the end*."[139] As the "time that remains between time and its end," messianic time is still a part of secular time, but it is secular time "which undergoes an entirely transformative contraction."[140] In essence, this is a return to a realized eschatology but as a part of a more radical, disruptive political project. This is because, as Agamben goes on to say, "the messianic vocation dislocates and, above all, nullifies" those who become identified with it.[141] Consequently:

> He [*sic*] who upholds himself in the messianic vocation no longer knows the *as if* [as per 1 Cor 7:31], he no longer has similitudes at his disposal. He knows that in messianic time the saved world coincides with the world that is irretrievably lost, and that, to use Bonhoeffer's words, he must now really live in a world without God. This means that he may not disguise this world's being-without-God in any way. The saving God is the God who abandons him, and the facts of representations (the fact of the *as if*) cannot pretend to save the appearance of salvation. The messianic subject does not contemplate the world as though it were saved. In Benjamin's words, he contemplates salvation only to the extent that he loses himself in what cannot be saved; this is how difficult it is to dwell in the calling.[142]

This paints an entirely different picture than that of Ratzinger or than that intended by Dodd. It is a picture that is compelling to others, especially

137. Agamben, *Time That Remains*.

138. Agamben, *Time That Remains*, 6–7.

139. Agamben, *Time That Remains*, 62.

140. Agamben, *Time That Remains*, 62, 64.

141. Agamben, *Time That Remains*, 41.

142. Agamben, *Time That Remains*, 42.

those studying Paulinism alongside of continental philosophy and social theory. Ted Jennings, for example, affirms Agamben's understanding of the messianic now time, even though he does wonder "whether it is really possible to live toward justice without the sense of impendingness, without the sense that the coming of what we hope for is not far off."[143] Larry Welborn also picks up on this sense of urgency in "Paul's 'now time'" which has no room for the future but is entirely focused upon the present.[144] Those who are waiting for something (anything) are, according to Welborn, too "enthralled by the future," and so never enter into the realization of the Pauline "today of salvation."[145] The *kairos*—a "temporal possibility that may be actualized in the moment when it is known"—is ever only marked by the now (*nun*) which enters into the present out of the past of the messianic event and thereby suspends *chronos* (secular time).[146] For Welborn, the intensity of this present realization of Pauline eschatology only increases as Paul ages.[147] Consequently, rather than being confronted with the purported problem of the delay of the *parousia*, in Paulinism we find "an *intensification* of expectation . . . the future hope of Paul's early years had become a present reality, to be grasped in a moment of awakening."[148]

It is interesting to observe the plurality of competing, contradicting, and overlapping positions that have developed in relation to the supposition of a realized Pauline eschatology. However, I remain unconvinced that this reading does justice to the apocalyptic eschatology of Paulinism. In most of these cases, positing a realized eschatology inserts foreign categories of thought into Paul's letters. Shifting the Pauline focus from history to eternity, from concrete actions to anthropology, and from cosmic events to existential personal encounters, are all examples of this.[149] By stating this, I am not asserting that the eternal, anthropological, and existential have no relation at all to Paulinism. They do—but they must be put into their *proper* places. In this regard, I am essentially in agreement with Cullmann, who strongly criticizes this perspective, especially as it is expressed by Bultmann.

143. Jennings, *Outlaw Justice*, 198; see also 136.

144. Welborn, *Paul's Summons to Messianic Life*, xv.

145. Welborn, *Paul's Summons to Messianic Life*, xv.

146. Welborn, *Paul's Summons to Messianic Life*, 11–15.

147. Welborn, *Paul's Summons to Messianic Life*, 48–51.

148. Welborn, *Paul's Summons to Messianic Life*, 52–53.

149. For further criticisms of this shift, see Sauter, *What Dare We Hope?* 98–99, 106; Moltmann, *Coming of God*, 24; Vos, *Pauline Eschatology*, 42–44.

Granted, Paul (like his coworkers) is fundamentally transformed by his personal encounters with Jesus and the Spirit, but an emphasis upon "salvation history" dominates Paulinism, and the Pauline faction always understands their role in relation to that history.[150] Thus, Cullmann rejects Bultmann's project of demythologization, in part, because Paul himself has already demythologizes mythic events and grounded them solidly in the historical life, death, and resurrection of Jesus.[151] In this way, Cullmann argues that "eschatology is determined primarily by its connection with historical events and not *vice versa* . . . Demythologizing in the biblical sense does not mean eliminating salvation history, but, on the contrary, deepening it."[152] Thus, he concludes (and I agree):

> Wherever eschatology is merely "desecularization," as in existential
> theology, we are no longer dealing with [Pauline] eschatology at all,
> and the expression has become meaningless . . . The abiding factor
> in eschatology is not the detemporalized situation of decision, but
> the retention of the tension, temporally understood.[153]

Finally, in this regard, I think even those influenced by Agamben are too heavily focused upon distancing themselves from seemingly problematical future-oriented expressions of hope to appreciate the *adventus* (as per Moltmann) towards which Paul and his coworkers are striving and within which their efforts are, in the now-time, beginning to bear fruit.

The Overlap of the Ages Expressed in Indicative and Imperative Tenses

Another crucial way of demonstrating the importance of the overlap of the ages within Paulinism is to turn to the role of the indicative and the imperative tenses within Pauline ethics. Bultmann is famous for highlighting the fact that the Pauline faction employs two tenses in their ethical material. At some point, the indicative is used and certain ethical actions appear to be the natural result of *who people are* in the Anointed. At other points, the imperative is used and people appear to have a *need to be commanded*, or

150. See Cullmann, *Salvation in History*, 115, 118. For passages that reflect this in Paul, see Rom 4; 5:12–14; 9–11, Gal 1:12–14; 3:6–4:7.

151. See Cullmann, *Salvation in History*, 140–42, 250. This is especially clear when it comes to the resurrection of the dead which is historicized in the resurrection of Jesus (see 1 Cor 15:12–14; Rom 8:29).

152. Cullmann, *Salvation in History*, 147, 150.

153. Cullmann, *Salvation in History*, 179, 181.

reminded, to act in certain ways. Thus, there appears to be an uncomfortable tension here—if certain actions result from who a person is, why must that person be told to engage in those actions? Likewise, if a person needs to be told to engage in certain actions, how can those actions really be the result of who that person already is? Consequently, since Bultmann, the relationship between the indicative and the imperative has been identified as a fundamental problem in interpreting Pauline ethics.[154] Indeed, some have suggested that this reveals a fundamental inconsistency within Paulinism.[155] However, possible resolutions to the problem exist.

Once again, Bultmann paved the way. He argued that the indicative and imperative in Pauline ethics contain two complimentary emphases. In the Anointed, people are *free* to obey and, in the Anointed, people are free *to obey*.[156] Thus, the imperative is grounded in the indicative—in faith and through the Spirit, a new possibility opens up to the Jesus loyalist, but it remains up to each individual person to make the existential decision required by each moment.[157] Thus, from the perspective of one's existence in faith, Pauline ethics are expressed in the indicative, but from the perspective of those outside (or prior to) faith, in the "age of sin," Pauline ethics are expressed in the imperative.[158]

While not all people are convinced by Bultmann's solution, most are convinced that the imperative is rooted in the indicative.[159] However, various (not always contradictory) solutions exist as to *how* the indicative is founded therein. For example, Willi Marxsen argues that because believers now exist in the Anointed they should act as the Anointed—but this also does not solve the problem raised (although, to be fair to Marxsen, he states that this is a tension that actually cannot be resolved).[160] David Horrell argues that people living in the Anointed have been changed and

154. See Furnish, *Theology and Ethics in Paul*, 9; Goguel, *Primitive Church*, 426; Barclay, *Obeying the Truth*, 225–27.

155. See Goguel, *Primitive Church*, 427–28.

156. See Bultmann, *Theology of the New Testament*, 2:203.

157. See Bultmann, *Theology of the New Testament*, 1:331–36. Goguel offers a slightly tempered version of Bultmann's hypothesis and argues that Paul's indicative and imperative reflect the tension he tries to negotiate between the ideal and the actual (*Primitive Church*, 428).

158. See Bultmann, *Theology of the New Testament*, 2:203.

159. Here, even Cullmann agrees (*Christ and Time*, 224; *Salvation in History*, 329).

160. See Marxsen, *New Testament Foundations*, 180–83, 213, 224.

so they are now required to live according to that change.[161] Thus, the "apparently paradoxical nature of the Pauline indicative-imperative formulations can, then, be resolved when the indicatives in question are seen not as statements which can be held to be either 'true' or not but as identity-descriptors and group norms which need to be constantly affirmed."[162] In a similar manner, Günther Bornkamm argues that the relationship between the indicative and the imperative can be described in this way: "Because God does everything, you too have everything to do."[163]

While each of these proposals has some merit, I believe that the use of the indicative and the imperative in Pauline ethics is explained when it is related to Pauline apocalyptic eschatology and the overlap of the ages that occurs between the Jesus-event and the *parousia* of the Anointed. Stated simply, the now and not-yet of Pauline apocalyptic eschatology, translates into the indicative and the imperative in Pauline ethics, and any form of realized eschatology, that does not account for this overlap, cannot sufficiently account for the usage of these tenses.[164] Therefore, according to Paul and his coworkers, because Jesus is now the risen Lord and because the Spirit has been poured out into the Jesus loyalists, a new way of being in the world (the indicative) has been made possible. However, because the world continues (for a time) to be dominated by death-dealing Powers—who still fight against God at cosmic, political, and personal levels—the members of the assemblies of Jesus loyalists must continue to consciously wage war (hence the imperative).[165] Leander Keck summarizes this well when he as-

161. See Horrell, *Social Ethos*, 80–81.

162. Horrell, *Solidarity and Difference*, 94.

163. Bornkamm, *Paul*, 201–2.

164. This is also a good reminder of the inextricable connection between Pauline "theology" and "ethics." See Dunn, *Theology of Paul the Apostle*, 627–29. Stephen Fowl comes close to expressing this point but does not employ the language of eschatology. Instead, he writes that the indicative and imperative demonstrate the relationship between Paul's "narrative theology" and his specific moral demands (Fowl, *Story of Christ*, 207–9). To this, one should add that Pauline narrative is rooted in apocalyptic eschatology. Schrage is a little further from this view, as he argues that the relation between the indicative and imperative expresses the relationship between Pauline soteriology and ethics (Schrage, *Ethics of the New Testament*, 168–72). Several others, apart from Dunn, take this view on the relationship between Paul's eschatology and ethics. See Brunner, *Eternal Hope*, 60; Sugai, "Paul's Eschatology," 132; Schnackenburg, *New Testament Theology*, 87–88; Cullmann, *Christ and Time*, 225; Keck, *Paul and His Letters*, 86–87; Cousar, *Letters of Paul*, 147–49.

165. See Beker, *Paul the Apostle*, 278; Sugai, "Paul's Eschatology," 119.

serts that Pauline ethics is marked by "anticipatory participation" in God's new age, as "Paul's imperative is not grounded simply in what *is* ("Become what you are!") but in what *is underway*."[166] Kümmel also states this well: those who are in the Anointed are called to battle Sin—in all its concrete manifestations—precisely because they have been freed from it and, although they live in the new age, they are constantly threatened by the old one.[167] Further, because all of this plays out in history—the circumstances of which are constantly changing—the choices that best reflect one's being in the Anointed are not always clear. Therefore, as Cullmann argues, the constant interplay between the indicative and the imperative reflects the ongoing negotiation of the historical situation in which the Pauline faction and the assemblies of Jesus loyalists find themselves.[168] Thus, the indicative reflects the eschatological "now" of their situation, and the imperative is a crucial reminder of the "not-yet," continually renegotiated in light of one's local circumstances.

We have now completed our description of one of Paul's key modifications of Judean apocalyptic eschatology—the establishment of an overlap between the two ages. However, the outpouring of the Spirit of Life, which has now been mentioned multiple times, is also a crucial aspect of this overlap and of Pauline apocalyptic eschatology.

The Apocalypse of God's Eschatological Spirit in Paul and the Assemblies of Jesus Loyalists

The Spirit of Life and of Jesus the Anointed plays a prominent role within Paul's personal life and the experiences and priorities of the Pauline faction more generally. Paul claims to have dramatically experienced the Spirit in his own life and the Pauline faction expected the presence of the Spirit to define the assemblies associated with them.[169] However, the point that needs to be emphasized here is that, within Second Temple Judaism(s) the coming of the Spirit was understood as an eschatological phenomenon—its

---

166. Keck, *Paul and His Letters*, 78.

167. Kümmel, *Theology of the New Testament*, 224–28.

168. Cullmann, *Salvation in History*, 331.

169. Gordon Fee's study, *God's Empowering Presence*, still remains the definitive study of the role of the Spirit in Pauline letters. Dunn also argues that "the *sine qua non* of belonging to Christ is possession of the Spirit of Christ" (*Beginning from Jerusalem*, 904).

outpouring was inextricably connected with the arrival of the new age.[170] Indeed, for the Pauline faction, the apocalypse of the Spirit signals the eschatological return of the God of Life to reign in a newly reconstituted Temple—the living bodies of individual believers now assembled as members of one larger body, which bursts the ethnic and nationalistic boundaries imposed by both Roman imperialism and Second Temple Judaism(s).[171] Therefore, it is important to realize that Pauline talk and experiences of the Spirit derives their significance from a foundation within the eschatology of the Judean Scriptures. It derives from passages like Ezekiel 37 and Joel 2 and not, as Boyarin has argued, from Pythagorean thought or, as others have argued, from Greco-Roman stoicism, gnosticism, or mysticism.[172]

However, because the apocalypse of the eschatological age did not occur as expected (i.e., it didn't happen all at once, but was inaugurated and awaited consummation), Pauline reflections upon the Spirit are appropriately nuanced. A focus upon the presence of the Spirit of Life as "the future present" can fall into an overly-realized eschatology, but this tendency is actively resisted.[173] Thus, Paul and his coworkers speak of the Spirit as a "deposit" or "down payment" and as the "first fruits" of life in the new age (2 Cor 1:22; 5:5; Rom 8:23). As such, the Spirit gives gifts (Rom 12:3–8; 1 Cor 12–14) and bears fruit in the lives of believers (Gal 5:22–24).[174] But this also

170. See Bruce, *Apostle of the Heart*, 140, Wright, *Paul*, 145–50; Davies, *Paul and Rabbinic Judaism*, 178–91, 202–24; Dunn, *Theology of Paul the Apostle*, 416–19; Fee, *Paul, the Spirit, and the People of God*, xv, 54–56, 180–84; Pate, *End of the Age*, 149–54; Vos, *Pauline Eschatology*, 159; Brunner, *Eternal Hope*, 59; Schnackenburg, *Moral Teaching*, 169.

171. See Pate, *End of the Age*, 151–52; Fee, *Paul, the Spirit, and the People of God*, 9–23. See Rom 12:2; 2 Cor 5:1–5.

172. Boyarin, *Radical Jew*, 53. Davies rejects the Hellenistic arguments in *Paul and Rabbinic Judaism*, 177–208.

173. The quotation is from Aune, *Cultic Setting*, 13, although it should be noted that Aune avoids this trap. It should also be noted that this is a tendency that spans from the charismatic experiences of the early Corinthian Jesus loyalists all the way to the present day in some charismatic expressions of Christianity. However, as I will argue, there are more factors that contribute to Spirit-focused components of an overly-realized eschatology—in Paul's day the Corinthians were surely influenced by the realized eschatology that was a part of Rome's propaganda campaign, and in our day a good many charismatics are influenced by the realized eschatology that accompanies the spread of global capitalism.

174. For a fuller discussion of these gifts and this fruit, see Pate, *End of the Age*, 154–58; Sampley, *Walking Between the Times*, 21–23; Vos, *Pauline Eschatology*, 160–63; Sauter, *What Dare We Hope?* 57–62.

clearly means that the life of the new age is not *fully* present. Thus, Pauline reflections upon the Spirit are deeply marked (even scarred) by the themes of struggle, suffering, and weakness. The Spirit-empowered participants in the assemblies continue to struggle with the Powers of the world who serve other ends. In their struggle, they inevitably suffer at the hands of those Powers, and thus come to know the Spirit of the Anointed in the concrete experience of cruciformity.[175] As Paul and his co-authors write in 2 Cor 12:8–10:

> Three times I appealed to the Lord about this, that it would leave me, but he said to me, "My grace is sufficient for you, for power is made perfect in weakness." So, I will boast all the more gladly of my weaknesses, so that the power of [the Anointed] may dwell in me. Therefore I am content with weaknesses, insults, hardships, persecutions, and calamities for the sake of [the Anointed]; for whenever I am weak, then I am strong.

We have already seen some of the socioeconomic and political implications of this in the previous chapter but it should also be noted that this Spirit-empowered cruciformity leads those loyal to Jesus to, individually and corporately, enter into solidarity with the sufferings of all creation—for, indeed, all creation suffered not only during the Roman civil wars but also through the rapacious (but legal) violence of Roman imperialism, conquest, and colonization. As Rom 8 makes clear, it is the Spirit that leads Paul and his peers to enter into the groaning of the world, in the company of all who suffer therein. This is a part of the eschatological birth-pangs of God's new age.[176] Thus, as Beker notes, Pauline experiences of the Spirit lead neither to triumphalism nor to sectarianism; instead, the Pauline faction neither destroy the world nor flee from it but, instead, "must show in the midst of—and in solidarity with—this world the new life that is God's design for the future of the created order."[177]

Understood in this way, it becomes immediately apparent that the role of the Spirit is vital for a Pauline approach to ethics. First, the Spirit becomes the norm and grounds of all ethical instructions.[178] Second, because the

---

175. Gorman, *Cruciformity*, 60; Fee, *Paul, the Spirit, and the People of God*, 107–8, 126–39, 140–51; Beker, *Paul the Apostle*, 278; Käsemann, *Perspectives on Paul*, 124.

176. See Käsemann, *Perspectives on Paul*, 125, 127, 136.

177. Beker, *Paul the Apostle*, 289–90.

178. See Cousar, *Letters of Paul*, 150–55; Kümmel, *Theology of the New Testament*, 217; Fee, *Paul, the Spirit, and the People of God*, xiii, 112–25; Martin, "Spirit in 2

Spirit acts as a person, she also becomes the key moral guide—constraining, directing, inspiring, and warning, Paul and other Jesus loyalists.[179] This means that all other guides, moral codes, traditions, rules, or laws (from the Judean law, to the Roman law, to the general rule of law), are relativized in light of the ongoing guidance and presence of the Spirit of Life.[180] Third, this all-encompassing guidance of the Spirit applies to every area of life—from liturgical practices (2 Cor 14), to the ways in which one treats one's body (Rom 12), to familial relations (Rom 8), to economic exchanges (2 Cor 9), there is no area of life that falls out of the purview of the Spirit.[181] Finally, the Spirit herself provides the Jesus loyalists with the power that they need in order to live an entirely new life now.[182] Here, the eschatological tension must be maintained.[183] Yes, the power of the Spirit is experienced in weakness, but it is still a powerful entity enabling new actions and new ways of sharing life together that are far more just (as we will see) than the ways of sharing life together imposed by Rome.[184]

Eschatology and Ethics: Questions of Pauline Sources

Having examined the narrative of eschatological tension found in Paulinism and the role played therein by the Spirit, we are now well equipped to pick up on some of the issues regarding the relationship between Pauline apocalyptic eschatology and Pauline ethics more generally. We will begin by looking at the question of sources.

Corinthians," 113–28; Sanders, *Paul and Palestinian Judaism*, 458; Schweitzer, *Mysticism of Paul the Apostle*, 125, 294–97; Furnish, *Moral Teaching of Paul*, 24.

179. See Barclay, *Obeying the Truth*, 219–20; Schnackenburg, *Moral Teaching*, 171.

180. See Cullmann, *Christ and Time*, 228–29; Fee, *Paul, the Spirit, and the People*, 52, 101–6, 114, 123; Scroggs, *Paul for a New Day*, 60–69; Theissen, *Fortress Introduction*, 87.

181. See Käsemann, *New Testament Questions*, 191–92; Sugai, "Paul's Eschatology," 103–6, 110.

182. See Schrage, *Ethics of the New Testament*, 177–81; Barrett, *Paul*, 136; Fee, *Paul, The Spirit, and the People of God*, 97–111; Schnackenburg, *Moral Teaching*, 172–74; Wright, *Simply Christian*, 218, 237.

183. Marxsen captures this well when he writes that "according to Paul, Christian ethics remain an impossible possibility *as well as* a possible impossibility" (*New Testament Foundations*, 197).

184. Theissen picks up on some of the implications of this when he argues that the Spirit becomes "the essential force leading to social innovation" (*Social Reality and the Early Christians*, 262).

Several scholars have argued that Pauline ethics are rooted in Hellenistic thought. This perspective gained some prominence at the end of the nineteenth and for the first part of the twentieth century CE. Over against prior (triumphalistic Christian) readings that argued that Pauline ethics arose as an historical *novum*, scholars of this period became increasingly aware of parallels between Pauline paraenesis and the teachings of contemporary Hellenistic philosophers. Once again, Bultmann was a powerful influence here (even if he himself was more nuanced than some who were inspired by him). Bultmann cautiously asserts that the Pauline faction derived their syncretistic ethics "in equal portions" from Jewish tradition, popular philosophers, and from the morals of the Hellenism.[185] However, Bultmann clearly favors rooting Paulinism in Hellenism. For example, he sees the Pauline approach to freedom as drawn from Stoicism, and he understands the pastorals and the *Haustafeln* in Ephesians and Colossians (which he regards as Pauline) as drawn from "the ideals of the Hellenistic bourgeoisie."[186] Pauline ethics actually mean "following such simple ethical demands as can be familiar to anyone . . . those demands in themselves require nothing which a heathen's judgement would not also acknowledge as good."[187] Thus, the Pauline faction simply takes over the moral vision of "popular philosophy" and "bourgeois morality."[188] Others, like Hans Conzelmann, Günther Bornkamm, and Howard Clark Kee fit into this trajectory, emphasizing Paulinism's close relation to bourgeois morality in general and Stoic detachment and natural law in particular.[189] This, then, has led a good many scholars to argue that the Pauline faction does not produce any new ethical *content*; rather, they provide the same content with a new "Christian" *motivation*.[190] Thus, for example, as with other Hellenistic philosophers, the Pauline faction highlights the importance of loving others, but the unique motivation for this is now said to be the example of the love demonstrated by Jesus the Anointed (see Phil 2:5–11).

However, around the middle of the twentieth century, the Jewishness of Paul began to be recovered. Thanks largely to the influential writings of

185. See Bultmann, *Primitive Christianity*, 177.

186. Bultmann, *Primitive Christianity*, 207, 185.

187. Bultmann, *Theology of the New Testament*, 2:225.

188. Bultmann, *Theology of the New Testament*, 2:226.

189. See Conzelmann, *Outline of the Theology*, 283; Bornkamm, *Paul*, 203–9; Kee, *Beginnings of Christianity*, 18–19.

190. See, for example, Schnackenburg, *Moral Teaching*, 303–6.

W. D. Davies and Hans-Joachim Schoeps, the scholarly consensus began to shift. While continuing to reject the older view of Christian ethics as a historical *novum*, Pauline ethics was said to be intimately rooted in the ethics of the Judaism of his day. Davies, like Bultmann, exercises some caution and warns the reader not to create a sharp dichotomy between "Jewish" and "Hellenistic" elements in Pauline writings, but then emphasizes Paul's continuity with Pharisaic or rabbinic Judaism.[191] Schoeps, too, argues that Paul is simply applying conservative Jewish social ethics to different diasporic contexts.[192] Thus, the debate after Davies and Schoeps has often revolved around the form of Judaism that influenced Paul (Palestinian or diasporic? Rabbinic or apocalyptic?) or the degree to which Paul deviates from this foundation. Regardless, Paulinism's ethical foundation in Judaism is now taken for granted by many.[193] Markus Bockmuehl is one prominent example of a scholar who further advances this position. He builds a strong case arguing that the halakhic Jewish teachings, teachings intended to govern Judean relationships with foreign nationals, were "remarkably similar" to Pauline paraenesis, especially when it comes to applying the Noachide commandments to foreign nationals and the Torah to the Judeans.[194]

Of course, as should be expected in the (unending) cycle of scholarship, there have also been some of who pushed back against the growth of this perspective. Abraham Malherbe notably rejects this view and continues to root Paul himself within Greek philosophy as a "*Paulus hellenisticus.*"[195] Malherbe draws together a number of parallel passages so that, at one moment, his Paul draws on the Cynics, at the next moment the Epicureans, then, at a third moment, the Moralists.[196] Thus, when Malherbe asks: "Was Paul a Hellenistic philosopher or a Christian pastor?" he provides the

191. Davies, *Paul and Rabbinic Judaism*, xxxvii, 321–34.

192. Schoeps, *Paul*, 210–11.

193. See Kümmel, *Theology of the New Testament*, 140; Meeks, *Moral World*, 97–98; Stauffer, *New Testament Theology*, 35–39; Crossan and Reed, *In Search of Paul*, 217–18.

194. See Bockmuehl, *Jewish Law in Gentile Churches*, 168–71, 236, and throughout.

195. Malherbe, *Paul and the Popular Philosophers*, 8, 74; Malherbe, *Social Aspects of Early Christianity*, 24.

196. Malherbe, *Paul and the Popular Philosophers*, 8–9. However, Malherbe does agree that there are a few distinctive elements about Paulinism—for example, Malherbe argues that Paul and his coworkers were more community-focused than the more individualistic Greek philosophers (*Paul and the Popular Philosophers*, 9, 67, 70–71).

following answer: "Paul is at once Hellenistic and Christian."[197] Noticeably absent here is any mention of Paul's Jewishness.

I remain unconvinced by Malherbe and the trajectory of thought he represents. Granted, there are a number of stylistic and syntactical parallels, or thematic points of resonance, that can be found between the Pauline texts and then contemporary philosophical schools, but these parallels should not blind us to: (a) the vast differences that exist between the anti-social political program of the Pauline faction (explored in volume 3 of this series) and the programs of those schools; nor should they (b) lead us to conclude that the Pauline faction actually relied upon those schools for the formation of their own ethics.[198] Indeed, rooting Paulinism within the Judaism of its day seems to make a good deal more historical sense of Paul himself—especially given his own autobiographical remarks about being rooted therein, and given the secondary account of Paul's life provided by the book of Acts.[199] Narrowly highlighting one or two topics in a search for parallels, while the bulk of Pauline material and other contexts wherein it resonates are neglected, seems bound to result in a misleading conception of sources.

That said, this does not mean that one must exclude everything Greek or Roman from being an influence upon Paulinism. Rather than simply locating Paul and his coworkers at two supposedly opposite poles (Greco-Roman philosophy or Second Temple Judaism), a good many scholars emphasize that Paul and his coworkers actually draw pragmatically from several sources for the formulation of their ethical arguments.[200] Not only this but the Pauline faction also draws on other sources in order to sub-vert them, reject them, overthrow them, or replace them. Thus, drawing

197. Malherbe, *Paul and the Popular Philosophers*, 76–77.

198. For example, in studying comparative religions one could draw attention to many similarities between the life and teachings of Jesus and the life and teachings of Prince Gautama. However, drawing attention to these similarities should not lead to the conclusion that Christianity and Buddhism are essentially teaching the same thing, nor should it lead to the assertion that Jesus's teachings relied upon, and repeated, the prior teachings of Gautama.

199. In this regard, I believe that Malherbe is actually susceptible to the charge of "parallelomania" that Seyoon Kim raises against counter-imperial readings of Paul (as already discussed above). The reason why I believe counter-imperial readings avoid the errors made by Malherbe, and raise appropriate parallels or points of contact between Pauline theory and praxis and Roman imperial theory and praxis will be related in the volumes that follow.

200. See, for example, Barrett, *Paul*, 138; Horrell, *Introduction to the Study*, 82–83.

together the three historical trends that have been mentioned here, Paulinism is said to draw its ethics from unique elements of the Jesus tradition, as well as from Second Temple Judaism and Greco-Roman culture. Some, like Deissmann, Dibelius, and Fitzpatrick argue that Paul does this in a largely acritical manner. In their opinion, Paul is a culturally-conditioned person who is simply impacted by, and interacting with, popular trends in the mixed milieu in which he lived.[201]

However, others who incline to a more overtly theological reading of Pauline paraenesis have argued that Paul's interaction with multiple sources is much more limited, critical, and selective. According to this perspective, Pauline ethics does not simply replicate that which came before, nor does it completely exclude those things—instead, Paul is seen as an innovator but one who found it unnecessary to develop an entirely new system.[202]

This, then, has led various people to posit different distinctive elements of Pauline ethics. James Dunn argues that it is the centrality of the Anointed, both as the Lord of the assemblies of Jesus loyalists and as the model for the behavior of those assembled therein, that accounts for the distinctive elements of Pauline ethics.[203] Others, like Theissen and Gad, argue that the Pauline faction simply incorporates external elements as a pragmatic missional tactic—their incorporation becomes a means of recruiting new members and a way of demonstrating that the Jesus loyalists outdo both the pagans and the Judeans in the moral codes they attempt to follow.[204] Alternatively, some folks look elsewhere for distinctive elements

201. See Deissmann, *Light from the Ancient East*, 310–12, 315–16; Dibelius, *Fresh Approach to the New Testament*, 219; Fitzpatrick, *Paul*, 103–4.

202. See Barclay, *Obeying the Truth*, 220–22; Bockmuehl, *Jewish Law in Gentile Churches*, 127–37; Scroggs, *Text and the Times*, 171–74; Roetzel, *Letters of Paul*, 46–47, 74–75.

203. Dunn, *Theology of Paul the Apostle*, 668, 673; Dunn, *Beginning from Jerusalem*, 108, 373. Of course, this then leads us down the trail of the Pauline understanding of the relation between the risen Anointed Lord Jesus and Jesus of Nazareth, and how this impacts Pauline ethics (see Bockmuehl, *Jewish Law in Gentile Churches*, 162; Horsley and Silberman, *Message and the Kingdom*, 158–60).

204. See Gad, "Paul and Adaptability," 17–41; Theissen, *Religion of the Earliest Churches*, 63 (even though, as Theissen notes, this effort to outdo others also leads to points of conflict with these others). Cerfaux has an interesting perspective on this. He argues that Paul first adopted the style of the popular philosophers but found that the "early Christians" too easily misunderstood this and so he abandons it for "le message Chrétien dans sa nudité [the naked Christian message, unadorned by other constructs]," which is the message of the cross and of (the) Anointed crucified (Cerfaux, "La Propagande," 32–33).

in Paul—for example, Victor Furnish emphasizes the more communal or social focus of Pauline syncretistic ethics, and Wayne Meeks, William Schrage, Willi Marxsen, and David Horrell return to the point that Paulinism provides a new motivation for an ethics that is now said to draw from multiple traditions.[205]

Given the proliferation of parallels that have arisen here, and the often-unclear methodology employed to evaluate them, others like Mark Strom argue that the search for a conscious dependence upon any specific classical school of thought is not worth pursuing.[206] Exegetes who lean towards literary or theological interpretations of the Pauline Epistles often tend to (implicitly or explicitly) agree with this. Given that other ethics were deeply interwoven with other theologies, a number of people simply focus on the relationship between Pauline ethics and Pauline theology.[207]

This, then, leads us back to our starting-point and rooting Pauline ethics in Judean apocalyptic eschatology now bookended by the Jesus-events (both past and future) and the present experience of the Spirit. Drawing from those who relate the (more explicitly) ethical passages of the Pauline letters to the (more explicitly) theological passages, we can see how both elements are deeply shaped by the apocalyptic eschatological narrative trajectory of Paulinism. Further, we have already seen how this arises out of the apocalyptic eschatology of Second Temple Judaism(s) and out of the Judean Scriptures (as emphasized by the likes of Davies and Schoeps). Finally, heeding those who highlight Paul's Greco-Roman context, we can see how the Pauline faction is still rooted in a particular context within the Roman Empire, and we can expect that this context will provide points of contact that can either be deployed acritically, pragmatically, or mocked and resisted by the Pauline faction itself.

205. See Furnish, *Theology and Ethics in Paul*, 29–48, 51–55, 66–67, 72, 75, 84; Meeks, *Origins of Christian Morality*, 69, 84; Schrage, *Ethics of the New Testament*, 198–201; Marxsen, *New Testament Foundations*, 214–19, 225–27; Horrell, *Solidarity and Difference*.

206. Strom, *Reframing Paul*, 10. Further, when looking at the methodology employed here, L. Michael White and John T. Fitzgerald, in their helpful survey of the history of the compilation of Pauline parallels in classical thought, raise the important question of looking at what motivates this compilation (White and Fitzgerald, "Quod Est Comparandum," 13–39).

207. See Cousar, *Letters of Paul*, 31–32; Bockmuehl, *Jewish Law in Gentile Churches*, 148–49. This, too, then leads us to posit a deeper connection between Pauline ethics and experiences, given the way in which encounters with Jesus and the Spirit shaped Pauline thinking (see Marxsen, *New Testament Foundations*, 145–67).

In sum, Pauline ethics are a description of what it concretely means—for specific people in a specific time and place—to live within the overlap of the ages.[208] This is very much a this-worldly and collaborative eschatology—it is crucial for the here-and-now as the Pauline faction and the members of the assemblies associated with them actively participate in the apocalypse of the new in the presence of the old.[209] Thus, while Dodd, Bultmann, and Barth do well to emphasize the critical importance of the present, they are wrong to lose sight of the historical-political domain as a locus where competing futures (that of the empire after the rise of Augustus and that of the assemblies' Jesus loyalists after the *anastasis* of the Anointed) struggle against one another. Conversely, while Schweitzer did well to recover the historico-political emphasis, he was wrong to think that the struggle was heroically fought and tragically lost long ago.

Eschatological Judgement

The mention of Schweitzer, however, does bring us back to some of the more obviously future-oriented elements of Pauline apocalyptic eschatology. The first element is the undeniable promise and threat of a future "Day of the Lord" when God will come to judge the living and the dead (see 1 Thess 3:13; 5:23; Gal 5:21; 6:6–9; 1 Cor 1:8, 12, 18–31; 3:1–5, 15, 17; 4:3–7; 6:9–10; 15; Rom 2:6–7; Phil 1:10, 28). When this theme is read in the context of the other themes mentioned above, it simply confirms the presence of the "now and not-yet" in Paulinism and mitigates against any blanket assertion of over-realized eschatology.

Yet the overlap of the ages holds even in relation to the specific moment of judgement. As N. T. Wright argues, "[t]he final judgement . . . will be anticipated in the present world through the Spirit-led work and witness

208. See Aune, *Cultic Setting*, 21; Beker, *Paul the Apostle*, 197; Hill, *In God's Time*, 197–98; Sampley, *Walking Between the Times*, 11–15, 23; Witherington, *Jesus, Paul and the End of the World*, 52–57; Yeo, *Chairman Mao*, 226; Moltmann, "Liberation of the Future," 266–67; Cullmann, *Christ and Time*, 79; Cullman, *Salvation in History*, 258; Wright, *Surprised by Hope*, xiii, 264; Davies, *Jewish and Pauline Studies*, 204–5; Gorman, *Apostle of the Crucified Lord*, 115; Longenecker, *Ministry and Message of Paul*, 100–102; Schnackenburg, *Moral Teaching*, 272; Hays, *Moral Vision*, 19–36; Schrage, *Ethics of the New Testament*, 172–74; Scroggs, *Paul for a New Day*, vii–viii; Sugai, "Paul's Eschatology," 157; Vos, *Pauline Eschatology*, 63; Taubes, *Occidental Eschatology*, 63.

209. See Witherington, *Jesus, Paul and the End of the World*, 228; Wright, *Surprised by Hope*, 46, 200, 213–30.

of Jesus' followers."[210] In this way, this element of Pauline eschatology is also connected to Pauline ethics. The affirmation of a future judgment influences the activities of the assemblies associated with the Pauline faction because members anticipate either a future reward or a future punishment.[211] Hence, as Maurice Goguel has stated, this results in an "ethic of gratitude" based on the hope of a future reward, and an "ethic of watchfulness" lest one fall into the sort of activity that merits punishment.[212] More importantly, however, and less frequently observed is the way in which this proleptic engagement of judgment is realized through practices oriented around justice and the refusal of unjust ways of structuring life together.[213]

The Parousia of Jesus the Anointed

The other prominent future-related element of Pauline eschatology, the *parousia* of Jesus Anointed, is the final point that we need to explore. Here we will look at questions related to the timing of the *parousia*—did the Pauline faction expect Jesus to return during their lifetime, or did they expect this at one point and then abandon this view later on, or did they not expect the *parousia* at any set time? Various parties have asserted each of these positions and each of these positions tends to favor different ethical implications.

THE ANOINTED'S IMMINENT RETURN
AND THE FORMULATION OF AN INTERIM ETHICS

The Pauline faction frequently mentions the *parousia* of Jesus (e.g., 1 Thess 2:19–20; 1 Cor 1:7; Phil 3:20; 1 Cor 7:29, 31; 15:58; 16:13; Phil 1:20; 2:16; 4:1, 4–9; 1 Cor 9:24–29; 15:15; 1 Thess 4:13; 5:1–11, 23). Much of

210. Wright, *Surprised by Hope*, 142. Other historical events—like the fall of Jerusalem anticipated by Jesus, and the fall of Rome anticipate in John's apocalypse—can be seen as moments of judgment that reflect this overlap.

211. See Dunn, *Theology of Paul the Apostle*, 672; Meeks, *Origins of Christian Morality*, 175, 179, 187–88; Schweitzer, *Mysticism of Paul the Apostle*, 310; Weiss, *Earliest Christianity*, 2:559–63; Kümmel, *Theology of the New Testament*, 228–32. It is interesting to note how a focus upon this theme in Pauline eschatology tends to wane over the twentieth century—as talk of reward and punishment becomes increasingly offensive to members of Western liberal democracies.

212. Goguel, *Primitive Church*, 429.

213. See volume 3 of this series for how this works out.

twentieth-century scholarship has understood these references to mean that they expected Jesus to return very soon and, as a result, Pauline ethics were only intended for a very short interim period prior to that return.

Schweitzer made a definitive mark here. Although Schweitzer emphasizes the here-and-now importance of Pauline "in-Christ mysticism," he argues, based upon the texts just mentioned, that Paul expected the return of the Anointed to occur in his lifetime.[214] Thus, he asserts that Paul's thinking is "always uniformly dominated by the expectation of the immediate return of Jesus."[215] This point is then widely accepted and employed by a number of scholars—for example, Deissmann, Conzelmann, Goguel, Davies, Meeks, Sanders, and Fredriksen.[216]

Because Paul expected the Anointed to return so soon, the argument is made that he never intended to formulate any sort of permanent or long-lasting ethics; rather, Paul simply formulates an "interim ethics" that is intended to guide Jesus loyalists through the (very short) state of exception in which they now live as they wait for the Anointed.[217]

There are two main ways in which this interim ethics has been understood. The more dominant perspective has tended to see this interim ethics as essentially conservative or sectarian—the current state of things is passing away any day and so, according to this Paul, the best thing to do is to go with the flow, not make any waves, and separate oneself from the worst aspects of the sinful world as one waits for the Lord.[218] This, then, is used to explain the supposedly conservative content written about social matters like slavery (1 Cor 7), the relation the assemblies should have to

214. Schweitzer, *Mysticism of Paul the Apostle*, 23–25.

215. Schweitzer, *Mysticism of Paul the Apostle*, 52.

216. See Deissmann, *New Testament*, 57; Conzelmann, *History of Primitive Christianity*, 108; Goguel, *Primitive Church*, 325, 329; Davies, *Jewish and Pauline Studies*, 296; Meeks, *First Urban Christians*, 190; Sanders, *Paul*, 21; Sanders, *Paul and Palestinian Judaism*, 447–79; Fredriksen, *From Jesus to Christ*, 56, 58, 62.

217. See Schweitzer, *Mysticism of Paul the Apostle*, 300; Bornkamm, *Paul*, 222, 226; Conzelmann, *Outline of the Theology*, 185; Dibelius, *Fresh Approach*, 219; Dibelius, *Paul*, 61–62, 86–88; Ladd, *Theology of the New Testament*, 572.

218. See Schweitzer, *Mysticism of Paul the Apostle*, 302; Barclay, *Mind of Saint Paul*, 220, 222; Barrett, *Paul*, 139; Davies, *Jewish and Pauline Studies*, 296; Dibelius, *Fresh Approach*, 219; Dibelius, *From Tradition to Gospel*, 30; MacDonald, *Pauline Churches*, 79; Kim, *Christ and Caesar*, 50–51; Judge, *Social Distinctives of the Christians*, 2–3; Ziesler, *Pauline Christianity*, 120; Keck and Furnish, *Pauline Letters*, 82, 85.

the ruling authorities (Rom 13), and the role of women in the assemblies (1 Cor 14).[219] This interim ethics is essentially passive.

The second perspective, which tends to be a minority view, argues that Paul's belief in the imminent return of Jesus leads to a more strenuous or urgent ethics.[220] Because Jesus is returning soon, one must do everything possible to be shaped in the image of the Anointed and Paul, himself, must do everything he can to extend the assemblies of Jesus loyalists in the time that remains.

In both cases, the point that tends to be emphasized is that the Pauline faction was clearly wrong about the timing of Jesus's return. This, then, creates a crisis related to the possible relevance of Pauline ethics outside of this time frame. Therefore, a good many of those already mentioned end up abandoning Pauline ethics and modifying his eschatology, while trying to retain other elements of his theology—say his Christology or pneumatology—which are then said to be the things that really matter in the Pauline Epistles.[221]

No Delay of the Parousia
and the Formulation of a Timeless Ethics

Others have pushed back against this conclusion. The first push-back is that presented by those who shift the focus from doctrines that have become problematical to the existential moment of decision-making. The realized eschatologies of Bultmann and Dodd mentioned above offer this solution. By changing the nature of the debate, Bultmann and Dodd sought to overcome the apparent problem of "the delay of the *parousia*" and its implications for contemporary appropriations of Pauline ethics. However, our prior rejection of Bultmann's and Dodd's positions, makes this solution untenable here.

For others, "the delay of the *parousia*" is not considered a problem at all. In many Christian faith communities, any Pauline talk related to the

219. I will return to these matters in volume 3 of this series. That said, Deissmann also argues that the sense of Jesus's imminent return leads to inconsistencies in Pauline ethics. Because Jesus is returning so soon, Deissmann argues that the Pauline faction does not systematize their thinking but simply write "with absolute abandon" as they urgently pursue the end-time mission given to them by God (*Light from the Ancient East*, 240–41).

220. See Cadoux, *Early Church and the World*, 86; Wright, *Paul*, 56.

221. See Schrage, *Ethics of the New Testament*, 181.

timing of the *parousia* has been (implicitly or explicitly) ignored and it is assumed that the Pauline faction was writing an eternal ethics that is just as applicable in the twenty-first century as it was in the first century. This view is buttressed by an affirmation of a "plain reading" of Scripture and by the evangelical slogan, "God said it, Paul wrote it, I believe [and do] it." This (accidental or willed) naïveté may work fine for many at a popular level, but there are some who have engaged the issue presented here more critically in order to overcome the problems raised by Schweitzer et al. Cullmann and Moltmann are two such people.

On the one hand, Cullmann agrees with Schweitzer and accepts the point that Paul was formulating an interim ethics.[222] However, unlike Schweitzer, Cullmann argues that Paul's talk about Jesus's return is not related to the *timing* of that event. Rather, Paul's focus is upon the *stages of history* and not the duration of those stages. Therefore, Cullmann argues, we continue to live in the same stage of history as Paul—wherein the ages overlap and Jesus loyalists enjoy the ongoing presence of the eschatological Spirit of Life—and so we live in the same interim as Paul.[223] This means that according to Cullmann, Paul's interim ethics continues to apply directly to the contemporary context. Thus, Cullmann sees concern over the delay of the *parousia* to be a modern "psychological mistake"—what is important is that the Anointed has come and won the decisive battle, and although the Anointed is guaranteed to come again, the timing of that coming is unimportant.[224]

Moltmann makes a similar point, even though, as we saw above, he rejects Cullmann's linear conception of time in favor of an ontological conception of time. Within his understanding of the past as the domain of the real, the future as the domain of the possible and the present as the moment when the possible is or is not realized, Moltmann understands Pauline talk of the imminence of the Anointed to be related to the intimacy one can now experience with "Abba Father."[225] Thus, Moltmann notes, talk of the

222. See Cullmann, *Salvation in History*, 331–33.

223. See Cullmann, *Christ and Time*, 213; Cullman, "Eschatology and Mission," 410–13.

224. See Cullmann, *Christ and Time*, 82, 86–90. Pate makes a similar point more generally (*End of the Age Has Come*, 217), as does Hans Urs von Balthasar (*Theology of History*, 86–87). Other biblical scholars who hold positions that are similar to Cullmann are Sampley (*Walking Between the Times*, 107–9) and Beker (*Paul the Apostle*, 113–14, 120, 272–78).

225. Moltmann, "Liberation of the Future," 265–66.

parousia takes place within a non-speculative paraenetic and eucharistic context with the intention of inspiring expectant creativity.[226] This, then, re-frames the imminence of the Anointed's return within a liturgical context.

PAUL CHANGED HIS MIND ABOUT
THE IMMINENCE OF THE ANOINTED'S RETURN

A third position that has gained some strength in scholarship is the view that a shift occurs in Paul's perspective on this issue. The (relative) abun-dance of Pauline references to the *parousia* in earlier letters is contrasted with the (relative) absence of those references in later letters, and this is taken as evidence of a shift in focus. Whereas the Pauline faction initially believed that the Anointed's return would occur within Paul's generation, the passage of time and the increasingly likelihood of Paul's death, is said to have caused them to think that the *parousia* would be delayed. Thus, from 1 Thessalonians to Philippians, the Pauline faction is said to undergo a major eschatological shift, as they are disappointed by the Anointed's delay.[227] Pas-sages that seem to recognize that there will be a delay are emphasized (see 1 Thess 4:15; 1 Cor 15:50ff; Rom 13:11; Phil 4:4; 1 Cor 5:1–11, 19) and this is further proof of a shift in Pauline expectations.

James Dunn can be seen as a particularly nuanced representative of this position. While agreeing that a shift does occur within the foci found in the Pauline letters, he argues that this may be more circumstantial than theological.[228] However, even given this circumstantial element, Dunn argues that Paul did begin with a sense of the Anointed's imminent return that he later "came either to regret or to modify significantly."[229] C. F. D. Moule takes a similar (but less certain) approach. While emphasizing the circumstantial nature of Pauline writings, he ends up with a conclusion that is vaguer than Dunn's. Thus, Moule concludes that "different formulations

226. Moltmann, *Way of Jesus Christ*, 338–41.

227. See Cadoux, *Early Church and the World*, 86; Schoeps, *Paul*, 102; read in con-junction with 122–23; Horsley and Silberman, *Message and the Kingdom*, 125–26, 131; Käsemann, *New Testament Questions of Today*, 109n1; Theissen, *Fortress Introduction*, 62, 67–68. Horrell feels the strength of this argument but believes that there is not enough evidence to sustain it and so, in relation to the delay of the *parousia*, he decides not to pick a side and feels that it is enough to simply emphasize the eschatological orientation of Pauline theology (*Introduction to the Study of Paul*, 70–73).

228. Dunn, *Theology of Paul the Apostle*, 302–13.

229. Dunn, *Beginning from Jerusalem*, 713; see 711–13.

[of Paul's eschatology] have to be enlisted in the service of different affirmations, all of which may prove to be simultaneous aspects of a single great conviction too large to be expressed coherently or singly."[230]

This position, like the first one described, creates some problems for the ongoing relevance of Pauline ethics. As Dunn notes, Paul, understood in this way, was not writing an ethics that would span generations and this is "a sobering conclusion to reach—especially for those who regard the earliest churches as models to be emulated by their modern successors, and especially for those who want to treat Paul's letters as timeless."[231] Therefore, one must carefully sift through the letters to see where and how ethical injunctions are impacted by the (earlier) belief in the imminent return of Jesus.

Hope Not Certainty: Further Qualifying the Pauline Sense of Imminence and its Ethical Implications

Having surveyed the above-mentioned perspectives, we are now situated to explore the position that I personally find most convincing. Briefly stated, this final push-back to the question of the delay of the *parousia* argues that Paul *hopes* for the return of Jesus to occur within his lifetime, but falls short of actually setting a time for the Anointed to return, recognizing that God's timing is often shrouded in mystery and impossible to calculate.

In many ways, Johannes Weiss is a precursor to those who currently hold this view. Weiss argues that Paul did expect an imminent end and that this expectation had "tremendous and far-reaching importance [for] every moral act."[232] However, Weiss also notes that at various points Paul's expectation of the imminence of this event fluctuates. In some passages, the Pauline faction appears to expect an imminent end (1 Thess 4:11–12; 1 Cor 7:29; Rom 13:11) but at other points the Pauline faction believes that a period of time must pass while current conditions are protracted (Phil 1:24–25; Rom 11:25; 15:24). Rather than explaining this fluctuation as Paul grappling with a supposed delay of the *parousia*, Weiss argues that we observe in Paul "that tense feeling on the one hand which expects the end at any moment, and on the other hand the conviction based upon tradition

---

230. Moule, *Essays in New Testament Interpretation*, 192; see also 184, 187–88.

231. Dunn, *Beginning from Jerusalem*, 712; see also Dunn, *Theology of Paul the Apostle*, 672.

232. Weiss, *Earliest Christianity*, 2:254; see also 254–57.

and revelation that a series of preordained events must still take place before Jesus can come again."[233] Thus, Weiss concludes that Paul "does not fix the time of the end"; instead, "[Paul's] only concern is, with the aid of these apocalyptic ideas, to set in motion ethical and religious forces, to suppress morbid unrest, to waken dull indifference, to spur on missionary zeal, to keep alive hope of the conversion of mankind."[234]

This, then, shifts the talk of the Pauline view of the timing of the Anointed's return from the domain of epistemological certainty to the domain of eschatological hope. Several others have followed Weiss in accepting this shift. Thus, Lohse argues that Pauline "eschatological hope is not dependent upon the calculation of some date, either in the immediate or distant future. Rather, the present is understood to exist under the sign of that which is to come."[235] Similarly, Herman Ridderbos sees the Pauline faction as holding onto the expectation of Jesus's imminent return with varying "degrees of intensity," Rudolph Schnackenburg describes this as "expectation" but not "dogma," Geerhardus Vos describes it as "an expectation and a wish," Schnabel describes it as "possible" but not as a given, and Calvin Roetzel argues that Paul only "dimly apprehended" the timing of Jesus's return thereby maintaining a tension that "avoided the eschatological disappointment of the enthusiasts and the easy conformity and surrender to the status quo of the traditionalists."[236] Thus, I believe that Frank Thielman is correct to assert that, from the first to last letter, Paul maintains the twin convictions that Jesus might come in his lifetime and that he might die before Jesus returns.[237]

Ben Witherington has probably done more than any other to drive this point home by means of careful exegesis.[238] After a detailed survey of the relevant passages, Witherington notes that the Pauline faction counsels both urgency and patience. Ethical injunctions are affected by the possible imminence of the Anointed's return, but they are not determined by that

233. Weiss, *Earliest Christianity*, 2:545.

234. Weiss, *Earliest Christianity*, 2:545.

235. Lohse, *Theological Ethics*, 43.

236. Ridderbos, *Paul*, 306; see also 489–93; Schnackenburg, *New Testament Theology*, 88–89; Schnackenburg, *Moral Teaching*, 189–92; Vos, *Pauline Eschatology*, 32–34; Schnabel, *Early Christian Mission*, 945; Roetzel, *Paul*, 37. Longenecker and Sugai employ descriptive terms similar to Roetzel here (see Longenecker, *Ministry and Message of Paul*, 102–4; Sugai, "Paul's Eschatology" 147–48, 151, 155–56, 167–68, 170, 187).

237. Thielman, *Theology of the New Testament*, 456.

238. See Witherington, *Jesus, Paul and the End of the World*, 26–33.

possibility.[239] The Pauline faction, then, holds three convictions: (1) the Anointed *will* return; (2) the Anointed *might* return at any moment; and (3) they *want* the Anointed to return soon.[240] Therefore, although the *parousia* will come as a surprise to many, it will not surprise the members of the assemblies associated with the Pauline faction—not because they know the timing of the Anointed's coming but because they know that the Anointed is coming and fervently hope that he is coming soon.[241]

This shift from certainty to hope offers the most satisfactory response to the question of the Pauline formulation of an interim ethics. What is important is the *nearness*, and not the timing, of the *parousia*. This, I think, demonstrates the superiority of this position over that taken by Cullmann. Cullmann, and others like him, simply treat the "when" of the Anointed's return as inconsequential. However, now the "when" is crucial. It is crucial, not because it gives a specific time, but because the answer to the question of "when?" is "Soon—perhaps even today!" Therefore, hope, longing, and eager anticipation—and perhaps even a willingness to abandon all that is treated as valuable in the present moment because of this—continue to be driving forces behind the actions taken by those who seek to live in the trajectory of Pauline apocalyptic eschatology.

Summary

In this section, I have explored the apocalyptic eschatology that provides the narrative framework for Paulinism. We have seen how it arises out of the apocalyptic eschatology of Second Temple Judaism(s), now reshaped based upon the Pauline faction's encounters with Jesus and the Spirit. In light of these things, the old age and the new age are said to exist in a state of tension, in an overlap that heightens the conflict between the God of Life and the death-dealing Powers of the world. In this conflict, the now-present eschatological Spirit of Life is apocalypsed as power in cruciform solidarity with those vanquished and left for dead by the empire. Ethics become about the way in which those loyal to Jesus are called to live within this moment in history as they both anticipate and await the *anastasis* of the dead, the judgment of all people, and the return of Jesus (which they hope will occur soon).

239. Witherington, *Jesus, Paul and the End of the World*, 28–29.
240. Witherington, *Jesus, Paul and the End of the World*, 23.
241. Witherington, *Jesus, Paul and the End of the World*, 25.

Summary and Conclusion

Before turning to a more thorough examination of how this apocalyptic eschatology engages the imperial ideo-theology of Rome, it is worth highlighting three points. The first point is that eschatology should be understood as a particular narration of history—one that highlights people, places, and events that are determined to be particularly important or decisive in light of the ultimate end or goal for which history is intended. Further, this goal-oriented history is narrated in order to make sense of one's current lived experiences and to call people to engage in actions that are taken to be historically meaningful. By this understanding, eschatology is more about one's material circumstances and less about the future state of one's soul.

Second, we have seen that an apocalyptic form of eschatology is one that is particularly pessimistic about the regnant (social, political, economic, and religious) Powers of the world. By dividing history into two ages—the past and present marked by the rule of death-dealing, anti-God forces, and the future marked by the just rule of the God of Life—history is seen as a domain of conflict and those who adhere to this view of history tend to be active agents in subverting, resisting, or militantly acting against the powers of the present evil age (whether by producing seditious literature or by participating in revolutionary movements, or both). This conflict is only further heightened given the ways in which apocalypticists tend to claim a special authority and a new revelation, which is often linked to the belief that something crucial is happening now (or soon) and so one must become involved in that happening.

Third, turning to Paulinism, we have seen how a christologically and pneumatologically reshaped apocalyptic eschatology provides the narrative framework for the efforts of the Pauline faction. In all of this, they are operating with history in mind and, just as importantly, they are operating with the perception of themselves as historical agents—as people who participate in actions and events that carry significance not just for themselves and the local assemblies of Jesus loyalists, but for all the nations of the world.

Given these things, it makes good sense to ask about the relation of these beliefs and practices to the Roman Empire and the way in which Roman imperial ideology understood history. Given that Rome and her emperor were situated at the pinnacle of the powers in Paul's day, one might suspect there to be a great deal of discomfort, conflict, and disconnection between Roman ideo-theology and Pauline apocalyptic eschatology—at both the theoretical and practical levels. As we will see in the next volumes, this suspicion is well-founded.

5

CONCLUSION

IN THIS VOLUME, I have covered the background material that is traditionally deployed to argue for this or that understanding of Pauline politics.
These are the factors that influence the plausibility of different perspectives
on the Pauline faction and readers will find different interpretations more
or less compelling based upon their understandings of these things. Often,
those who explicitly engage with the theme of "Paul and politics" simply
assume or take for granted this or that position related to this background
material. This is fine if one simply wishes to speak with other like-minded
people but it has a very limited utility if one wishes to engage in a conversation or confrontation with people situated in very different (and sometimes
oppositional) perspectives. Therefore, I have spent a considerable amount
of time addressing these matters because I am interested in not only encouraging others who understand Pauline politics in the way that I do, but
because I wish to make other understandings of Paulinism less compelling
to a broad spectrum of people who are reading Paul today. I believe there
is a certain urgency to this task. Paul is, yet again, being quoted to justify
the practices of neo-fascist government bodies and the relentlessly death-
dealing corporations who profit from their laws. For example, the former
Attorney General of the United States Jeff Sessions recently quoted Rom 13
in order to try and quell opposition to the development of multi-million-
dollar concentration camps for racialized and criminalized migrant children
in the territories colonized by the US. That Sessions felt that quoting Rom
13 in this context was a beneficial strategic move, and that many Americans
would have trouble countering (or even wanting to counter) Sessions's use
of that passage, suggests that we very much need to engage in the kind of

comprehensive engagement with the Pauline faction that I attempt in this series. Thus, it is my hope that this series will, in its own small way, not only help to inspire those who actively resist the death-dealing rulers of our day, but that it will both convert some of those who serve Death to the service of Life, and provide those who are troubled by Sessions's use of Rom 13 (but who do not know how to articulate why it bothers them or understand how to counter it), with a compelling argument that gives them the foundation they are seeking for an alternative interpretation and praxis. Of course, not everyone needs this kind of exegetical work to jump into the fray—and I remain convinced that the best way to learn Paulinism is to do what the liberation theologians have urged us to do and seek the company of the Spirit of *anastasis* Life in solidarity with the left-for-dead—but I recognize that many people do need this kind of exegetical work to allay their fears and inspire them to jump. In my context, many of these people are "my people" (i.e., generally cishet, middle-class, settlers of Christian and European descent) and, even if I recognize the truth of William Stringfellow's assertion that "my people is the enemy," I am still responsible to and for my people.[1] As tempting as it might be to dissociate myself from my people, in order to build my so-called "radical" brand status and make myself feel as if I am not like "those violent, oppressive people over there," this kind of dissociation tends to have more to do with my desire to feel virtuous (and thereby "sleep the sleep of the just"), and has less to do with concretely changing the oppressive structure that shape our life together. It strikes me as a rebranded form of personal pietism that has more to do with how I feel about myself than it is about participating in the kinds of actions that bring about socioeconomic and political transformation. Sometimes I worry that so-called "radical" scholars, comfortably situated with their peers in the academy, are engaging in this kind of self-oriented virtue-signalling—especially when they welcome criticisms from those to the Right of them (because this reaffirms the identity they wish to have) but become extremely defensive when they are faced with any criticisms from those to the Left of them (because this challenges the identity they wish to have). Yet the increase of violence we are seeing in our world—from mainstream Islamophobia, to newly public celebrations of murderous violence against women, to the rise of neo-fascism and the increase in racialized violence it brings, to the ongoing structural war capitalism wages on the commons, Indigenous peoples, and workers—suggests to me that the stakes are far too high to engage in

1. Stringfellow, *My People is the Enemy*.

this kind of self-affirming siloing. Angry White men do not become any less angry when we abandon them to surround ourselves with people who make us feel good about ourselves. In fact, these seem to just become angrier.[2] And the same goes for imperialistic and death-dealing expressions of Christianity. It is not enough for us to simply flee or fight against these people. If they are your people—as they are mine—then we must also try to convert them.

Now, granted, seriously trying to engage in this task may seem like a fool's errand (as we will see in volume 3, the Pauline faction has a great appreciation for this kind of folly), but to give up on my people and resign myself to hopelessness (as I did for several years) seems, to me, to be a symptom of privilege. I can give up on this task because I am not the one most adversely affected by the death-dealing practices of our day. It is not my children who are being raped and disappeared in Wal-Marts that have been converted into concentration camps. Hopeless resignation costs me very little (only my youthful idealism, not the health, wealth, or well-being of myself or my family members). Precisely on this point, I am reminded of the words of Malcolm X, when he was approached by well-meaning White people who desired to help him in his efforts. Essentially, Malcolm explained, the Black community did not need any more White saviors bombing in to show them the way—the Black community was full of intelligent, committed, strong, and resilient people who could take care of their own. Instead, Malcolm said, these well-meaning White people should go back to the White community and deal with their own people who, after all, were the root of the problem. You just cannot deal with White supremacy if you do not deal with White people. I have tried to take this injunction seriously in my own work.

In this volume, I explored the background material that generally influences how plausible we find various political understandings of Paulinism. By now, it should be clear that there is no such thing as an apolitical perspective on Paulinism—for even disavowing politics has serious political consequences. In this exploration, I found that people consistently

2. Here, I appreciate Michael Kimmel's analysis in *Angry White Men*, even if I disagree with his conclusion (prior to the rise of Trumpism) that they are a dying breed. I feel that Carol Anderson's book, *White Rage*, offers a better analysis of why angry White men persist. More generally, I think Roger Griffin's study, *Modernism and Fascism*, does an excellent job of demonstrating the persistent appeal of fascism to my people, although the lengthy history of resistance to fascism should also be recalled (see, for example, Bray, *Antifa*; Testa, *Militant Antifascism*; and Ross, *Against the Fascist Creep*).

based conclusions upon an absence of evidence—and conclusions that I feel are actually unwarranted based upon the evidence we do have. These are conclusions that individual scholars or camps find compelling based upon their own socioeconomic and theopolitical contexts and preferences. When dealing with the evidence, it seems to me that the conservative understanding of Paulinism is most strongly undercut (at this point, not thoroughly discredited—although I believe it will be thoroughly discredited by the end of this series) and the counter-imperial understanding of Paulinism becomes much more plausible. However, this picture is still far from complete. To begin with, our examination of apocalypticism is incomplete. I have focused on literary motifs associated with apocalyptic eschatology but we need to spend considerably more time dealing with apocalypticism as a grassroots uprising that takes place in the context of oppressive empires. Furthermore, we need to examine the imperial propaganda—what I refer to as the ideo-theology of Rome—that was the most dominant and rapidly growing system of beliefs and practices spreading throughout the eastern portion of the Roman Empire at the time when the Pauline faction was active. To try and understand the politics of the Pauline faction, without carefully and thoroughly engaging the political ideology (and its concomitant socioeconomic practices) that was ubiquitous and central to all of the locations we associate with the Pauline faction—Corinth, Philippi, Rome, Thessalonika, and so on—is inexcusable at this point. Therefore, this further examination of apocalypticism and of the ideo-theology of Rome will be the topic of volume 2. By the end of volume 2, the stage will be set for a sustained examination of the central themes and practices of Paulinism. This will be the subject of volume 3. Onwards, then.

BIBLIOGRAPHY

Adams, Sean A. "Crucifixion in the Ancient World: A Response to L. L. Welborn." In *Paul's World*, edited by Stanley E. Porter, 111–29. Pauline Studies 4. Leiden: Brill, 2008.

———. "Paul the Roman Citizen: Roman Citizenship in the Ancient World and Its Importance for Understanding Acts 22:22–29." In *Paul: Jew, Greek, and Roman*, edited by Stanley E. Porter, 309–26. Pauline Studies 5. Leiden: Brill, 2008.

Agamben, Giorgio. *The Time That Remains: A Commentary on the Letter to the Romans.* Translated by by Patricia Dailey. Meridian: Crossing Aesthetics Series. Stanford: Stanford University Press, 2005.

Anderson, Carol. *White Rage: The Unspoken Truth of our Racial Divide.* New York: Bloomsbury, 2016.

Ando, Clifford. *Imperial Ideology and the Provincial Loyalty in the Roman Empire.* Berkeley: University of California Press, 2000.

Aune, David E. *Apocalypticism, Prophecy, and Magic in Early Christianity: Collected Essays.* Grand Rapids: Baker Academic, 2008.

———. *The Cultic Setting of Realized Eschatology in Early Christianity.* Leiden: Brill, 1972.

———. *Prophecy in Early Christianity and the Ancient Mediterranean World.* Grand Rapids: Eerdmans, 1983.

Badiou, Alain. *Being and Event.* Translated by Oliver Feltham. Bloomsbury Revelations. London: Bloomsbury Academic, 2005.

———. *St. Paul: The Foundations of Universalism.* Translated by Ray Brassier. Cultural Memory in the Present Series. Stanford: Stanford University Press, 2003.

Bammel, Ernst. "Romans 13." In *Jesus and the Politics of His Day*, edited by Ernst Bammel and C. F. D. Moule, 363–85. Cambridge: Cambridge University Press, 1984.

Barclay, John M. G. "Deviance and Apostasy: Some applications of deviance theory to first century Judaism and Christianity." In *Modelling Early Christianity: Social-scientific studies of the New Testament in its context*, edited by Philip F. Esler, 114–27. London: Routledge, 1995.

———. "Diaspora Judaism." In *Religious Diversity in the Graeco-Roman World: A Survey of Recent Scholarship*, edited by Dan Cohn-Sherbrook and John M. Court, 47–64. Sheffield: Sheffield Academic Press, 2001.

———. *Obeying the Truth: A study of Paul's Ethics in Galatians.* Studies in the New Testament and Its World Series. Edinburgh: T. & T. Clark, 1988.

Barclay, William. *The Mind of Saint Paul.* New York: Harper & Row, 1975.

Bardacke, Frank. *Tramping Out the Vintage: Cesar Chavez and the Two Souls of the United Farm Workers*. New York: Verso, 2012.

Barrett, C. K. *Paul: An Introduction to His Thought*. Louisville: Westminster John Knox, 1994.

Barth, Karl. *Church Dogmatics 3.1: The Doctrine of Creation*. Translated by J. W. Edwards, O. Bussey, and H. Knight. Edited by G. W. Bromiley and T. F. Torrance. London: T. & T. Clark International, 2004.

Bauckham, Richard. *The Bible in Politics: How to Read the Bible Politically*. Louisville: Westminster John Knox, 1989.

———, ed. *God Will be All In All: The Eschatology of Jürgen Moltmann*. Edinburgh: T. & T. Clark, 1999.

Baudrillard, Jean. *Simulacra and Simulation*. Translated by Sheila Faria Glaser. Ann Arbor: University of Michigan Press, 1994.

Beker, J. Christiaan. *Paul's Apocalyptic Gospel: The Coming Triumph of God*. Philadelphia: Fortress, 1982.

———. *Paul the Apostle: The Triumph of God in Life and Thought*. Philadelphia: Fortress, 1984.

Betz, Hans Dieter. *Galatians: A Commentary on Paul's Letter to the Churches in Galatia*. Hermeneia Series. Philadelphia: Fortress, 1979.

Blanton, Ward. *A Materialism for the Masses: Saint Paul and the Philosophy of Undying Life*. Insurrections: Critical Studies in Religion, Politics, and Culture. New York: Columbia University Press, 2014.

Bloom, Joshua and Waldo E. Martin Jr. *Black Against Empire: The History and Politics of the Black Panther Party*. Berkeley: University of California Press, 2013.

Bockmuehl, Markus. *Jewish Law in Gentile Churches: Halakhah and the Beginning of Christian Public Ethics*. Grand Rapids: Baker Academic, 2000.

Boff, Leonardo, and Clodovis Boff. *Introducing Liberation Theology*. Translated by Paul Burns. Maryknoll: Orbis, 1992.

Boff, Clodovis, and George V. Pixley. *The Bible, the Church, and the Poor*. Translated by Paul Burns. Theology and Liberation Series. Maryknoll, NY: Orbis, 1989.

Bornkamm, Günther. *Early Christian Experience*. Translated by Paul L. Hammer. The New Testament Library Series. London: SCM, 1969.

———. *Paul: Paulus*. Translated by D. M. G. Stalker. New York: Harper & Row, 1971.

Bourgois, Philippe, and Jeffrey Schonberg. *Righteous Dopefiend*. Berkeley: University of California Press, 2009.

Boyarin, Daniel. *A Radical Jew: Paul and the Politics of Identity*. Berkeley: University of California Press, 1994.

Bray, Mark. *Antifa: The Anti-Fascist Handbook*. Brooklyn: Melville House, 2017.

Bruce, F. F. *Paul: Apostle of the Heart Set Free*. Grand Rapids: Eerdmans, 1990.

Brueggemann, Walter. *The Prophetic Imagination*. Minneapolis: Fortress, 1978.

———. *Texts Under Negotiation: The Bible and Postmodern Imagination*. Minneapolis: Fortress, 1993.

Brunner, Emil. *Eternal Hope*. Translated by Harold Knight. London: Lutterworth, 1954.

Bryan, Christopher. *Render to Caesar: Jesus, the Early Church, and the Roman Superpower*. Oxford: Oxford University Press, 2005.

Buck-Morss, Susan. *Hegel, Haiti, and Universal History*. Pittsburgh: Pittsburgh University Press, 1999.

Bultmann, Rudolph. *Existence and Faith: Shorter Writings of Rudolph Bultmann*. Edited and Translated by Schubert M. Ogden. London: Collins Clear-Type, 1964.

———. "History and Eschatology in the New Testament." *New Testament Studies* 1 (1954) 5–16.

———. *History and Eschatology: The Gifford Lectures 1955*. Edinburgh: Edinburgh University Press, 1957.

———. *Primitive Christianity: In its Contemporary Setting*. Translated by R. H. Fuller. London: Thomas and Hudson, 1956.

———. *Theology of the New Testament*. Vol. 1. Translated by Kendrick Grobel. London: SCM, 1952.

Cadoux, Cecil John. *The Early Church and the World: A History of the Christian Attitude to Pagan Society and the State Down to the Time of Constantinus*. Edinburgh: T. & T. Clark, 1955.

Callahan, Allen Dwight. "Paul, Ekklesia, and Emancipation in Corinth: A Coda on Liberation Theology." In *Paul and Politics: Ekklesia, Israel, Imperium, Interpretation. Essays in Honor of Krister Stendahl*, edited by Richard A. Horsley, 216–23. Harrisburg: Trinity Press International, 2000.

Campbell, William S. *Paul and the Creation of Christian Identity*. Library of New Testament Studies. London: T. & T. Clark, 2006.

Carter, Craig A. *Interpreting Scripture with the Great Tradition: Recovering the Genius of Premodern Exegesis*. Grand Rapids: Baker Academic, 2018.

Carter, Warren. *John and Empire: Initial Explorations*. New York: T. & T. Clark, 2008.

———. "Matthew Negotiates the Roman Empire." In *In The Shadow of Empire: Reclaiming the Bible as a History of Faithful* Resistance, edited by Richard A. Horsley, 117–36. Louisville: Westminster John Knox, 2008.

———. *The Roman Empire and the New Testament: An Essential Guide*. Nashville: Abingdon, 2006.

———. "Vulnerable Power: The Roman Empire Challenged by the Early Christians." In *Handbook of Early Christianity: Social-Science Approaches*, edited by Anthony J. Blasi et al., 453–88. New York: Altamira, 2002.

Case, Shirley Jackson. *The Social Origins of Christianity*. New York: Cooper Square, 1923.

Casey, P. M. *From Jewish Prophet to Gentile God: The Origins and Development of New Testament Christology*. Louisville: Westminster John Knox, 1991.

Cerfaux, Lucien. *The Church in the Theology of St. Paul*. Translated by Geoffrey Webb and Adrian Walker. London: Herder and Herder, 1959.

———. "La Propagande Du Christ Et Des Apôtres." In *Christianisme et Propagande: Idées directrices et suggestions pratiques*, edited by E. Nauwelaerts, 23–37. Études de Pastorale 3. Louvain: Publications Universitaires, 1948.

Chadwick, Henry. *The Early Church: The Story of Emergent Christianity*. London: Penguin, 1992.

Churchill, Ward. *Pacifism as Pathology: Reflections on the Role of Armed Struggle in North America*. Winnipeg: Arbeiter Ring, 1998.

Cicero, Marcus Tulius. *Cicero: Political Speeches*. Translated by D. H. Berry. Oxford World's Classics. Oxford: Oxford University Press, 2006.

———. *The Orations of Marcus Tulius Cicero*. Translated by C. D. Yonge. London: George Bell and Sons, 1891. http://www.perseus.tufts.edu/hopper/text?doc=Cic.%20Balb.

Clarke, Andrew D. "Jew and Greek, Slave and Free, Male and Female: Paul's Theology of Ethnic, Social and Gender Inclusiveness in Romans 16." In *Rome in the Bible and the Early Church*, edited by Peter Oakes, 103–25. Carlisle: Paternoster, 2002.

Coggan, Donald. *Paul: Portrait of a Revolutionary.* London: Hodder and Stoughton, 1984.

Collins, John J. *The Apocalyptic Imagination: An Introduction to Jewish Apocalyptic Literature.* Grand Rapids: Eerdmans, 1998.

Conzelmann, Hans. *History of Primitive Christianity.* Translated by John E. Steely. New York: Abingdon, 1973.

———. *An Outline of the Theology of the New Testament.* Translated by John Bowden. New Testament Library Series. London: SCM, 1969.

Countryman, Louis William. *The Rich Christians in the Church of the Early Empire: Contradictions and Accommodations.* New York: Edwin Mellen, 1980.

Cousar, Charles B. *An Introduction to the New Testament: Witnesses to God's New Work.* Louisville: Westminster John Knox, 2006.

———. *The Letters of Paul.* Interpreting Biblical Texts. Nashville: Abingdon, 1996.

Crossan, John Dominic. *God and Empire: Jesus Against Rome, Then and Now.* San Francisco: HarperSanFrancisco, 2007.

Crossan, John Dominic, and Marcus J. Borg. *The First Paul: Reclaiming the Radical Vision Behind the Church's Conservative Icon.* New York: HarperOne, 2009.

Crossan, John Dominic, and Jonathan L. Reed. *In Search of Paul: How Jesus's Apostle Opposed Rome's Empire with God's Kingdom. A New Vision of Paul's Words & World.* San Francisco: HarperSanFrancisco, 2004.

Cullmann, Oscar. *Christ and Time: The Primitive Christian Conception of Time and History.* Translated by Floyd V. Filson. Philadelphia: Westminster, 1964.

———. "Eschatology and Mission in the New Testament." In *The Background of the New Testament and its Eschatology: Studies in Honour of C. H. Dodd*, edited by William Davis Davies and D. Daube, 409–21. Cambridge: Cambridge University Press, 1964.

———. *Salvation in History.* Translated by Sidney G. Sowers. New Testament Library. London: SCM, 1967.

Dahl, Nils Alstrup, and Paul Donahue. *Studies in Paul: Theology for the Early Christian Mission.* Minneapolis: Augsburg, 1977.

Daniélou, Jean. *The Lord of History: Reflections on the Inner Meaning of History.* Translated by Nigel Abercrombie. New York: Meridian, 1958.

Davies, William David. *Jewish and Pauline Studies.* Philadelphia: Fortress, 1984.

———. *Paul and Rabbinic Judaism: Some Rabbinic Elements in Pauline Theology.* Philadelphia: Fortress, 1980.

Dawson, Christopher. "The Christian View of History." In *God, History and the Historians: An Anthology of Modern Christian Views on History*, edited by C. T. McIntire, 29–45. Oxford: Oxford University Press, 1979.

Deissmann, Adolf. *Light from the Ancient East: The New Testament Illustrated by Recently Discovered Texts of the Graeco-Roman World.* Translated by Lionel R. M. Strachan. Grand Rapids: Baker, 1978.

———. *The New Testament in Light of Modern Research: The Haskell Lectures, 1929.* London: Hodder & Stoughton, 1929.

———. *Paul: A Study in Social and Religious History.* Translated by William E. Wilson. New York: George H. Doran, 1926.

———. *The Religion of Jesus and the Faith of Paul: The Selly Oak Lectures, 1923, On the Communion of Jesus with God & the Communion of Paul with Christ*. Translated by William E. Wilson. London: Hodder & Stoughton, 1923.

Deleuze, Gilles, and Félix Guattari. *Anti-Oedipus: Capitalism and Schizophrenia*. Vol. 1. Translated by Robert Hurley, Mark Seem, and Helen R. Lane. Preface by Michel Foucault. Minneapolis: Minneapolis University Press, 1983.

Dewey, Arthur J. "EIS THN SPANIAN: The Future and Paul." In *Religious Propaganda and Missionary Competition in the New Testament World: Essay Honoring Dieter Georgi*, edited by Lukas Bormann, Kelly del Tredici, and Angela Standhartinger, 321–49. Leiden: Brill, 1994.

Dibelius, Martin. *A Fresh Approach to the New Testament and Early Christian Literature*. London: Nicholson & Watson, 1937.

———. *From Tradition to Gospel*. Translated by Bertram Lee Woolf. London: Redwood, 1971.

———. *Paul*. Edited and completed by Werner Georg Kümmel. Translated by Frank Clarke. Philadelphia: Westminster, 1953.

Dodd, C. H. *The Apostolic Preaching and Its Development. Three Lectures with an Appendix on Eschatology and History*. London: Hodder & Stoughton, 1963.

———. *The Coming of Christ*. Cambridge: Cambridge University Press, 1954.

———. "The Ethics of the Pauline Epistles." In *The Evolution of Ethics*, edited by E. H. Sneath. New Haven: Yale University Press, 1927.

———. *History and the Gospel*. London: Hodder & Stoughton, 1964.

Donfried, Karl P. "The Imperial Cults of Thessalonica and Political Conflict in 1 Thessalonians." In *Paul and Empire: Religion and Power in Roman Imperial Society*, edited by Richard A. Horsley, 215–23. Harrisburg: Trinity Press International, 1997.

Dumbrell, William J. *The Search for Order: Biblical Eschatology in Focus*. Grand Rapids: Baker, 1994.

Dunn, James D. G. *Beginning from Jerusalem*. Christianity in the Making 2. Grand Rapids: Eerdmans, 2009.

———. "Diversity in Paul." In *Religious Diversity in the Graeco-Roman World: A Survey of Recent Scholarship*, edited by Dan Cohn-Sherbok and John M. Court, 107–23. Sheffield: Sheffield Academic Press, 2001.

———. *The Epistles to the Colossians and to Philemon*. New International Greek Text Commentary. Grand Rapids: Eerdmans, 1996.

———. *The Theology of Paul the Apostle*. Grand Rapids: Eerdmans, 1998.

Eagleton, Terry. *After Theory*. London: Penguin, 2003.

———. "The Critic as Partisan: William Hazlitt's radical imagination." *Harper's Magazine* 318 (2009) 77–82.

Ehrman, Bart D. *Jesus: Apocalyptic Prophet of the New Millennium*. Oxford: Oxford University Press, 1999.

———. *Jesus, Interrupted: Revealing the Hidden Contradictions of the Bible (and Why We Don't Know About Them)*. New York: HarperOne, 2009.

Elias, Jacob W. *Remember the Future: The Pastoral Theology of Paul the Apostle*. Waterloo: Herald, 2006.

Elliott, Neil. *The Arrogance of Nations: Reading Romans in the Shadow of Empire*. Paul in Critical Contexts. Minneapolis: Fortress, 2008.

———. *Liberating Paul: The Justice of God and the Politics of the Apostle*. Maryknoll, NY: Orbis, 1994.

———. "Paul and the Politics of Empire: Problems and Prospects." In *Paul and Politics: Ekklesia, Israel, Imperium, Interpretation. Essays in Honor of Krister Stendahl*, edited by Richard A. Horsley, 17–39. Harrisburg: Trinity Press International, 2000.

———. "Strategies of Resistance and Hidden Transcripts in the Pauline Communities." In *Hidden Transcripts and the Arts of Resistance: Applying the Works of James C. Scott to Jesus and Paul*, edited by Richard A. Horsley, 97–122. Semeia Studies 48. Atlanta: Society of Biblical Literature, 2004.

Engberg-Pedersen, Troels. *Paul and the Stoics*. Edinburgh: T. & T. Clark, 2000.

Engler, Yves, and Anthony Fenton. *Canada in Haiti: Waging War on the Poor Majority*. Vancouver: Fernwood, 2005.

Erikson, Millard J. *Christian Theology*. Grand Rapids: Baker, 1998.

Esler, Philip F. *Conflict and Identity in Romans: The Social Setting of Paul's Letter*. Minneapolis: Fortress, 2003.

———. *The Early Christian World*. Vol. 1. London: Routledge, 2000.

———. *New Testament Theology: Communion and Community*. Minneapolis: Fortress, 2005.

Fee, Gordon D. *God's Empowering Presence: The Holy Spirit in the Letters of Paul*. Peabody, MA: Hendrickson, 1994.

———. *Paul, the Spirit, and the People of God*. Peabody, MA: Hendrickson, 1996.

Finley, M. I. *The Ancient Economy*. Sather Classical Lectures 43. Berkeley: University of California Press, 1973.

Fitzgerald, John T., et al. *Early Christianity and Classical Culture: Comparative Studies in Honor of Abraham J. Malherbe*. Leiden: Brill, 2003.

Fitzpatrick, Joseph P. *Paul: Saint of the Inner City*. New York: Paulist, 1990.

Foucault, Michel. *The Archaeology of Knowledge and the Discourse on Language*. Translated by A. M. Sheridan Smith. New York: Pantheon, 1972.

———. *Discipline and Punish: The Birth of the Prison*. Translated by Alan Sheridan. New York: Vintage, 1995.

———. *Power/Knowledge: Selected Interviews & Other Writings. 1972-1977*. Edited by Colin Gordon. Translated by Colin Gordon, Leo Marshall, John Mepham, and Kate Soper. New York: Pantheon, 1980.

Fowl, Stephen E. *The Story of Christ in the Ethics of Paul: An Analysis of the Function of the Hymnic Material in the Pauline Corpus*. Journal for the Study of the New Testament Supplement Series 36. Sheffield: JSOT, 1990.

Fowl, Stephen E., and L. Gregory Jones. *Reading in Communion: Scripture and Ethics in Christian Life*. Grand Rapids: Eerdmans, 1991.

Fredriksen, Paula. *From Jesus to Christ: The Origins of the New Testament Images of Jesus*. New Haven: Yale University Press, 2000

Friesen, Steven J. "Injustice or God's Will: Explanations of Poverty in Proto-Christian Texts." In *Christian Origins: A People's History of Christianity, Volume 1*, edited by Richard A. Horsley, 240–60. Minneapolis: Fortress, 2005.

———. "Paul and Economics: The Jerusalem Collection as an Alternative to Patronage." In *Paul Unbound: Other Perspectives on the Apostle*, edited by Mark D. Given, 27–54. Peabody, MA: Hendrickson, 2010.

Fukuyama, Francis. *The End of History and the Last Man*. New York: Avon, 1992.

Furnish, Victor Paul. *The Moral Teaching of Paul: Selected Issues*. Nashville: Abingdon, 1979.

———. *Theology and Ethics in Paul*. Nashville: Abingdon, 1968.

Gad, Clarence E. "Paul and Adaptability." In *Paul in the Greco-Roman World: A Handbook*, edited by J. Paul Sampley, 17–41. New York: Trinity Press International, 2003.

Garnsey, Peter, and Richard Saller. *The Roman Empire: Economy, Society and Culture*. Berkeley: University of California Press, 1987.

Gelderloos, Peter. *The Failure of Nonviolence*. Seattle: Left Bank, 2013.

———. *How Nonviolence Protects the State*. Cambridge, MA: South End, 2007.

Georgi, Dieter. *Theocracy: In Paul's Praxis and Theology*. Translated by David E. Green. Minneapolis: Fortress, 1991.

Gibbs, Nancy and John F. Dickerson. "Person of the Year." *TIME Magazine*. December 19, 2004. http://content.time.com/time/magazine/article/0,9171,1009927,00.html

Goguel, Maurice. "Le Caractere, À La Fois Actuel Et Futur, Du Salut Dans La Théologie Paulinienne." In *The Background of the New Testament and Its Eschatology: Studies in Honour of C. H. Dodd*, edited by William Davis Davies and D. Daube, 322–41. Cambridge: Cambridge University Press, 1964.

———. *The Primitive Church*. Translated by H. C. Snape. London: Allen & Unwin, 1964.

Goldberg, David Theo, ed. *Multiculturalism: A Critical Reader*. Oxford: Oxford University Press, 1994.

González, Justo L. *Faith and Wealth: A History of Christian Ideas on the Origin, Significance, and Use of Money*. San Francisco: HarperSanFrancisco, 1990.

Gorman, Michael J. *Apostle of the Crucified Lord: A Theological Introduction to Paul & His Letters*. Grand Rapids: Eerdmans, 2004.

———. *Cruciformity: Paul's Narrative Spirituality of the Cross*. Grand Rapids: Eerdmans, 2001.

———. *Reading Paul*. Cascade Companions. Eugene, OR: Cascade, 2008.

Gorringe, Timothy. "Eschatology and Political Radicalism: The Example of Karl Barth and Jürgen Moltmann." In *God Will be All in All: The Eschatology of Moltmann*, edited by Richard Bauckham, 87–114. Edinburgh: T. & T. Clark, 1999.

Grant, F. C. "The Economic Background of the New Testament." In *The Background of the New Testament and its Eschatology: Essays in Honour of C. H. Dodd*, edited by William Davis Davies and D. Daube, 96–114. Cambridge: Cambridge University Press, 1964.

Grant, Robert M. *Early Christianity and Society: Seven Studies*. San Francisco: Harper & Row, 1977.

Green, Joel B. *The Gospel of Luke*. New International Commentary on the New Testament. Grand Rapids: Eerdmans, 1997.

Griffin, Roger. *Modernism and Fascism: The Sense of a Beginnin Under Mussolini and Hitler*. New York: Palgrave MacMillan, 2007.

Grubačić, Andrej, and Denis O'Hearn. *Living at the Edges of Capitalism: Adventures in Exile and Mutual Aid*. Oakland: University of California Press, 2016.

Gutierrez, Gustavo. *The Power of the Poor in History*. Translated by Robert R. Barr. Maryknoll, NY: Orbis, 1983.

———. *A Theology of Liberation: History, Politics and Salvation*. Translated and Edited by Sister Caridad Inda and John Eagleson. Maryknoll, NY: Orbis, 1973.

———. *We Drink from our Own Wells: The Spiritual Journey of a People*. Translated by Matthew J. O'Connell. Maryknoll, NY: Orbis, 2003.

Hallward, Peter. *Damming the Flood: Haiti, Aristide, and the Politics of Containment*. London: Verso, 2008.

Hanisch, Carol. "The Personal is Political." http://www.carolhanisch.org/CHwritings/PIP. html.

Hanssen, Ryan. Messianic or Apocalyptic? Engaging Agamben on Paul and Politics." In *Paul, Philosophy, and the Theopolitical Vision: Critical Engagements with Agamben, Badiou, Žižek, and Others,* edited by Douglas Harink, 198–223. Theopolitical Visions Series. Eugene, OR: Cascade, 2010.

Hardin, Justin K. *Galatians and the Imperial Cult: A Critical Analysis of the First-Century Social Context of Paul's Letter.* Wissenschaftliche Untersuchungen zum Neuen Testament 2. Reihe 237. Tubingen: Mohr Siebeck, 2008.

Harink, Douglas. *Paul Among the Postliberals: Pauline Theology Beyond Christendom and Modernity.* Grand Rapids: Brazos, 2003.

Harink, Douglas, ed. *Paul, Philosophy, and the Theopolitical Vision: Critical Engagements with Agamben, Badiou, Žižek, and Others.* Theopolitical Visions Series. Eugene, OR: Cascade, 2010.

Harland, Philip A. "Connections with Elites in the World of the Early Christians." In *Handbook of Early Christianity: Social-Science Approaches.* Edited by Anthony Blasi, J. Jean Duhaime and Paul André Turcotte, 385–408. New York: Altamira, 2002.

Harrill, J. Albert. *Slaves in the New Testament: Literary, Social, and Moral Dimensions.* Minneapolis: Fortress, 2006.

Hays, Richard B. *The Moral Vision of the New Testament: A Contemporary Introduction to New Testament Ethics.* San Francisco: HarperSanFrancisco, 1996.

Hill, Craig C. *In God's Time: The Bible and the Future.* Grand Rapids: Eerdmans, 2002.

Hill, Gord. *The 500 Years of Resistance Comic Book.* Vancouver: Arsenal Pulp, 2012.

Hoehner, Harold. *Ephesians: An Exegetical Commentary.* Grand Rapids: Baker, 2002.

Holmberg, Bengt. *Sociology and the New Testament: An Appraisal.* Minneapolis: Fortress, 1990.

Hopkins, Keith. *A World Full of Gods: Pagans, Jews and Christians in the Roman Empire.* London: Weidenfeld & Nicholas, 1999.

Horrell, David G. ""Becoming Christian": Solidifying Christian Identity and Content." In *Handbook of Early Christianity: Social-Science Approaches,* edited by Anthony Blasi, Paul André Turcotte, and Jean Duhaime, 309–35. New York: Altamira, 2002.

———. "Introduction—Social-Scientific Interpretation of the New Testament." In *Social-Scientific Approaches to New Testament Interpretation,* edited by David G. Horrell, 3–27. Edinburgh: T. & T. Clark, 1999.

———. *An Introduction to the Study of Paul.* T. & T. Clark Approaches to Biblical Studies. London: T. & T. Clark, 2006.

———. *The Social Ethos of the Corinthian Correspondence: Interests and Ideology from 1 Corinthians to 1 Clement.* Studies of the New Testament and Its World. Edinburgh: T. & T. Clark, 1996.

———. *Solidarity and Difference: A Contemporary Reading of Paul's Ethics.* London: T. & T. Clark International, 2005.

Horsley, Richard A. *Covenant Economics: A Biblical Vision of Justice for All.* Louisville: Westminster John Knox, 2009.

———. *Jesus and Empire: The Kingdom of God and the New World Disorder.* Minneapolis: Fortress, 2003.

———. *The Liberation of Christmas: The Infancy Narratives in Social Context.* Eugene, OR: Wipf & Stock, 1989.

———. *Religion and Empire: People, Power, and the Life of the Spirit*. Facets Series. Minneapolis: Fortress, 2003.

Horsley, Richard A., ed. *Christian Origins: A People's History of Christianity*. Vol. 1. Minneapolis: Fortress, 2005.

———. *Hidden Transcripts and the Arts of Resistance: Applying the Works of James C. Scott to Jesus and Paul*. Semeia Studies 48. Atlanta: Society of Biblical Literature, 2004.

———. *Paul and Empire: Religion and Power in Roman Imperial Society*. Harrisburg: Trinity Press International, 1997.

Horsley, Richard A., and Neil Asher Silberman. *The Message and the Kingdom: How Jesus and Paul Ignited a Revolution and Transformed the Ancient World*. Minneapolis: Fortress, 1997.

Howard-Brook, Wes. *Empire Baptized: How the Church Embraced What Jesus Rejected 2nd-5th Centuries*. Maryknoll, NY: Orbis, 2016

Howard-Brook, Wes, and Anthony Gwyther. *Unveiling Empire: Reading Revelation Then and Now*. Forward by Elizabeth McAlister. The Bible and Liberation Series. Maryknoll, NY: Orbis, 1999.

Hurtado, Larry. *Destroyer of the Gods: Early Christian Distinctiveness in the Roman World*. Waco, TX: Baylor University Press, 2016.

James, C. L. R. *The Black Jacobins: Toussaint L'Ouverture and the San Domingo Revolution*. New York: Vintage, 1989.

Jeffers, James S. *The Greco-Roman World of the New Testament Era: Exploring the Background of Early Christianity*. Downers Grove, IL: InterVarsity, 1999.

Jennings, Theodore W., Jr. *Outlaw Justice: The Messianic Politics of Paul*. Stanford: Stanford University Press, 2013.

Jerome. *De Virus Illustibus*. http://www.newadvent.org/fathers/2708.htm.

———. *St. Jerome's Commentaries on Galatians, Titus, and Philemon*. Translated by Thomas P. Scheck. Notre Dame: University of Notre Dame Press, 2010.

Jewett, Robert. *Romans: A Commentary*. Hermeneia Series. Minneapolis: Fortress, 2007.

———. *The Thessalonians Correspondence: Pauline Rhetoric and Millenarian Piety*. Foundations and Facets. Philadelphia: Fortress, 1986.

Judge, Edwin A. "Did the Churches Compete with Cult Groups?" In *Early Christianity and Classical Culture: Comparative Studies in Honor of Abraham J. Malherbe*, edited by John Fitzgerald, Thomas Olbricht, and L. Michael White, 501–24. Leiden: E. J. Brill, 2003.

———. *Social Distinctives of the Christians in the First Century: Pivotal Essays by E. A. Judge*. Edited by David M. Sholer. Peabody, MA: Hendrickson, 2008.

Juvenal. "Satires." In *Juvenal: The Sixteen Satires*, translated with an introduction and notes by Peter Green, 65–297. Penguin Classics. London: Penguin, 1967.

Kahl, Brigitte. *Galatians Re-Imagined: Reading with the Eyes of the Vanquished*. Paul in Critical Contexts Series. Minneapolis: Fortress, 2010.

Käsemann, Ernst. *New Testament Questions of Today*. Translated by W. J. Montague. Philadelphia: Fortress, 1969.

———. *Perspectives on Paul*. Translated by Margaret Kohl. London: SCM, 1971.

Kautsky, Karl. *Foundations of Christianity*. Translated by Henry F. Mins. New York: S. A. Russell, 1953.

Keck, Leander E. *Paul and His Letters*. Edited by Gerhard Krodel. Philadelphia: Fortress, 1988.

Keck, Leander E., and Victory Paul Furnish. *The Pauline Letters.* Edited by Lloyd R. Bailey Sr. and Victor P. Furnish. Interpreting Biblical Texts Series. Nashville: Abingdon, 1984.

Kee, Howard Clark. *The Beginnings of Christianity: An Introduction to the New Testament.* London: T. & T. Clark, 2005.

———. *Christian Origins in Sociological Perspective: Methods and Resources.* Philadelphia: Westminster, 1980.

———. *The Renewal of Hope.* New York: Association, 1959.

Keresztes, Paul. *Imperial Rome and the Christians: From Herod the Great to about 200 A.D.* Vol. 1. New York: University Press of America, 1989.

Kim, Seyoon. *Christ and Caesar: The Gospel and the Roman Empire in the Writings of Paul and Luke.* Grand Rapids: Eerdmans, 2008.

Kim, Yung Suk. *Christ's Body in Corinth: The Politics of a Metaphor.* Paul in Critical Contexts. Minneapolis: Fortress, 2008.

Kimmel, Michael. *Angry White Men: American Masculinity at the End of an Era.* New York: Nation, 2017.

Klein, Naomi. *The Shock Doctrine: The Rise of Disaster Capitalism.* Toronto: Alfred A. Knopf Canada, 2007.

Koch, Klaus. *The Rediscovery of Apocalyptic.* Studies in Biblical Theology Second Series 22. London: SCM, 1972.

Koester, Helmut. *Introduction to the New Testament Volume 1: History, Culture, and Religion of the Hellenistic Age.* Berlin: De Gruyter, 1995.

Kümmel, Werner Georg. *Introduction to the New Testament.* Translated by Howard Clark Kee. Nashville: Abingdon, 1975.

———. *The Theology of the New Testament According to Its Major Witnesses: Jesus—Paul—John.* Nashville: Abingdon, 1973.

Ladd, George Eldon. *The Blessed Hope.* Grand Rapids: Eerdmans, 1956.

———. "The Place of Apocalypticism in Biblical Religion." *Evangelical Quarterly* 30.2 (1958) 25–85.

———. *The Presence of the Future: The Eschatology of Biblical Realism.* Grand Rapids: Eerdmans, 1974.

———. *A Theology of the New Testament.* Edited by Donald A Hagner. Grand Rapids: Eerdmans, 1993.

Lietzmann, Hans. *The Beginnings of the Christian Church.* Translated by Bertram Lee Woolf. London: Lutterworth, 1953.

Lohse, Eduard. *The New Testament Environment.* Translated by John E. Steely. Nashville: Abingdon, 1976.

———. *Theological Ethics of the New Testament.* Translated by M. Eugene Boring. Minneapolis: Fortress, 1991.

Longenecker, Bruce W. *Remember the Poor: Paul, Poverty, and the Greco-Roman World.* Grand Rapids: Eerdmans, 2010.

Longenecker, Richard N. *The Ministry and Message of Paul.* Grand Rapids: Zondervan, 1971.

———. *New Testament Social Ethics for Today.* Grand Rapids: Eerdmans, 1984.

———. *Paul, Apostle of Liberty: The Origin and Nature of Paul's Christianity.* Grand Rapids: Baker, 1976.

Luther, Martin. *Galatians.* Edited by Alister McGrath and J. I. Packer. The Crossway Classic Commentaries Series. Wheaton, Il.: Crossway, 1998.

MacDonald, Margaret Y. *The Pauline Churches: A Socio-historical Study of Institutionalization in the Pauline and Deutero-Pauline Writings*. Society for New Testament Studies Monograph Series 60. Cambridge: Cambridge University Press, 1988.

MacMullen, Ramsay. *Changes in the Roman Empire: Essays in the Ordinary*. Princeton: Princeton University Press, 1990.

Maier, Harry O. *Picturing Paul in Empire: Imperial Image, Text and Persuasion in Colossians, Ephesians and the Pastoral Epistles*. London: Bloomsbury T. & T. Clark, 2013.

Malherbe, Abraham J. *The Letters to the Thessalonians*. Anchor Bible Commentary 32B. New York: Doubleday, 2000.

———. *Paul and the Popular Philosophers*. Minneapolis: Fortress, 1989.

———. *Social Aspects of Early Christianity*. Philadelphia: Fortress, 1983.

Malina, Bruce J. "Social Levels, Morals and Daily Life." In *The Early Christian World: Volume 1*, edited by Philip F. Esler, 369–400. London: Routledge, 2000.

Malina, Bruce J., and John J. Pilch. *Social-Science Commentary on the Letters of Paul*. Minneapolis: Fortress, 2006.

Malka, Haim. *Gaza's Health Sector Under Hamas: Incurable Ills?* A Report of the CSIS Global Health Policy Center. Washington: Center for Strategic and International Studies, 2012.

Marshall, I. Howard. *A Concise New Testament Theology*. Downers Grove, IL: InterVarsity, 2008.

Martin, Clarice J. "The Eyes Have It: Slaves in Communities of Christ-Believers." In *Christian Origins: A People's History of Christianity, Volume 1*, edited by Richard A. Horsley, 221–39. Minneapolis: Fortress, 2005.

Martin, Ralph. "The Spirit in 2 Corinthians in Light of the 'Fellowship of the Spirit' in 2 Corinthians 13:14." In *Eschatology and the New Testament: Essays in Honor of George Raymond Beasley-Murray*, edited by W. Hulitt Gloer, 113–28. Peabody, MA: Hendrickson, 1988.

Martyn, J. Louis. *Theological Issues in the Letters of Paul*. Nashville: Abingdon, 1997.

Marxsen, Willi. *New Testament Foundations for Christian Ethics*. Translated by O. C. Dean Jr. Minneapolis: Fortress, 1993.

Matera, Frank J. *New Testament Ethics: The Legacies of Jesus and Paul*. Louisville: Westminster John Knox, 1996.

Meeks, Wayne A. *The First Urban Christians: The Social World of the Apostle Paul*. New Haven, CT: Yale University Press, 1983.

———. *In Search of the Early Christians: Selected Essays*. Edited by Allen R. Hilston and H. Gregory Snyder. New Haven, CT: Yale University Press, 2002.

———. *The Moral World of the First Christians*. Library of Early Christianity. Philadelphia: Westminster, 1986.

———. *The Origins of Christian Morality: The First Two Centuries*. New Haven, CT: Yale University Press, 1993.

———. *The Writings of St. Paul*. A Norton Critical Edition. New York: W. W. Norton & Company, 1972.

Meggitt, Justin J. *Paul, Poverty and Survival*. Studies of the New Testament and Its World. Edinburgh: T. & T. Clark, 1998.

Merkley, Paul. *The Greek and Hebrew Origins of our Idea of History*. Toronto Studies in Theology 32. Lewiston, NY: Edwin Mellen, 1987.

Miranda, José Porfirio. *Marx and the Bible: A Critique of the Philosophy of Oppression.* Translated by John Eagleson. Maryknoll, NY: Orbis, 1974.

Moltmann, Jürgen. "The Bible, The Exegete and The Theologian: Response to Richard Bauckham." In *God Will be All in All: The Eschatology of Jürgen Moltmann*, edited by Richard Bauckham, 227–32. Edinburgh: T. & T. Clark, 1999.

———. *The Coming of God: Christian Eschatology.* Translated by Margaret Kohl. Minneapolis: Fortress, 1996.

———. *Experiences in Theology: Ways and Forms of Christian Theology.* Translated by Margaret Kohl. Minneapolis: Fortress, 2000.

———. *God in Creation: A New Theology of Creation and the Spirit of God.* Translated by Margaret Kohl. Minneapolis: Fortress, 1993.

———. "The Liberation of the Future and Its Anticipation in History." In *God Will be All in All: The Eschatology of Jürgen Moltmann*, edited by Richard Bauckham, 265–89. Edinburgh: T. & T. Clark, 1999.

———. *Theology of Hope: On the Ground and Implications of a Christian Eschatology.* Translated by James W. Leitch. New York: Harper & Row, 1967.

———. *The Way of Jesus Christ: Christology in Messianic Dimensions.* Translated by Margaret Kohl. Minneapolis: Fortress, 1990.

Moule, C. F. D. *Essays in New Testament Interpretation.* Cambridge: Cambridge University Press, 1982.

Moxnes, Halvor. "Introduction." In *Constructing Early Christian Families: family as social reality and metaphor*, edited by Halvor Moxnes, 1–12. London: Routledge, 1997.

Moxnes, Halvor, ed. *Constructing Early Christian Families: family as social reality and metaphor.* London: Routledge, 1997.

Munck, Johannes. *Paul and the Salvation of Mankind.* Translated by Frank Clarke. London: SCM, 1959.

Neusner, Jacob. *The Christian and Judaic Invention of History.* AAR Studies in Religion 55. Atlanta: Scholars, 1990.

Neyrey, Jerome. *Paul, In Other Words: A Cultural Reading of His Letters.* Louisville: Westminster John Knox, 1990.

Nordman, Alfred. *Wittgenstein's Tractatus: An Introduction.* Cambridge Introductions to Key Philosophical Texts. Cambridge: Cambridge University Press, 2005.

Oakes, Peter. "Methodological Issues in Using Economic Evidence in Interpretation of Early Christian Texts." In *Engaging Economics: New Testament Scenarios and Early Christian Reception*, edited by Bruce W. Longenecker and Kelly D. Liebengood, 9–34. Grand Rapids: Eerdmans, 2005.

———. *Philippians: From People to Letter.* Society for New Testament Studies Monograph Series 110. Cambridge: Cambridge University Press, 2001.

———. *Reading Romans in Pompeii: Paul's Letter at Ground Level.* Minneapolis: Fortress, 2009.

Oakes, Peter, ed. *Rome in the Bible and the Early Church.* Carlisle, UK: Paternoster, 2002.

O'Brien, Peter T. *The Letter to the Ephesians.* Pillar New Testament Commentary. Grand Rapids: Eerdmans, 1999.

Osiek, Carolyn. "Family Matters." In *Christian Origins: A People's History of Christianity, Volume 1*, edited by Richard A. Horsley, 201–20. Minneapolis: Fortress, 2005.

Pannenberg, Wolfhardt. *Revelation as History.* London: Macmillan, 1968.

Pate, C. Marvin. *The End of the Age has Come: The Theology of Paul.* Grand Rapids: Zondervan, 1995.

Perrin, Norman. *The New Testament: An Introduction. Proclamation and Parenesis, Myth and History*. New York: Harcourt Brace Jovanovich, 1974.

Pickett, Ray. "Conflicts at Corinth." In *Christian Origins: A People's History of Christianity, Volume 1*, edited by Richard A. Horsley, 113–37. Minneapolis: Fortress, 2005.

Pilgrim, Walter. *Uneasy Neighbors: Church and State in the New Testament*. Overtures to Biblical Theology. Minneapolis: Fortress, 1999.

Price, Simon R. F. *Rituals and Power: The Roman imperial cult in Asia Minor*. Cambridge: Cambridge University Press, 1984.

Räisänen, Heikki. *Paul and the Law*. Wissenschaftliche Untersuchungen zum Neuen Testament 29. Tübingen: Mohr Siebeck, 1983.

Rancière, Jacques. *The Ignorant Schoolmaster: Five Lessons in Intellectual Emancipation*. Translated with an introduction by Kristin Ross. Stanford: Stanford University Press, 1991.

Ratzinger, Joseph. *Eschatology, Death, and Eternal Life*. Edited by Aidan Nichols. Translated by Michael Waldstein. Washington: Catholic University of America Press, 1988.

Remus, Harold. "Persecution." In *Handbook of Early Christianity: Social-Science Approaches*, edited by Anthony Blasi, Paul André Turcotte, and Jean Duhaime, 431–52. New York: Altamira, 2002.

Renshaw, Patrick. *The Wobblies: The Story of the IWW and Syndicalism in the United States*. Chicago: Ivan R. Dee, 1999.

Reynolds, Frank E., and David Tracy, eds. *Myth and Philosophy*. Albany: State University of New York Press, 1990.

Rhoads David, David Esterline, and Jae Won Lee, eds. *Luke-Acts and Empire: Essays in Honor of Robert L. Brawley*. Princeton Theological Monograph Series 151. Eugene, OR: Pickwick, 2011.

Richards, E. Randolph. *Paul and First-Century Letter Writing: Secretaries, Composition and Collection*. Downers Grove, IL: InterVarsity, 2004.

Richardson, Peter. *Paul's Ethic of Freedom*. Philadelphia: Westminster, 1979.

Ricoeur, Paul. *The Symbolism of Evil*. Translated by Emerson Buchanan. New York: Harper & Row, 1969.

Ridderbos, Herman. *Paul: An Outline of His Theology*. Translated by John Richard De Witt. Grand Rapids: Eerdmans, 1975.

Roetzel, Calvin J. *The Letters of Paul: Conversations in Context*. Louisville: Westminster John Knox, 1998.

———. *Paul—A Jew on the Margins*. Louisville: Westminster John Knox, 2003.

Ross, Alexander Reid. *Against the Fascist Creep*. San Francisco: AK, 2017.

Rostovtzeff, M. *The Social and Economic History of the Hellenistic World*. Vol. 2. Oxford: Clarendon, 1941.

Rowe, C. Kavin. *World Upside Down: Reading Acts in the Graeco-Roman Age*. Oxford: Oxford University Press, 2009.

Saller, Richard P. *Personal Patronage Under the Early Empire*. Cambridge: Cambridge University Press, 1982.

Sampley, J. Paul. *Walking Between the Times: Paul's Moral Reasoning*. Minneapolis: Fortress, 1991.

Sanders, E. P. *The Historical Figure of Jesus*. London: Penguin, 1993.

———. *Jesus and Judaism*. Philadelphia: Fortress, 1985.

———. *Paul*. Past Masters Series. Oxford: Oxford University Press, 1991.

———. *Paul: The Apostle's Life, Letters, and Thoughts.* Minneapolis: Fortress, 2015.

———. *Paul and Palestinian Judaism: A Comparison of Patterns of Religion.* Minneapolis: Fortress, 1977.

Sauter, Gerhard. *What Dare We Hope? Reconsidering Eschatology.* Theology for the Twenty-First Century. Harrisburg: Trinity Press International, 1999.

Schnabel, Eckhard J. *Early Christian Mission, Volume 2: Paul and The Early Church.* Leicester: Apollos, 2004.

Schnackenburg, Rudolf. *The Moral Teaching of the New Testament.* Translated by J. Holland-Smith and W. J. O'Hara. London: Burns & Oates, 1967.

———. *New Testament Theology.* Translated by David Askew. Montreal: Palm, 1963.

Schnelle, Udo. *Apostle Paul: His Life and Theology.* Translated by M. Eugene Boring. Grand Rapids: Baker, 2005.

Schoeps, H. J. *Paul: The Theology of the Apostle in the Light of Jewish Religious History.* Translated by Harold Knight. Philadelphia: Westminster, 1961.

Schottroff, Luise. "'Not Many Powerful': Approaches to a Sociology of Early Christianity." In *Social-Scientific Approaches to New Testament Interpretation*, edited by David G. Horrell, 275–87. Edinburgh: T. & T. Clark, 1999.

Schrage, Wolfgang. *The Ethics of the New Testament.* Translated by David E. Green. Philadelphia: Fortress, 1988.

Schreiner, Thomas R. *Paul: Apostle of God's Glory in Christ.* Downers Grove, IL: InterVarsity, 2001.

———. *Romans.* Baker Exegetical Commentary on the New Testament. Grand Rapids: Baker, 1998.

Schüssler-Fiorenza, Elisabeth. *In Memory of Her: A Feminist Theological Reconstruction of Christian Origins.* New York: Crossroad, 1994.

———. "Paul and the Politics of Interpretation." In *Paul and Politics: Ekklesia, Israel, Imperium, Interpretation. Essays in Honor of Krister Stendahl*, edited by Richard A. Horsley, 40–57. Harrisburg: Trinity Press International: 2000.

———. *Rhetoric and Ethic: The Politics of Biblical Study.* Minneapolis: Fortress, 1999.

Schweitzer, Albert. *The Mysticism of Paul the Apostle.* Translated by William Montgomery. London: Black, 1931.

———. *Paul and His Interpreters: A Critical History.* Translated by W. Montgomery. London: Black, 1912.

———. *The Quest for the Historical Jesus: A Critical Study of Its Progress from Reimarus to Wrede.* London: Black, 1911.

Scott, James C. *The Art of Not Being Governed: An Anarchist History of Upland Southeast Asia.* Yale Agrarian Studies Series. New Haven, CT: Yale University Press, 2009.

———. *Domination and the Arts of Resistance: Hidden Transcripts.* Yale: Yale University Press, 1992.

———. *Weapons of the Weak: Everyday Forms of Peasant Resistance.* Yale: Yale University Press, 1987.

Scroggs, Robin. *Paul for a New Day.* Philadelphia: Fortress, 1977.

———. *The Text and the Times: New Testament Essays for Today.* Minneapolis: Fortress, 1993.

Segundo, Juan Luis. *The Humanist Christology of Paul.* Edited and Translated by John Drury. Jesus of Nazareth Yesterday and Today 3. Maryknoll, NY: Orbis, 1986.

Shaw, Brent D. "The Myth of Neronian Persecution." *Journal of Roman Studies* 105 (2015) 73–100.

Sherwin-White, A. N. *The Roman Citizenship*. Oxford: Clarendon, 1973.

Sinclair, Upton. *The Jungle*. Penguin Classics. With an Introduction by Ronal Gottesman. London: Penguin, 1986.

Smith, Abraham. ""Unmasking the Powers": Toward a Postcolonial Analysis of 1 Thessalonians." In *Paul and the Roman Imperial Order*, edited by Richard A. Horsley, 47–66. Harrisburg: Trinity Press International, 2004.

Smith, Linda Tuhiwai. *Decolonizing Methodologies: Research and Indigenous Peoples*. London: Zed, 2012.

Sobrino, Jon. *No Salvation Outside the Poor: Prophetic-Utopian Essays*. Translated by Orbis Books. Maryknoll, NY: Orbis, 2008.

Stauffer, Ethelbert. *Christ and the Caesars: Historical Sketches*. Translated by K. and R. Gregor Smith. London: SCM, 1955.

———. *New Testament Theology*. Translated by John Marsh. London: SCM, 1955.

Stendahl, Krister. *Paul Among Jews and Gentiles and Other Essays*. Philadelphia: Fortress, 1976.

Strabo. *The Geography of Strabo*. Translated with notes by H. C. Hamilton Esq. and W. Falconer. London: Bell & Sons, 1903. http://www.perseus.tufts.edu/hopper/text?doc =Perseus:text:1999.01.0239.

Stringfellow, William. *My People is the Enemy: An Autobiographical Polemic*. Eugene, OR: Wipf & Stock, 2005.

Strom, Mark. *Reframing Paul: Conversations in Grace & Community*. Downers Grove, IL: InterVarsity, 2000.

Suetonius Trannquillus, C. *The Twelve Caesars*. Translated by Robert Graves. London: Folio Society, 2005.

Sugai, Yasko. "Paul's Eschatology and his Ethical Thought in Relation to It." Master's thesis, Regent College, Canada, April 1982.

Taubes, Jacob. *Occidental Eschatology*. Translated by David Ratmoko. Cultural Memory in the Present Series. Stanford: Stanford University Press, 2009.

———. *The Political Theology of Paul*. Cultural Memory in the Present Series. Edited by Aleida Assmann and Jan Assmann, in confunction with Horst Folkers, Wolf-Daniel Hartwich, and Christoph Schulte, and translated by Dana Hollander. Stanford: Stanford University Press, 2004.

Tawney, R. H. *Religion and the Rise of Capitalism: A Historical Study*. New York: Harcourt, Brace & World, 1963.

Tellbe, Mikael. *Paul Between Synagogue and State: Christians, Jews, and Civic Authorities in 1 Thessalonians, Romans, and Philippians*. Coniectanea Biblica New Testament Series 34. Stockholm: Almqvist & Wiksell, 2001.

Tenney, Merrill C. *New Testament Times*. London: Lowe & Brydone, 1965.

Testa, M. *Militant Anti-Fascism: A Hundred Years of Resistance*. San Francisco: AK, 2015.

Theissen, Gerd. *Fortress Introduction to The New Testament*. Translated by John Bowden. Minneapolis: Fortress, 2003.

———. *The Religion of the Earliest Churches: Creating a Symbolic World*. Translated by John Bowden. Minneapolis: Fortress, 1999.

———. *Social Reality and the Early Christians: Theology, Ethics, and the World of the New Testament*. Translated by Margaret Kohl. Minneapolis: Fortress, 1992.

———. *The Social Setting of Pauline Christianity: Essays on Corinth*. Edited and translated with introduction by John H. Schütz. Philadelphia: Fortress, 1982.

Thielman, Frank. *Theology of the New Testament: a canonical and synthetic approach.* Grand Rapids: Zondervan, 2005.

Thiselton, Anthony C. *The Living Paul: An Introduction to the Apostle's Life and Thought.* Downers Grove, IL: InterVarsity Academic, 2009.

Troeltsch, Ernst. *The Social Teachings of the Christian Churches.* Vol. 1. Translated by Olive Wyon with introduction by H. Richard Niebuhr. New York: Harper & Row, 1960.

Trouillot, Michel-Rolph. *Silencing the Past: Power and the Production of History.* Boston: Beacon, 1995.

Valencia, Sayak. *Gore Capitalism.* Translated by John Pluecker. Semiotext(e) Intervention Series 24. South Pasadena, CA: Semiotext(e), 2018.

Venturi, Franco. *Roots of Revolution: A History of the Populist and Socialist Movements in 19th Century Russia.* Translated by Francis Haskell. Introduction by Isaiah Berlin. London: Phoenix, 2001.

Vergilius Maro, Publius. *The Aeneid.* Translated by Robert Fitzgerald. Vintage Classics. New York: Vintage, 1990.

von Balthasar, Hans Urs. *A Theology of History.* San Francisco: Ignatius, 1994.

von Campenhausen, Hans. *Ecclesiastical Authority and Spiritual Power in the Church of the First Three Centuries.* Translated by J. A. Baker. Stanford: Stanford University Press, 1969.

Vos, Geerhardus. *The Pauline Eschatology.* Grand Rapids: Eerdmans, 1972.

Walsh, Brian J., and Sylvia C. Keesmaat. *Colossians Remixed: Subverting the Empire.* Downers Grove, IL: InterVarsity, 2004.

Way, David. *The Lordship of Christ: Ernst Käsemann's Interpretation of Paul's Theology.* Oxford Theological Monographs. Oxford: Oxford University Press, 1991.

Weber, Max. *The Protestant Ethic and the Spirit of Capitalism.* Translated by Talcott Parsons. Introduction by Anthony Giddens. New York: Routledge, 2006.

Weiss, Johannes. *Earliest Christianity: A History of the Period A.D. 30–150.* Vol. 1. Translated by Frederick C. Grant and Arthur Haire Forster. Gloucester, MA: Peter Smith, 1970.

———. *Earliest Christianity: History of the Period A.D. 30–150.* Vol. 2. Completed by Rudolf Knopf. Translated by Frederick C. Grant and Paul Stevens Kramer. Gloucester, MA: Peter Smith, 1970.

———. *Paul and Jesus.* Translated by H. J. Chaytor. London: Harper & Brothers, 1909.

Welborn, L. L. *Paul's Summons to Messianic Life.* Insurrections: Critical Studies in Religion, Politics, and Culture. New York: Columbia University Press, 2015.

———. *Paul, the Fool of Christ: A Study of 1 Corinthians 1–4 in the Comic-Philosophic Tradition.* Early Christianity in Context Series. Published under the Journal for the Study of the New Testament Supplement Series 293. London: T. & T. Clark International, 2005.

———. "That There May Be Equality: The Context and Consequences of a Pauline Ideal." *New Testament Studies* 59.1 (2013) 73–90.

Wengst, Klaus. *PAX ROMANA and the Peace of Jesus Christ.* Translated by John Bowden. London: SCM, 1987.

Westerholm, Stephen. *Perspectives Old and New on Paul: The "Lutheran" Paul and His Critics.* Grand Rapids: Eerdmans, 2004.

White, L. Michael, and John T. Fitzgerald. "Quod Est Comparandum: The Problem of Parallels." In *Early Christianity and Classical Culture: Comparative Studies in Honor of Abraham J. Malherbe.* Edited by John T. Fitzgerald, Thomas Olbricht, and L. Michael White, 13–39. Leiden: Brill, 2003.

Wilkens, Ulrich. "The Understanding of Revelation Within the History of Primitive Christianity." In *Revelation as History*, edited by Wolfhart Pannenberg, 55–121. London: Macmillan, 1968.

Wink, Walter. *Engaging the Powers: Discernment and Resistance in a World of Domination.* Minneapolis: Fortress, 1992.

———. *Naming the Powers: The Language of Power in the New Testament.* Philadelphia: Fortress, 1984.

———. *Unmasking the Powers: The Invisible Forces that Determine Human Existence.* Philadelphia: Fortress, 1986.

Winter, Bruce W. *After Paul Left Corinth: The Influence of Secular Ethics and Social Change.* Grand Rapids: Eerdmans, 2001.

———. *Divine Honours for the Caesars: The First Christians' Responses.* Grand Rapids: Eerdmans, 2015.

———. "Roman Law and Society in Romans 12-15." In *Rome in the Bible and the Early Church*, edited by Peter Oakes, 67–102. Carlisle: Paternoster, 2002.

———. *Seek the Welfare of the City: Christians as Benefactors and Citizens.* First Century Christians in the Graeco-Roman World. Carlisle: Paternoster, 1994.

Witherington, Ben, III. *Jesus, Paul and the End of the World: A Comparative Study in New Testament Eschatology.* Downers Grove, IL: InterVarsity, 1992.

———. *The Paul Quest: The Renewed Search for the Jew of Tarsus.* Downers Grove, IL: InterVarsity, 1998.

Wrede, W. *Paul.* Translated by Edward Lummis. London: Elsom, 1907.

Wright, N. T. *The Climax of the Covenant: Christ and the Law in Pauline Theology.* Minneapolis: Fortress, 1993.

———. *Jesus and the Victory of God.* Christian Origins and the Question of God 2. Minneapolis: Fortress, 1996.

———. *Justification: God's Plan and Paul's Vision.* Downers Grove, IL: InterVarsity, 2009

———. *New Tasks For A Renewed Church.* London: Hodder & Stoughton, 1992.

———. *The New Testament and the People of God.* Christian Origins and the Question of God 1. Minneapolis: Fortress, 1992.

———. *Paul: In Fresh Perspective.* Minneapolis: Fortress, 2005.

———. "Paul's Gospel and Caesar's Empire." In *Paul and Politics: Ekklesia, Israel, Imperium, Interpretation. Essays in Honor of Krister Stendahl*, edited by Richard A. Horsley, 160–83. Harrisburg: Trinity Press International, 2000.

———. *Simply Christian: Why Christianity Makes Sense.* San Francisco: HarperSanFrancisco, 2006.

———. *Surprised by Hope: Rethinking Heaven, the Resurrection, and the Mission of the Church.* New York: HarperOne, 2008.

———. *What Saint Paul Really Said: Was Paul of Tarsus the Real Founder of Christianity?* Grand Rapids: Eerdmans, 1997.

Yeo, Khiok-Khng. *Chairman Mao Meets the Apostle Paul: Christianity, Communism, and the Hope of China.* Grand Rapids: Brazos, 2002.

Ziesler, John A. *Pauline Christianity.* Oxford Bible Series. Oxford: Oxford University Press, 1983.

Žižek, Slavoj. *First as Tragedy, Then as Farce.* London: Verso, 2009.

———. *On Belief.* Thinking in Action Series. London: Routledge, 2001.

————. *The Puppet and the Dwarf: The Perverse Core of Christianity*. Short Circuits. Cambridge, MA: MIT Press, 2003.

Zola, Émile. *Germinal*. Translated with an introduction by Leonard Tancock. Penguin Classics. London: Penguin, 1954.

CPSIA information can be obtained
at www.ICGtesting.com
Printed in the USA
BVHW031922150221
600174BV00009B/221